**Monographs of the
American Association on Mental Retardation, 11**

Michael J. Begab, Series Editor

Parents
for
Children,
Children
for Parents

The
Adoption
Alternative

by
Laraine Masters Glidden
St. Mary's College
of Maryland

Published by
American Association on Mental Retardation
1719 Kalorama Road, NW
Washington, DC 20009

No. 11, Monographs of the American Association on Mental Retardation (ISSN 0895-8009)

Library of Congress Cataloging-in-Publication Data

Glidden, Laraine Masters, 1943-
    Parents for children, children for parents.

    (Monographs of the American Association on Mental Retardation, 0895-8009;11)
    Bibliography: p.
    1. Adoption—England—Case studies. 2. Developmentally disabled children—England—Family relationships—Case studies. 3. Parents of handicapped children—England—Case studies. I. Title. II. Series.
    HV875.58.G72E544   1989   362.7'34'0942   98-188
    ISBN 0-940898-20-9

Printed in the United States of America

Dedication

To my mother, who left this world just as this book was coming into it. In ways I will never fully understand, it would not have been written without her influence.

Contents

Contents

Foreword

To someone like me who entered the field of mental retardation in 1942, this book is a reminder of how the world has changed! Place children who are mentally retarded out for adoption? Anyone suggesting that would have risked commitment to a state hospital. Indeed, most people, including professionals in the field, believed that children with handicaps were better off in institutions than in their home communities.

There are several reasons we are in debt to Dr. Glidden. First, she documents how the world has changed and how those changes have affected adoption practices, especially regarding youngsters with retardation. Second, in a most clear and incisive way she tells us of the difficulties encountered in interpreting studies about who adopts and why, about satisfactory and unsatisfactory outcomes, about short and long term criteria of these outcomes. Better than anyone else, Dr. Glidden has identified the methodological issues that future researchers will be unable to ignore. Third, this book contains a well–executed study of families who adopted children with mental retardation. The quantitative data are clear and understandable (no small feat) and enrich the sensitive, compelling case material. Reviews of literature and presentation of quantitative data are too frequently dry and soporific, draining interest from the clinical-human issues they are intended to illuminate. This book is a refreshing exception.

There can no longer be any doubt that most families who adopt these youngers find it a rewarding experience. To many people that conclusion will still be hard to comprehend. This book will help them to understand better why that conclusion should not be surprising. There is one finding from Dr. Glidden's study that I wish to emphasize because it concerns a finding that one of my students obtained in a smaller sample similar to that used by Dr. Glidden. Because the sample was small we were understandably hesitant to make much of it. I refer to Dr. Glidden's finding about the important role of religious attitudes and beliefs in a significant minority of her families.

It is my hope that this book will receive the attention it deserves from researchers, clinicians, and policymakers. More than that, it can profitably be read by the general public because it is an engrossing document of the best in people.

Seymour B. Sarason

ix

Acknowledgments

Hundreds of individuals were influential in the development and production of this book, and deciding which of them to acknowledge evokes its own existential crisis! Certainly, those persons who were directly responsible must be mentioned by role, if not by name. The families who were the respondents and gave uncomplainingly of their time and thoughts and feelings were, first and foremost, responsible for this book. As I traveled to their homes, and cut a small slice out of their lives, I came to realize how much I owed to them.

Close behind were the agency workers who cooperated with me and were unfailingly courteous and helpful in making initial contacts with the families, answering my questions, and allowing me access to background information. Although there are dozens of women and men in that category, Phillida Sawbridge, director of Parents for Children, deserves to be mentioned as a prototype. I went to her first and she provided me with a great deal of general information as well as more respondents than any other single agency. She deserves credit and praise for her many years of service to furthering the adoption of handicapped children.

During my year of data collection, I was a visiting professor at the London Hospital Medical College working at its Family Research Unit. I have fond memories of all my colleagues there, but two especially helped bring this project to fruition: Stephen Wolkind, head of the unit and author of an earlier study on adoption of children with medical problems, provided tangible resources and less tangible psychological support. Sue Kruk did a wonderful job of interviewing families and providing insightful observations.

There were many individuals at my home institution, St. Mary's College of Maryland, who contributed to this book. Students helped with data analysis, library searches and other tasks. Most notably, Patti Parkinson, Sandra Herbert, Shaun McGarvey, Niki Valliere, and Jean Pursley worked extensively and intensively. My colleagues in the Division of Human Development and across the college offered continuing psychological support. Elaine Ormond and Linda Vallandingham smilingly performed numerous secretarial duties that helped bring the book to completion. And the administration believed enough in the value of this effort to grant me a semester's leave of absence to prepare the manuscript. Financial support was provided by faculty development grants over a several-year period, and additional research that informed the current work was supported by Grant No. HD 21993-01 from the National Institute of Child Health and Human Development.

Finally, enduring gratitude goes to my family. My husband, Bill, was supportive throughout, even when I did not deserve it. My children, Danny and Trina, were patient and uncomplaining, accepting the lack of attention to them that accompanied this project. My foster daughter, Maria, helped in many tangible ways to decrease my domestic burdens.

This book belongs to all of these persons, named and unnamed. It exists only because of their efforts.

Chapter 1
Introduction
Conception,
Conceptualization,
and Methodology

Alice Welker is 50 years old. She runs a boardinghouse in a small industrial city, where she and her daughter Elizabeth live.

❑   ❑   ❑

Cynthia and William Fenton, married more than 30 years, have raised eight children, several of whom are still living with them. This task, plus the working of their farm and their daily church activities, keeps them busy.

❑   ❑   ❑

Frank and Carol Garner are young and recently married. College educated, they both work fulltime at jobs they enjoy. They also both take pleasure in their infant daughter, Penelope.

❑   ❑   ❑

The people described above, although different in age, occupation, and other characteristics, share one very important life event: they have adopted a child who is retarded. This kind of adoption is a relatively rare occurrence, as is research that investigates it. Very little is known about why individuals or families decide to adopt a child who is handicapped and how they view that adoption and its effects months and years later.

These issues and others are discussed in this book. In this introduction, however, three other, related objectives are primary. First, the origin of the research, how and why it was conceived, is important. This conception will lead naturally to the second objective, conceptualization. The context of the research, the theoretical framework from which it derives and with which it can be interpreted, is described. Finally, a number of methodological features are considered, along with their possible impact on the relevance and generalizability of the present results to other research in the domain of function and dysfunction in families with children who are handicapped.

THE CONCEPTION

As reviewed in detail in the next chapter, until very recently the psychological and medical literature had adopted an almost invariant treatment of families with children who are handicapped. The entrance of such a child into the family was viewed as an occasion for stress and distress, crisis, deterioration, and disintegration. Families were frequently advised to institutionalize their children rather than risk destroying their own lives and the lives of their other children. This literature is quite familiar to students and professionals in the field of exceptionality.

However, another literature also exists, a more anecdotal literature. It consists primarily of first-person accounts, usually those of parents who had reared or were in the process of rearing children with handicaps (MacDonald & Oden, 1978; Trainer, 1975). While these accounts are far from storybook, romanticized, happy-ending narratives, they do tend to emphasize the joys, the rewards, the positive aspects of having a handicapped child. The reader is led toward a message of lifelong impact, but not necessarily of lifelong sorrow. Rather than crisis, the themes are of adaptation and renewal, of acquired meaning and identity, of opportunity for growth and development.

How, then, to reconcile these two literatures? Why did some parents write so positively about an event regarded by psychologists, sociologists, and health practitioners as negative. Were both accounts true but opposite faces of the same existential coin? Were there differing reactions for different people, the one that occurred depending on individual circumstance, personality, life history? Or were the professionals viewing a life event from a very limited, short-term perspective, perhaps seeing the families only during periods of crisis and therefore failing to recognize that for much of the time adaptation was good? Did their theoretical orientation cause them to look only for negative effects and to ignore positive ones?

Any or all of these explanations may be valid. Further, it is likely that the initial experiences of the family both with professionals and with significant others in their lives do, in part, determine later experiences. It was the belief in the importance of these initial experiences and the ways in which individuals reacted to them and emerged from them that led to the conception and the conceptualization of the present research.

THE CONCEPTUALIZATION

There is no doubt, then, that having a child who is mentally retarded can be a positive experience for a family. However, most families do not consider it from that perspective when the child is initially diagnosed.

Rather, the initial diagnosis usually precipitates reactions of shock, grief, and guilt, as well as existential crises, as described in detail in the next chapter. These existential crises include feelings of disillusionment, aloneness, vulnerability, inequity, and loss of immortality, among other responses (Roos, 1985). They involve the questioning of life's meaning, of one's own identity and values. It is only after an individual emerges from these existential crises that he or she may be able to confront the reality of rearing the child, a reality that may have its own difficulties, but that also may have rewards.

Further, the experience of the existential crisis itself may determine how the parent responds to the reality burdens. Mothers and fathers who are still mourning for their lost "perfect" child and suffering from feelings of aloneness and vulnerability may find it very difficult to assume the caretaking burdens of a child who is developmentally delayed and may have accompanying medical problems. Thus, the reality of caring for a child with handicaps is perceived differently by persons who have undergone different existential crises. Parents who feel guilty, embittered, grieving, and angry are not going to react to reality crises in the same way as

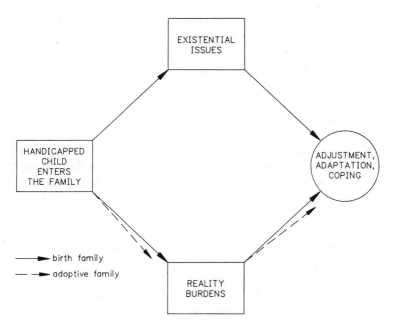

FIGURE 1-1. Adjustment model for families with children who are handicapped. The adoptive family usually experiences only the bottom pathway. Birth families experience both pathways.

parents who are not experiencing these emotions. In order to get a reasonably pure measure of reality concerns, it is necessary to study the adjustment to the child without the confounding factor of existential crises.

However, disentangling existential and reality crises is difficult. In the biological family, the reality crises begin almost immediately upon diagnosis of handicap, while the family is still embroiled in the acute stages of its existential crises. Figure 1-1 shows the flow of events, with the biological family experiencing both existential and reality difficulties beginning as soon as the child enters the family, and with both contributing to the adjustment that the family must make. Because the reality crises begin before the existential crises have ended, and because the presence of existential crises may even increase the burden of the reality crises, adjustment may be problematic. This temporal simultaneity also makes the two types of burdens difficult to disentangle.

One technique for separate study of existential and reality concerns is to manipulate the existential crisis as an independent variable and to examine its relationship to the reality crisis. For example, if one could rate the family as to intensity and duration of distress following the diagnosis of handicap and then also measure the amount of stress and strain involved in actually caring for the child, the relationship between the two might be clarified. The obvious prediction is that families who suffer more severe existential crises would also be more likely to experience more severe reality crises. However, the two types of stresses may not be related in such a simple, linear fashion. Only research addressed to a more specific quantification of both existential and reality crises will uncover the relationship between the two.

The strategy chosen for the current research is a variant of the approach described above. Rather than manipulate the intensity of the existential crisis as an independent variable, an attempt was made to hold it constant by studying families who did not experience existential crises. Such families are probably extremely rare, perhaps nonexistent among the biologic parents of children who are retarded. They should be the norm, however, among families who have adopted children with mental retardation.

In recent years more and more children who are mentally retarded have been adopted. Little research, however, has been done on the family adjustment of those who have adopted these children. They seem a perfect population to use to disentangle existential and reality crises. Adoptive families have made a conscious and voluntary decision to rear a child who is handicapped, making it unlikely that they will suffer existential crises. They will have known about the handicap and will have some information about how to cope with it prior to the beginning of their reality concerns. Thus, whatever crises adoptive parents experience should be a consequence of the reality of caring for a difficult child and not a result of unresolved existential crisis. In Figure 1-1, adoptive families presumably follow only the lower pathway. When the child enters the family, they must begin to deal with reality burdens that will affect family adjustment. However, because adoptive families should not have to deal with existential crises, they should provide a good vehicle for disentangling the existential and reality burdens from one another.

The research described in this book is really a beginning in trying to understand the events that take place in families with children who are handicapped. Adoptive families are studied in part as a vehicle for also understanding what occurs in birth families. Families who adopt children with retardation are interesting, however, not only because they are families with children who are handicapped, but also because they are families who have adopted. The motivation for adopting a child who is retarded, the process by which the child entered the family, and the adjustment of the family to the child are all relevant issues for understanding adoption as well as for relating to birth families of children with handicaps.

Thus, this book has a two-pronged thrust. It relates both to the field of exceptionality and the families of exceptional children and to the field of adoption. This double thrust is illustrated by the orientations of the next two chapters. Chapter 2 is a review of the reactions of families with children who are handicapped at birth. Chapter 3 is a historically oriented review of adoption, ending with recent research on the adoption of children with handicaps. In other chapters as well, generalizations are made to both the domain of adoption and the domain of families of children with handicaps. Ultimately, however, the objective is singular: to come to a clearer understanding of family relationships, regardless of the way in which the family is formed or the characteristics of the individuals in it. The domains of adoption and exceptionality are both relevant to this objective.

Finally, to understand the contributions that the current research can make, it is necessary to know its methodology along with some of the limitations of that methodology. In the next section, an overview of methods is provided, along with some explanations of how to interpret those methods. Methodological issues are also introduced within the book at places appropriate to their consideration. Appendices provide supplementary information, including the measuring instruments that were used, for those readers interested in the fullest understanding of the procedures.

METHODOLOGY

Sample

The final sample of respondents consisted of 42 families, mostly married couples, who had adopted or were long-term fostering at least one child with mental retardation. No distinction is made in this book between families who had adopted and those who were long-term fostering because all of the families had made long-term commitments to their children. Frequently, the only reason a family long-term fostered rather than adopted was because the child was not legally free for adoption. In addition, many of the families were technically in a fostering arrangement until the adoption was finalized. Because judicial and legal intricacies sometimes delayed adoptions for months or even years, the official status was far less important than were the family's intentions.

All of the families but five were identified through the adoption agencies that had been instrumental in placing the children. The remaining five families were referred by other families in the sample. Once referred, the participation rate was very high. Only one family who had been referred refused to participate when contacted. The reason given was that they had begun to feel as if they were on display, having been interviewed many times since the adoption several years before.

Despite this high participation rate, the sample may not be totally representative, random, or unbiased. A number of factors operated to introduce possible bias into the sample. First, limitations of time and money caused recruitment of a sample that was close to a high-density population center (London). Thus, the large majority of respondents lived within a 100-mile radius of London. Although the population base of this area is large, London-area adopters may not be representative of adopters in general. Although this bias is probably minimal, and it exists in almost all but the largest scale research projects, it should be considered when generalizing to the entire population of adopters.

The second type of bias is even more limiting for generalizations to the population of all adopted children who are retarded. Almost all of the children who were adopted in the present sample were retarded because of a definite organic etiology (e.g., Down syndrome, cerebral palsy, brain damage). This type of retardation is usually more severe and accounts for, at most, only about 20% of all mental retardation. Scientists generally ascribe the causes of the other 80% of retardation to cultural-familial factors. Cultural-familial retardation is generally milder, associated with a disadvantaged environment (cultural aspect), and linked to lower general intellectual functioning in other family members (familial aspect).

This bias toward more severe and organically based mental retardation derives from two sources. Agencies with a reputation for placing hard-to-place children were contacted first in recruiting respondents. Because children with more severe handicaps are usually more difficult to place, these children constituted many of the initial referrals. The second source of bias, however, comes from the agencies themselves, who tended to do some screening before referring families. At least occasionally, agencies did not refer children who were retarded on the basis of IQ scores, but whose retardation, it was firmly believed, was the result of environmental deprivation. One agency worker explicitly stated that she was not referring such a child because agency workers expected the child's intellectual functioning to improve dramatically once she was with her adoptive family, and because they had never used the term "mentally handicapped" in describing this child to her adoptive family. They did not want a psychologist intervening in the placement and labeling the child as mentally retarded.

Other agency screening may have occurred, introducing yet a third type of bias. Agencies may not have referred families who were having difficulties adjusting. Although there were some families with adjustment problems in the sample (see Chapter 9), it is possible that others were "protected" from intrusion. How much, if any, of this protection occurred is unknown. One worker did mention that she would not have referred a particular family 6 months before, when they were experiencing some traumas. Other agencies, however, referred all appropriate clients.

This type of bias, if present, represents the most serious limitation for interpretation of the results. If, indeed, families undergoing difficulties were specifically excluded, then the positive outcomes achieved by sample families must be regarded with suspicion and caution. Discussions with the social workers who were the contact people lead to the conclusion that little or no screening of this sort went on. However, it should be cataloged as a cautionary note, and certainly future research should guard carefully against this selective screening.

Interview Procedures

The primary source of information was obtained from a semi-structured interview with the mother, either alone or together with the father. Fathers were present for all or part of the interview in 61% of the families where there was an adoptive father. Because there are substantially less first-hand data on the fathers, the results with respect to fathers should be treated as more speculative. Sometimes, wives reported about their husbands. These reports should be regarded with the same caution that any second-hand data would be.

Because there are more data on the mothers, this book focuses on them. This focus does not imply that fathers are unimportant; although fathers have sometimes been treated as "invisible" parents, current psychological research has begun to focus on the father's contribution to the family (Dworetzky, 1984; Gallagher, Cross, & Scharfman, 1981; Lamb, 1981; Parke, 1981). The design of the present study, however, focuses on mothers because they were either the primary caretakers or equal to the father as caretaker. Time and budget constraints prevented the conduct of separate interviews with the father, as would have been optimally desirable. Throughout the book whenever the term respondent or any other similar generic word is used, the reader should assume that the data are from mothers unless otherwise indicated.

Scoring Procedures

All of the interviews were tape recorded and then, except when equipment malfunction or experimenter error precluded it, transcribed for scoring. Complete notes were also taken during the interviews, and transcriptions were used for reliability checks on the interview notes. Two different people conducted the interviews, and an additional two individuals scored the interviews and transcripts. All items requiring subjective judgments on the part of the scorers were checked for interrater reliability. If at least 80% reliability was not achieved, then scoring procedures were discussed and modified until reliability was 80% or greater, or the item was abandoned. Thus, all the data reported in this book met commonly accepted requirements for reliability.

Questionnaires

In addition to the interviews, mothers and fathers filled out two questionnaires. One, referred to as "the Farber" because it was adapted from Farber (1959), consisted of 10 multiple choice items that assessed functioning of the respondent following the placement of the child in the family. (See Appendix C.) This short questionnaire was completed by all mothers and by those fathers who were present at the interview immediately following the interview. Other fathers were asked to return it by mail. The response rate for mothers, therefore, was 100%. The response rate for fathers was 97%.

The other measuring instrument used was the Holroyd (1974, 1985) Questionnaire on Resources and Stress (QRS), which is reproduced in Appendix B. It consists of 285 true-false statements that can be analyzed along different dimensions and factors relating to family functioning, parental problems, and child characteristics. Since its development in the early 1970s, the QRS has been used extensively by Holroyd and others (Friedrich & Friedrich, 1981; Holroyd, 1974; Holroyd & Guthrie, 1979; Salisbury, 1985) and now has a substantial data base to support its reliability and validity. The manual (Holroyd, 1985) reports on the details of scoring, reliability, validity, norming populations, and various shortened forms that are currently being developed and tested. It differentiates well between functioning in families with a handicapped child and in families with nonhandicapped children, as well as among different types of handicaps. Although Holroyd and others have suggested different ways of analyzing the results, only analyses along the 15 different dimensions that Holroyd originally specified are presented here. These dimensions are presented in Appendix B and in Chapter 8, where the QRS results are first discussed at length.

Because of their length, the QRS forms along with a stamped, addressed envelope were left for both mothers and fathers to complete and return at their leisure. Completed questionnaires were received from 93% of the mothers and 92% of the fathers.

Sample Size Differences

Although 42 families were interviewed, the sample size for different variables is frequently not 42. Sometimes these differences are a result of less than total questionnaire return rate, as in the case of the QRS. Other differences are the result of considering units other than the family as the unit of analysis. For example, when all children are the unit, the sample size increases to 56, but when only currently living fathers are considered, the sample size decreases to 36. When percentages are provided in the text, they are always based on the total sample size for the appropriate unit of analysis.

Personal Accounts and Confidentiality

Vignettes are used at the beginning of each chapter to introduce some of the chapter's important themes. With the exceptions of Chapters 2 and 3, these stories are based on actual families and children from this study. The vignettes in Chapters 2 and 3 are fictional, but are derived from typical events that have been described by others.

Although the stories are based on study subjects, information that could be identifying but is unimportant to the theme has been changed. Similarly, throughout the book identifying information is changed in the anecdotes and illustrations. Names, of course, are different, as may be the sex and age of the child, the jobs of family members, the number of other children in the family, where they live, how long they have been married, etc. These changes were made with two important criteria in mind. Protecting the privacy and confidentiality of the persons involved was foremost. Although these individuals may in some cases recognize themselves if they remember saying some of what is quoted, most of the time even they might not be sure. Certainly no one else will recognize them.

The second criterion related to the verity of the research project and its results. The objective in making changes was always that the description still characterize the results in the same way as the original had. The illustrations, therefore, while protecting confidentiality, remain consistent with the underlying themes and findings of the research.

The personal accounts are meant to be both engrossing and edifying. In the end, this book is about people, about an important life decision that they made, how they came to it, and the consequences for them and others connected with them. The personal basis should coexist with the scientific importance of the research.

ORGANIZATION OF THE BOOK

Following the introduction, the second and third chapters of the book provide both historical and theoretical overviews of the two domains to which the current research relates: families with children who are handicapped, and adoption. These two chapters attempt a thorough, though not exhaustive, review of the literature in those two fields. Those readers already familiar with these literatures may want to skim the material in these chapters. Beginning with Chapter 4, the present project and its results are described, focusing on the family characteristics in Chapter 4, on the processes involved in the adoption in Chapters 5 and 6, and on the children who were adopted in Chapter 7. Chapters 8 and 9 are the most data-filled chapters, providing an answer to one of the primary research questions: What are the results for the families of adopting a child who is mentally retarded?

Chapter 10 summarizes, generalizes, and speculates about the meaning of the findings and what important research questions should be addressed next. Although Chapter 10 may be regarded as the end, as with most research the end is really only the road to another beginning. As with the snakes of the serpent-haired Gorgons, "killing" one question usually only breeds several more. This proliferation is particularly true with this research, which is so new in its conception. The questions that remain to be explored far outnumber the ones that have been answered. This book will have served its heuristic purpose if it stimulates that exploration.

Chapter 2

A Child
is Born

Brenda woke up, disoriented and in pain. Suddenly, the recollections came flooding back: the early labor, the decision to do a C-section because of fetal distress. She remembered being wheeled into the OR, the gentle reassurances of the surgical nurses and the doctor, Nathan in his surgical mask, and not much else. She had a vague recollection of a long moment of silence when they lifted out the baby, followed by a blustery, "Well, she's got all her fingers and all her toes, hasn't she, Nate?" from Dr. Toutmond.

But now she felt alert, even though she hurt a lot. She looked around her hospital room. Where was her daughter? Why wasn't she in the crib next to her bed like the other babies were? "Nurse," Brenda called, "Nurse, can you tell me where my baby is?" The nurse looked a bit worried and stammered, "Just a minute, let me find out for you." Moments later, the doctor strode in, Nate following closely behind. They both looked very tired, and not at all jubilant. Brenda knew immediately that something was wrong.

"Brenda, I'm afraid we have some bad news for you," Dr. Toutmond began in a hushed voice. "What is it? It's the baby, isn't it? She's dead, isn't she, Nate? She's dead, isn't she?" Nate looked as if he were about to cry. Dr. Toutmond said hurriedly, "No, no, it's nothing like that, is it, Nate?" Nate shook his head no. "What is it then?" Brenda demanded. "What's wrong?"

Dr. Toutmond cleared his throat. "Have you ever heard of a condition called Down syndrome, Brenda?" Brenda shook her head. "I don't think so." "Some people call it mongolism." Brenda looked up quickly, thinking back to that article she had read about having children when you're older. That was one of the defects. "But that can't be my baby. That's only if you're old, like over 40."

11

"You're right, Brenda, it is associated with older mothers; but it can occur regardless of the age of the parents. In fact, more Down's babies are born to women under 30 than to women over 40, because women under 30 have so many more children . . ."

Dr. Toutmond's voice droned on. Brenda thought about how professional he sounded, how distant. She stopped listening to the words, words like congenital heart defect *and* severe mental retardation. *One thought came to her again and again: "This can't be happening to me. It's all a bad dream. I'll wake up any minute now, and my baby, my little girl, will be lying right next to me. She'll be whole, she'll be normal."*

❑   ❑   ❑

Brenda and Nate are at the beginning of an experience that will affect them and their newborn daughter for the rest of their lives. How they react to the realization that they are the parents of a child who is retarded can, in part, determine how they will cope with this event throughout their lifespan. Although each family will respond to the diagnosis of mental retardation somewhat differently, similar reactions have been noted by many writers (Drotar, Baskiewicz, Irwin, Kennell, & Klaus, 1975; Parks, 1977; Schild, 1971). These reactions include an initial profound and pervasive sense of confusion and shock. The initial shock may be accompanied by an attempt to deny the problem or, at least, to believe that the retardation is not as serious or as incurable as it may, indeed, be. Crises of personal values, existential crises, frequently follow the confusion and shock. Parents may question their own identity, their fate, their religious values, their life goals (Roos, 1985).

Persons may emerge from these existential crises with a steadfastness and with a remarkable ability to cope with the reality of caring for a child who is handicapped. Alternatively, parents may have great difficulty in resolving their existential crises and therefore in coping with the realities of rearing a possibly difficult-to-rear child. In this chapter, the responses that different families may have to the birth of a child who is retarded are described. The chapter also examines those characteristics identified by researchers and clinicians as important in leading to a positive, well-adjusted, coping response in contrast to a negative, disruptive, rejecting response. Brenda and Nate will help personalize this review through descriptions of the first days and months of their adjustment to being the parents of a child with retardation. First, the way in which they were told of the diagnosis and their reactions to it will be compared with the results of research and clinical reports.

INITIAL DIAGNOSIS

The way in which parents are told that their child is handicapped is known to affect their perception and interpretation of that handicap (Lipton & Svarstad, 1977; Lyon & Preis, 1983). When the parents are told, how the information is relayed, and what information is actually given are all components of the initial diagnostic interview and will contribute toward the interview's success or failure.

When

For some parents, as for Brenda and Nate, the diagnosis and its communication come very soon after the birth of the child. The immediacy of the diagnosis is related to the type of handicap. With a condition such as Down syndrome, where many of the physical stigmata are obvious even to the untrained observer, diagnosis usually occurs early. In instances of a mild developmental disability with no particular risk factors such as low birthweight or perinatal distress, diagnosis may not come until the child is a toddler, a preschooler, or even in primary school, where the delay becomes more obvious in comparison with peers who perform at their chronological age level.

However, even in the obvious cases the parents are not always informed as soon as the diagnosis is known. Obstetricians and pediatricians are sometimes reluctant to convey the information that a child is not normal (Darling, 1979). Many physicians state that the mother is not emotionally ready or not educated enough to appreciate the implications of the handicap. Others state that they wait until the parents have formed an attachment to the infant before advising them of the handicap (Cunningham, Morgan, & McGucken, 1984).

In contrast, parents almost universally report that they want to be told as soon as the handicap is recognized or even suspected. Based on interviews with 30 parents, Cunningham and Sloper (1977) formulated a set of recommendations that included informing parents of the diagnosis quickly and doing so when they were together. Similarly, in a study of 59 families interviewed about the disclosure that their newborns had Down syndrome, 58% expressed dissatisfaction. Parents frequently perceived disclosures as occurring too late or without both parents present.

Even if the initial diagnostic interview is correctly timed, it may suffer from other problems. The manner in which the informer communicates the facts, and what facts and recommendations he or she provides, influence parental feelings about the child.

How and What

The attitude that the informer displays is of prime importance, and parents tend to remember it (Koch, Graliker, Sands, & Parmelee, 1959; Rubin & Rubin, 1980). For example, one mother expressed resentment toward the pediatrician who called her daughter, who had Down syndrome, "funny-looking." The mother said that she thought the baby was lovely (Cunningham et al., 1984). In another study of 121 mothers of children with Down syndrome, doctors were reported as making comments such as "a child with Down syndrome is the best kind of idiot to have!" (Murdoch, 1984b).

Just as dissatisfied parents list the physician's attitude as important, so do satisfied parents. In a study of 24 mothers (Rubin & Rubin, 1980), those satisfied with the diagnostic interview said that the physician's attitude was one of concern for both child and family. Physicians communicated their feelings that the child was a valuable person and answered questions in a complete and unhurried fashion.

The attitude of the physician is undoubtedly related to what he or she tells the parents. Although it is no longer usual for physicians to warn parents against becoming attached to their infant or to routinely recommend institutionalization, both kinds of advice are still given (Poznanski, 1984; Springer & Steele, 1980). For example, the parents of one infant with Down syndrome were advised to go home, forget about this child, and have another one (Bernheimer, Young, & Winton, 1983). Given that physicians readily admit that they have negative attitudes about retardation (Darling, 1979), this type of advice should not be surprising.

Whereas many parents get upset about the negative advice described above, they do appreciate receiving extensive information about the child's diagnosis and prognosis. The initial diagnostic interview, however, may not be the best time for this information. Several studies point to the need for follow-up work so that parents can ask additional questions and assimilate more information about the baby's condition (Cunningham et al., 1984; Cunningham & Sloper, 1977; Rubin & Rubin, 1980). Unfortunately, in these same studies many parents report that their physician was uninformed, that follow-up meetings were not scheduled, or that they were of limited value.

Summary and Conclusions

Many features of the diagnostic interview were illustrated in Brenda and Nate's story. Dr. Toutmond told them that their daughter had Down syndrome almost immediately, a positive aspect of the disclosure, but he apparently told Nate first, and without Brenda. He also lapsed into intellectualism, giving them technical information that was not important to them right then. The baby was not with them at the time of the telling, and Brenda withdrew, beginning to deny the information that she needed to assimilate. If Dr. Toutmond is sensitive to her reaction and experienced in dealing with parents in this situation, he will recognize that he has made an error and that he must help the parents to focus on the immediate reality of caring for their child. One of the most important functions that he can serve at this point is as a resource person, giving Brenda and Nate the information that they need and also putting them in contact with others, both professionals and parents, who are knowledgeable about children with mental retardation.

In conclusion, many parents report that the disclosure is the most critical and stressful event that they experience in the parental role (Bray, Coleman, & Bracken, 1981). Most studies have found that the majority of parents interviewed were dissatisfied with the way in which the initial diagnosis was conveyed. However, when parents are informed immediately, in private, and with both parents present, by a knowledgeable, sympathetic professional, satisfaction is high. Follow-up interviews where questions are answered forthrightly are also important. This kind of treatment may avoid some of the difficulties associated with the existential crises described in the next section.

EXISTENTIAL CRISES

Regardless of how well the disclosure of the handicap is handled, parents who have just given birth to a child who is retarded will be upset. In addition to shock and denial, a variety of other emotional reactions have been reported. Grief, isolation and inability to share feelings, a need to ascribe blame, guilt, shame, embarrassment, lowered self-esteem, and uncertainty and lack of self-confidence are among the reactions that parents may manifest soon after the birth of a child who is retarded (Blacher, 1984; Burden, 1978). Professionals must recognize that both mothers and fathers may be in a period of mourning when the defective child that was born replaces their fantasized perfect child (Solnit & Stark, 1961). Indeed, some writers have maintained that many of these feelings never really disappear and that the parents of a child who is retarded experience chronic sorrow as they continue to mourn for the expected, but lost, normal child (Olshansky, 1962).

The intensity, pervasiveness, and duration of these emotional reactions are important in determining the eventual resolution of the existential crises that they precipitate. Although initial feelings of emotional and physical rejection of the child are quite common (Darling, 1979; Graliker, Parmelee, & Koch, 1959), they usually turn into acceptance and love. For example, Drotar et al. (1975) described several mothers talking about the unique and especially close attachments that they had with their handicapped children. Graliker et al. (1959) say that 48% of the 67 parents of children who were retarded in their sample expressed initial rejection of the children, but only two of these children were given up for foster care placement. In another study, only 14% of 119 mothers of babies with Down syndrome had any doubt that they would take the babies home, and some of these doubts may have been caused by uncertainty that the baby would survive. Also, in approximately 7% of these cases the hospital had advised either institutionalization or foster care (Murdoch, 1984a).

Hill's A-B-C-X Model of Crisis

Despite the low incidence of total rejection, the resolution of existential crises and the adjustment to the child are not usually easy. Parents almost always define the birth of a baby who is retarded as tragic and crisis provoking. This subjective definition is one of four components that determine a family's experience of stress according to Hill's classic A-B-C-X model. Hill (1949, 1958) maintained that the stressor event interacts with the family's resources and its definition of the event to produce a crisis. If the family were not to define an event as traumatic then a crisis would not occur, regardless of the objective nature of the event. In addition, if the family's coping resources are excellent, then the family is to some degree inoculated against the crisis.

Important family resource factors include prior mental health, intensity of religious beliefs, marital satisfaction, family patterns of interaction, extended family cohesion and contact, and friendship networks (Wikler, 1986). Problem-solving abilities are an additional resource that can lessen the effect of stress (Patterson & McCubbin, 1983). These factors are also important in determining how a family will *define* the stressor event; they are, therefore, doubly critical in determining the extent to which existential crises are experienced and the ease with which they are resolved. For example, if a person's religious or world view incorporates the belief that all human life is worthy, regardless of individual abilities and achievements, that person may not define the birth of a child who is handicapped as a severe stressor. In addition, this religious or world view may also be a coping resource that will provide the individual with strength to tolerate whatever stresses do occur.

Specific Existential Reactions

Loss of self-esteem. Many investigators have studied these initial reactions and resultant existential crises. In recent research, Mintzer, Als, Tronick, and Brazelton (1985) followed five families over a 2-year period to assess how each family had adapted to the birth of a child with a defect. The researchers concluded that parental reactions were influenced by a number of variables, including the parents' views of themselves as parents and the nature of the marital relationship. They found a loss of self-esteem to be especially critical in delaying adaptation to the child. Until the parents could view the infant as a separate individual rather than as an extension of their own inadequacies, they could not reestablish self-esteem.

This loss of self-esteem may be related to the many narcissistic and utilitarian reasons for wanting a child (Chapter 5, this volume; Gordeuk, 1976). Glory to self, benefit to community, social competition, and accomplishment are all frustrated motives when parents produce a defective child. If these motives predominate over more altruistic motivations such as a genuine affection and concern for children, they may hinder adaptation to the child.

Fear. Featherstone (1980) wrote eloquently from both first-person and professional perspectives of the reactions she and her family had to the diagnosis that her son was blind, hydrocephalic, retarded, cerebral palsied, and epileptic. She described the initial responses of fear, anger, loneliness, guilt, and self-doubt. Fear is an especially strong emotional reaction, with both the child and the self as object. Fears for the child focus on present day concerns, including survival itself. And they may reach out to the future, to the prospect of institutionalization or to some other barren environment that may not satisfy either physical or emotional needs.

The fear for the self that Featherstone described captures the essence of existential crises. She proposed that the child who is handicapped disrupts the natural rhythm of the life cycle, thus leading a parent into thinking about the future and old age in despairing rather than hopeful terms. The following excerpt reinforces this view. It is from a father's description of his encounter with mortality as a result of his life with his seriously ill, severely retarded daughter:

I began to have an awareness of the reality of death that drew me closer to my 80-year-old grandfather than to any of my friends. Whatever remained of my youth, with its innocent faith in immortality, ended abruptly and forever (Searl, 1978, p. 127).

Capacity for love. A child with a handicap also forces the parent to question his or her own capacity for love. Parents may ask themselves whether they can love a child who is grossly disfigured, or even just slightly different. Darling (1979) cited a mother's comment regarding her initial reaction to her daughter: "I was kind of turned off. I didn't want to go near her. It was like she had a disease or something and I didn't want to catch it. I didn't want to touch her . . ." (p. 135). Parents may also question their ability to love someone who in economic terms may be regarded by society as worthless. This questioning of one's own capacity for love may lead to guilt, which can then magnify the original fears that generated it.

Guilt. Guilt may be generated by self-doubt or by self-blame for producing a child who is handicapped. Although responsibility for the handicap can rarely be assigned to one or both parents, they frequently feel it (Parks, 1977; Schild, 1971). Mothers, especially, often look to the pregnancy period for behaviors that might have caused the handicap (Roskies, 1972). Some parents will not be able to resolve their sense of guilt and failure until they are able to produce a nonhandicapped baby (Silcock, 1984). Others maintain that the child is a punishment for past sins committed (Robinson & Robinson, 1976). Obviously, regardless of the reality basis for the guilt, parents need to work through it in order to make an effective adjustment.

Anger. Parents also feel anger at the injustice to which they have been subjected. The "Why me?" question arises repeatedly. Parents describe a feeling of being "ripped off," cheated out of something that they had planned for, worked for, had every reason to expect—a normal child. The sense that an injustice has been done may cause some parents to question even deeply held religious convictions (Massie & Massie, 1973). Other parents may use religious symbols as a vehicle for venting anger, as did the mother who said, as she raised a clenched fist: "I don't even believe in God, but sometimes I look up and tell Him that I hate Him" (Featherstone, 1980, p. 49).

Sometimes the anger that parents feel is turned inward; sometimes it is directed at the child; sometimes it is directed at others in the family; and sometimes it is directed at people outside the family, including professionals (Jackson, 1974). Regardless of the focus, parents must learn to handle the anger constructively in order to resolve their existential crises (Huber, 1979; Kennedy, 1970).

Loneliness. Loneliness can be another result of having a child who is handicapped (Featherstone, 1980; Firth, Gardner-Medwin, Hosking, & Wilkinson, 1983; Leyendecker, 1982; Mandelbaum, 1967). Parents may feel they are different because their child is different. This difference can create social isolation in part because other people avoid them and in part because they avoid others. This loneliness and isolation may then exacerbate other emotional reactions such as fear and anger, which can lead in turn to greater isolation.

Depression. The intensity and enormity of these emotional reactions may lead to depression. In one interview study of 37 mothers prior to the beginning of a home-based therapy program, 57% said that they often felt miserable and depressed (Burden, 1980). Feelings of inadequacy at reproduction and the grief and mourning that accompany the birth of the child with a handicap may be precursors of depression. Withdrawal from social contacts and social isolation are likely to aggravate depressive feelings. Clinicians advise that in the stage following shock and denial, parents usually seem depressed. It is at this point that professionals and friends may have to be especially understanding, sympathetic, and patient with the family (Miller, 1969).

Pearl Buck, a famous mother of a child with retardation, wrote one of the most poignant descriptions of an existential crisis. In her extraordinarily moving account of her own experiences with her daughter, Buck spoke of her sorrow and despair in *The Child Who Never Grew.*

There was no more joy left in anything. All human relationships became meaningless. Everything became meaningless. I took no more pleasure in the things I had enjoyed before; landscapes, flowers, music were empty. Indeed, I could not bear to hear music at all. It was years before I could listen to music. Even after the learning process had gone very far, and my spirit had become nearly reconciled through understanding, I could not hear music. I did my work during this time: I saw that my house was neat and clean, I cut flowers for the vases, I planned the gardens and tended my roses, and arranged for meals to be properly served. We had guests and I did my duty in the community. But none of it meant anything. My hands performed their routine . . . the despair into which I had sunk when I realized that nothing could be done for the child and that she would live on and on had become a morass into which I could easily have sunk into uselessness. Despair so profound and absorbing poisons the whole system and destroys thought and energy (Buck, 1950, pp. 29–31).

This eloquent description captures the essence of the existential crisis—a pervasive sense of meaninglessness and despair.

Criticisms and Conclusions

The preceding review demonstrates that substantial personal, clinical, and research attention has been directed toward the initial negative reactions and existential crises of parents who give birth to a child who is handicapped. As early as 1967, Wolfensberger was able to write of the "flood of papers" on this topic. Despite this extensive amount of study and the seemingly unanimous agreement that these emotional reactions and crises do exist, there is little general consensus as to how profound and long lasting they are and precisely how parental, child, or circumstantial factors operate to ameliorate or prolong them.

For example, Olshansky (1962) stated emphatically that parents of children who are mentally retarded suffer chronic sorrow as a lifelong response to a tragic fact, but offered little substantive data to support this statement. His original paper was an essay based on personal clinical experience, and others have written from a similar perspective (Ballard, 1978; Wright, 1976).

Drotar et al. (1975) provided a stage model that included an estimate of both the intensity and duration of reactions, but these were described only in very general and relative terms. The authors admitted that it was difficult to determine the length of particular stages of parental reactions. Other investigators have maintained that the greatest distress is at the initial diagnosis of mental retardation and, although existential concerns do occur later, they tend to be experienced periodically rather than continuously (Berry & Zimmerman, 1983; Wikler, Wasow, & Hatfield, 1981).

Regardless of the various views on the exact nature of the existential crises, however, all writers agree that most parents come to accept the child, become attached to it, and begin to meet its needs as well as those of the rest of the family. If and when this adjustment is made, it precipitates crises of a different sort, those involved in the reality of caring for a child whose needs are far greater than those of the nonhandicapped child.

REALITY CRISES

Brenda rocked Melanie gently back and forth, singing softly to her. Melanie's eyes were closing and Brenda thought back to the first time she had seen those eyes and how strange looking their almond shape had seemed. Now they were beautiful to her, as was Melanie's fine, straight, blonde hair and her pudgy, soft, little body. "If only her muscles had more tone," thought Brenda, as she gently placed Melanie in her crib, "she'd be so much easier to handle, and I bet she'd at least be sitting up by herself already, and maybe even crawling."

Brenda mentally reviewed Melanie's accomplishments and deficiencies, as she did regularly. Melanie was 10 months old now, and the pediatrician said that she was performing at about the 6-month age level. Of course, she had been premature, and the open heart surgery she'd had to correct the congenital defect had set her back a bit. So, all in all, she wasn't doing badly.

It had been a struggle, though. The realization that they were the parents of a child who was retarded hadn't come immediately. They hadn't really thought of her as theirs, at first. There were so many problems to deal with: medical crises, genetic testing to determine whether one of them was a carrier, economic difficulties when their insurance company said that this or that procedure wasn't covered, the way their friends and family reacted to them. Nate's father hadn't even wanted to come and visit, and when he finally did he just sat in the corner the whole time and wouldn't even look at or touch Melanie.

But they had come through it. And somehow she felt that she and Nate were stronger and closer to each other than they had been. Oh, they'd quarreled a lot, at first. They had both felt so tired and stressed at the beginning, when Melanie had first come home. Her sucking reflex had been weak, and she had had to feed every couple of hours. They had taken turns waking up and feeding her, and neither of them had had any energy during those months. But now Melanie was sleeping through the night, or at least until 5:30 or so. That wasn't any different from their friends with normal babies. Anyway, after she and Nate had survived those months, they had both felt that they could go through anything together. Of course, they had always been able to talk to each other. "Good communication links" is what the counselors called it. Well, they had them, and it was a good thing they did, because she wasn't sure she would have been able to face all of this alone.

Caregiving Demands

Brenda's musings reflect the resolution of existential crises, and also the difficulties in caring for a child with mental retardation. Regardless of whether existential crises are resolved quickly, slowly, or not at all, the family with a child who is handicapped must quickly assume a burden of care that far exceeds that required in rearing a nonhandicapped child. Initially, lifesaving medical interventions may separate the parents and child, causing disruption of the bonding process (Sugarman, 1977). Hospitalizations may destroy months of developmental progress and disrupt family routine, making an already difficult child even more difficult (Trout, 1983). For the child at home, prescribed techniques and procedures may necessitate exorbitant amounts of time and energy, as in the case of very frequent feedings or exercise routines (Sloper, Cunningham, & Arnljotsdottir, 1983).

Personal and behavioral characteristics of the child can influence the breadth and depth of the reality crises caused by caregiving demands. Children who are less socially responsive, who engage in repetitive behavior patterns, or who are temperamentally difficult create more stress in the caregiver (Beckman, 1983; Trout, 1983). Children who are limp or tense when held, not demanding of attention, who seldom smile or vocalize, or who fail to establish good eye contact when held may reduce or delay the development of attachment behaviors in the caregiver (Stone & Chesney, 1978).

Many of the child's characteristics may be related to the severity of the handicap and whether the retardation is accompanied by additional physical or emotional problems. In a study of the daily lives of families with developmentally delayed children and families with nonhandicapped children, few overall differences emerged between the two groups. However, parents of the most severely delayed children reported the most problems of physical management and demands on resources (Wishart, Bidder, & Gray, 1980).

Holt (1958) studied more than 200 families who were caring at home for children who were retarded. She reported a pattern of unremitting caretaking for many of the children. Some required constant supervision and nursing. Some could not walk or talk or feed or dress themselves. Some were destructive and aggressive. Some required attention at night. Parents occasionally resorted to extreme measures to fulfill their mission of care. For example, one mother carried a bucket from room to room for her own toileting needs in order never to leave her child unattended. It is surprising that only 19% of the mothers in Holt's study reported that they were exhausted. It is not surprising, however, that in another study mothers said that they desperately wanted help in the form of respite care, schooling, or occupational training (Schonell & Watts, 1956). When this research was conducted almost three decades ago, very few of those services were available in most communities.

Routine burdens of care such as feeding, diapering, bathing, and dressing will persist much longer with a child who is retarded. In addition, specialized information and routines may have to be mastered. Although this mastery may ultimately be for the good of the child, it can also interfere with establishing and maintaining a normal relationship. Tyler and Kogan (1977) reported on mothers who had been trained to do therapy with their young children who had cerebral palsy. The mothers were so concerned with achieving the stated therapeutic goal that they were less positive toward their children, a phenomenon that the authors called "affect turn-off." Mothers had to be specifically instructed in positive interaction techniques in order to prevent affect turn-off.

Family and Friends

People outside the immediate family can help ease caretaking demands, as well as help resolve existential crises. However, they can also be another source of stress. The attitude of Nate's father, for example, contributed to Brenda and Nate's feeling of being damaged and socially isolated. Waisbren's (1980) data demonstrated that support from the husband's parents was an important determinant of the adjustment of both mother and father. Mothers who felt that their in-laws were not supportive had more negative feelings about their children. Fathers who felt that their parents were not supportive tended to engage in fewer activities with their children, did not sense any personal change for the better since the child's birth, and were less willing or able to plan for the future.

Sometimes other family members will strongly advocate decisions that are not necessarily in the best interests of the child or the family. Sieffert (1978) described a case in which other family members were pressuring the parents of a girl with Down syndrome into placing her in an institution. The parents were not comfortable with this decision, but expressed their discomfort in anger toward, and rejection of, the child. Only brief intervention was necessary to resolve this reality crisis. The counselor informed them of the inappropriateness of the institution for their healthy and responsive daughter and referred them to a variety of supportive services available to them in their community.

Financial Burdens

Support services and a variety of benefits ease the caretaking and economic burden of rearing a child with special needs. Nonetheless, financial concerns are frequently a component of the reality crises for the family (Buckle, 1984; Lyon & Preis, 1983). Lower income families are particularly susceptible to this crisis. Eheart and Ciccone (1982) studied the needs of low-income mothers of children who were developmentally delayed. Many mothers who had planned to return to work after the child's birth did not do so, thus contributing to the family's financial problems. Some mothers cited medical bills and the need for specialized equipment as sources of worry over finances.

Similar findings were reported in a study of predominantly rural and poor families in Alabama. Money problems ranked behind only excessive time demands in a list of difficulties associated with raising a child who is handicapped (Dunlap & Hollinsworth, 1977). Indeed, the reality crises of economic and time demands are not unrelated. A family with discretionary income can afford to buy more services, such as long- and short-term respite care, that will ease the continuous demands on their time. The low-income family does not have the option of purchasing these services and must make do with whatever is provided by subsidized programs. Because these families are also less likely to be aware of the existence of such programs or to be able to negotiate the labyrinth of social service networks, they may do without for long periods of time.

Professional Services

On the whole, however, parents are entitled to, and utilize, aid from various institutions and agencies in coping with their reality-based needs. Parents encounter a kaleidoscope of services offered by government as well as private agencies (McGown, 1982). They meet and have to interact with medical personnel such as resident doctors and nurses, midwives, obstetricians, pediatricians, surgeons, psychologists, speech therapists, physical therapists, occupational therapists, and radiologists. They may have to discuss their child with social workers, remedial teachers, educational psychologists, staff in day care centers, lawyers, legal aides, and numerous other professional or staff people that comprise the gigantic network of service that the child and family may require. It is no wonder that McGown's families said that they needed help with professional workers: how to contact the appropriate ones, how to understand them, and how to cooperate with them.

Relief. These services, for the most part, greatly alleviate the burden of care for the family. For example, in Minnesota a Mental Retardation Family Subsidy Program begun in 1976 was designed to enable families to care at home for their children who are severely mentally retarded. The subsidy provided to families permits them to buy a continuum of services they would not otherwise be able to afford. Parents perceive the program very favorably and find purchase of respite care and babysitting services particularly effective in improving family functioning and the ability to cope (Zimmerman, 1984).

Although more community-based services are available currently than in the past, programs have been designed and implemented for decades. For example, Schonell and Rorke (1960) described an occupational training center for children and adolescents who are retarded. An evaluation of the program and its auxiliary benefits showed greatly improved functioning for the children and their families after a minimum of 6 months in the program. Mothers were particularly grateful for the opportunity to meet with other parents and discuss common problems and concerns. This particular reaction is neither time nor culture bound. In Norway, one program offers information and support to families with children who are disabled. Parents travel to a center near Oslo to attend lectures, private consultations with professionals, and formal and informal discussions with other parents who have children with the same disability. Recently, participants gave the program excellent evaluations. The opportunity to talk with other families trying to cope with similar problems was especially valued, with about 75% of both mothers and fathers giving it the highest possible rating (Fossen, 1983).

Other researchers have described similar positive results of professional intervention. For example, Matheny and Vernick (1969) provided brief intervention to 40 families seen at a mental retardation clinic. They gave information and recommendations relevant to residential and educational placement, as well as long-term prognosis for the child. They concluded that the intervention was effective in making parental expectations, goals, and behavior more realistic. Their final recommendation was that clinics serving children who are retarded and their families should focus on communication of precise information, which parents desperately need. This recommendation is supported by other interview data. Mothers of children with mild, moderate, and severe delays all responded that their greatest need was for information that would help them to better understand their children's development (Eheart & Ciccone, 1982).

The importance of competent professionals in dealing with a child's needs was illustrated in a personal account given by one relieved mother talking about her son's special education placement:

> I'm a different person. There were times when I would feel like I couldn't handle him anymore. I'm going to pack my bags and walk completely out of here. But he's had some successes and I think that's what we really feel good about . . . I didn't have the feeling that I had to supplement what was going on in the day because I felt he was getting what he needed (Winton & Turnbull, 1981, p. 15).

Source of stress. Although services can provide relief they can also become another source of reality crisis for the family. Parents sometimes feel that professionals do not understand their needs, do not recognize the realities of day-to-day living with a child who is handicapped (Darling, 1979). Retrospective interviews with nine families about their experiences in finding and utilizing services for their children indicated general dissatisfaction with human service institutions and personnel (Halpern & Parker-Crawford, 1982). The families reported a variety of difficulties, including professionals who lacked both information and compassion, lack of coordination of services, no clear entry point into the service system, and no effective outreach programs that would ensure that families would be made aware of the services that might help their children.

Other data corroborate this view. In a study of 30 families with children of 18 months or younger who were developmentally disabled, Waisbren (1980) found no significant relationship between the availability of public services and positive outcome measures. She attempted to explain this unexpected result by speculating that parents did not use the services available because they did not know about them, were ineligible, or found the services unsuited to their current needs. Her interview data suggest an additional explanation: Parents may have been too proud or too embarrassed to request the services that might have helped them.

Parental experiences with services may also depend greatly on the nature of the child's handicapping condition. For example, one study compared stress in parents of children who either had Down syndrome or were diagnosed as developmentally delayed with uncertain etiology (Bernheimer et al., 1983). Whereas the children who had Down syndrome were diagnosed very early in life, the children with developmental delays were not diagnosed until, on average, 21 months. These parents frequently had to actively seek the diagnosis, often against the advice of professionals who thought they were being overly anxious. For example, one mother suspected her child's delay because of behavioral lag in sitting, grasping, etc. When she voiced her suspicions her family doctor told her, "Eileen's just a beautiful dumb blond. She's not interested. She doesn't want to do these things yet" (Booth, 1978, p. 213).

Initial services were provided much later for the children with developmental delays than for the children with Down syndrome in the Bernheimer et al. (1983) study. But parents of both types of children felt that the professional making the diagnosis was not a very helpful resource in directing them to services and intervention. The parent had to turn into a "professional" in order to make informed decisions about the child's training and education.

In addition, parents must learn to adapt to changing trends and ideologies among professionals who are giving them advice in the rearing of their children. Current advice is for independence of the person who is retarded, for normalization in education, residence, employment, and sexuality (Dickerson, 1982). Twenty years ago, professionals routinely advised parents to place children who were retarded in institutions and return the family to a "normal" life. Parents who followed this advice may suffer new existential and reality crises when their children are deinstitutionalized. Their feelings of betrayal and confusion are understandable. In good faith, they followed the advice of one professional only to learn some years later that they did the wrong thing in the view of another professional.

Summary

Reality crises, then, begin to affect the family as soon as the child with a handicap is born. They coexist with, but may also extend beyond, the family's existential crises. As proposed in Chapter 1, reality and existential difficulties may interact to affect overall immediate and long-term adaptation. Regardless of the nature and intensity of these crises, some kind of equilibrium and long-term adjustment to the child does occur for most families.

LONG-TERM ADJUSTMENT

Nonetheless, there seems to be little agreement among investigators as to whether long-term adjustment is generally positive or negative. Some see it as replete with rewards and satisfactions, differing little from the adjustment that any family must face. Others regard families with children who are handicapped as families who are handicapped, suffering in both private and public purgatories with their burden.

Methodological Problems

This lack of consensus has been fostered by genuine individual differences among families and by the lack of sophisticated modeling to account for these differences. There has also been a general tendency to treat tentative and unreplicated findings as conclusive and to overstate the negative impact of the child who is retarded. For example, the work of Farber, regarded as classic in this field, is usually cited as indicating a far more negative reaction to a child with severe retardation than the data warrant. Farber (1959) compared the marital integration of families who had institutionalized their children with the integration of those who kept the children at home. The only near significant result he found was that institutionalizing a boy was associated with higher marital integration than keeping the boy at home if the parents had low marital integration before the child was born. The finding did not pertain for girls nor did it hold true for families with high marital integration prior to the birth of the retarded child. Similarly, in Farber (1960b) there were no overall significant differences in mean marital integration scores of parents with a child living in an institution and parents with a child living at home.

In addition, Farber's (1959) work is frequently cited as an example of the negative impact children with retardation have on their nonhandicapped siblings. He did find that the maternal ratings of personality traits of normal sisters were significantly higher if the child with retardation had been institutionalized. However, this effect held only if the child with retardation was under 10 years of age. Also, the effect was reversed for normal brothers: their personality ratings were higher when the child with retardation stayed at home. These qualifications of the negative effect are rarely reported. Further, because none of Farber's work used nonretarded controls, it is impossible to draw conclusions about stress and negative adjustment in comparison to what the normative family experiences.

Other early work suffers from the same problem of lack of controls. One survey revealed many long-term economic, social, and emotional negative effects of children who are retarded on their families (Schonell & Watts, 1956). Mothers blamed instances of paternal alcoholism and marital separation on the presence of the child. Without a control group, however, these results are difficult to interpret. It is to the authors' credit that they were extremely cautious in their conclusions. Indeed, they emphasized that the parents had received little help from outside sources, with none of the children even attending school or a training center. The outcome for these families might have been considerably different if programs and facilities had been available and utilized.

Negative Impact

Some studies conducted more recently have used controls. For example, Friedrich and Friedrich (1981) compared 34 families of children who were mentally or physically handicapped with a control group of 34 families matched for family income, maternal age, and family size who had nonhandicapped children of similar ages. Most of the 19 different dependent variables showed more negative adjustment by the mothers of children with handicaps. These mothers reported less satisfactory marriages, more parent problems, less psychological well-being, more limits on family opportunity, and a variety of other difficulties of a psychosocial nature.

Adjustment data are also available for 30 families with children who have Down syndrome in comparison with matched families with a nonhandicapped target child (Gath, 1977). Although the parents of the babies with Down syndrome had the usual initial reactions and existential crises, other indices of adjustment such as physical health, psychiatric illness, and family activity were comparable for the two groups 2 years after the birth of the target children. There was a significantly higher rate of marital breakdown or serious marital disharmony among the families of the children with Down syndrome, however.

Longer term adjustment is reported in an 8-year follow-up of this sample (Gath & Gumley, 1984). Of the intact marriages, there was no significant difference in quality of the relationships between families with and without children who are retarded. Similarly, serious psychiatric illness occurred with equal frequency in the families of control children and children with Down syndrome. Minor psychiatric illness was more common among the parents of children with Down syndrome, however.

Positive Impact

Despite some evidence of negative long-term effects on the family giving birth to and rearing a child who is mentally retarded, there is also ample evidence of positive impact. In Gath's (1977) data, positive measures of the marital relationship were actually higher among parents of children with Down syndrome. Almost half of those parents indicated that their marriage had become stronger rather than weaker following the birth of the child who was handicapped. Similarly, interviews with the families revealed warmth, affection, fun, and enjoyable family life as frequently in these families as in the control families (Gath & Gumley, 1984).

Another investigator explained that her original research plan, comparing parents who approved with parents who disapproved of their children with handicaps, had to be reconceptualized because she could not find any parents who did not seem to be loving and accepting of their children. These positive feelings tended to grow over time, as stated by one of the mothers: "It's taken me two years to adjust to her. I've come a long way emotionally. . . . Now I wouldn't trade her for any child in the world" (Darling, 1979, p. 169). Wishart et al. (1980) also reported data that suggested a consistent trend toward parents viewing their children with retardation more favorably with time.

Along with acceptance, personal growth can emerge from the crises associated with a child who is handicapped. Parents may experience an enhanced appreciation of learning and development; a reexamination of feelings and attitudes about handicap and differences; a creation of bonds; and an increase of nurturance, gentleness, kindness, humanity. They may also cast off false values and adopt real ones, as did a woman who was overly concerned about her physical appearance before the birth of her child (Featherstone, 1980, p. 229). In many cases, the event gives direction to the lives of those who become professionally involved with handicap as a result of their personal experiences.

Summary

In conclusion, the long-term impact of a child with retardation on the family may have both positive and negative aspects. Whether the ultimate adjustment is a good one depends on both preexisting parental characteristics and environmental support systems, as discussed in the sections on existential and reality crises (Farran, Metzger, & Sparling, 1986). Belsky (1984) has woven these characteristics into a process model depicting the determinants of parenting. In his model, parental developmental history, parental personality, marital relations, social networks, and work characteristics are critical dimensions that interact with child characteristics to produce parenting outcomes.

Although Belsky discusses his model in the context of predicting extremes of parental behavior such as child abuse and neglect, it is equally applicable to the present context of reactions to parenting a child who is handicapped. The relative probability of effective parental functioning is dependent on parental personality and psychological well-being, on the contextual systems of support, and on the child's characteristics. Assuming that children with handicaps are more likely to have negative characteristics, it is still possible to function as a highly competent parent if parental personality and psychological well-being, as well as contextual systems of support, are at a high level. Individual differences in families on these variables must be thoroughly investigated in order to formulate a complete model of family adjustment to a child who is retarded.

In spite of these individual differences in long-term adjustment, most parents would not voluntarily choose this role. The woman who wrote the following letter to Ann Landers is clearly an exception to this generalization:

I just finished reading the letter from "Down about Down's" and I am thoroughly disgusted with the woman who wrote it. She felt that life had cheated her because her child was not "normal." That insensitive mother should get down on her hands and knees and thank the good Lord she has a child.

My husband and I have been wanting a baby for eight years. If God sent us a Down's syndrome child we would be thrilled. My sister and her husband have a Down's child. She is the sweetest, most adorable 11-month-old I have ever seen. The youngster never cries. She has a golden disposition and goes to everyone in the family without a minute's fuss. I've seen her cuddled by at least 15 different people in an evening and she just loves it.

I believe God sent us Down's children for a reason. These special youngsters teach us so much about compassion and real love. The gentleness of the little darlings is a model that many adults could learn from (R.S.T. in Quebec, 1985, p. D8).

This book is about people who are exceptions. They all have chosen to rear children who are retarded. They have chosen a role that most other individuals would not choose, if given the opportunity. Therefore, the research on families who give birth to children who are retarded is relevant to adoptive families only in some dimensions, and is inapplicable in others. Nonetheless, studying adoptive families provides a window to the adjustment process in all families, whether formed by adoption or by birth. Reality crises and adjustments to them, unobscured by existential reactions, may be seen more clearly through this window than through any other.

People have started to choose to adopt children with retardation only recently because of changed ideology and practices concerning both handicaps and adoption. In Chapter 3, the origins of these changes are traced and historical trends that have resulted in greater societal acceptance of families who are different are described.

Chapter 3

Children for Parents or Parents for Children?

Ruth Arneson looked at the calendar: June 8, 1947. It was a momentous day, one that she would never forget. "I must call Everett," Ruth thought excitedly, "and tell him what the social worker said about the baby that is waiting for us." It was the girl that they had wanted, born eight weeks earlier. The baby had been targeted for them even then, but the agency had wanted to be certain that there was nothing wrong with her. Not that there was any reason for doubt, Mrs. Flintwood had assured them, but it was agency policy not to place newborns. After all, they wanted to make sure that this was exactly the right baby for the Arnesons, one that would fit their family as if she had been born into it.

And to Ruth, it sounded exactly as if that is what they were getting. Mrs. Flintwood said that she was blue-eyed, with fair skin, and even had the reddish-blonde curly hair that was Everett's distinguishing feature. How much closer a match could they have gotten? Probably, someone unfamiliar with their daughter's origins would never even guess that she was adopted.

Ruth felt a little twinge of regret at that thought. It had taken them some time to make the decision to adopt. After years of trying to have their own child, they had finally accepted the inevitable—but not without trepidation. Ruth's mother had warned her, "There's nothing like blood, you know. You'll never be able to love someone else's like your own." Ruth had fought against her mother's admonitions, but even as she was denying them out loud, inside she felt their ring of truth. Maybe her mother was right. Maybe she never would be able to have the same feelings for an adopted child. Maybe she wouldn't be able to love her as much. After all, she was still afraid of what other people's reactions would be when they found out that their child was adopted. Although

33

she and Everett had agreed with Mrs. Flintwood that they must
be honest with the child and never try to hide the adoption from
her, she still wasn't so sure that that was the right thing to do.
Why make her feel different? Why create this barrier between them?
It would be so easy to treat her as if she had been born to them.

But for now, Ruth shook off these thoughts. She did not want
them to spoil her excitement, her joy in finally becoming a mother.
The nursery had been finished for months, now, waiting for a small
body to occupy it. She looked around at the newly papered walls,
at the crib that they had rescued from her parents' attic and
repainted just the right shade of yellow to match the flowers in
the paper. Nothing would diminish these wonderful feelings she
was having today. Time enough to deal with all those troublesome
issues when Susan was older. Time enough to decide what to do
in years to come.

❑   ❑   ❑

Bob and Linda looked at each other meaningfully. They had
been vaguely aware of the information that they were receiving
now from the social worker, but they had wanted to deny its truth.
The words echoed in the small room: three-year waiting period,
no guarantee even then, declining numbers of white babies
available for adoption. Had they considered other alternatives?
"What kinds of alternatives?" Bob asked. "Well," said Miss Jessup,
"it is 1968, and times have changed considerably from what they
were even ten years ago. We have quite a few couples who are
willing to consider adopting a baby of a different race. If that kind
of adoption were of interest, we would be able to start working
with you immediately. For example, we have several biracial
children, mixed Negro and white, that are available for adoption
right now. We also work cooperatively with an agency that
specializes in adoption from Korea. If you think that either of those
options is a possibility for you in creating your family, you could
probably have a baby within 6 to 9 months. Otherwise, it's either
a very long wait, or an older child, one that is at least two or three."

Bob and Linda turned to each other again. Each knew what
the other was thinking. They would have to talk about this situation
before they could answer Miss Jessup. As if reading their thoughts,
Miss Jessup added, "Of course, this information is probably all a
surprise to you, and you'll need to think it over, talk it over between
yourselves. That's the way most of our couples react. They usually
are not aware of the present status of adoption. They have an image
that's about 20 years old, of being able to walk into an orphanage,

and choose among half a dozen bright-eyed, curly-haired, adorable babies. Of course, even 20 years ago that wasn't quite the way it worked, but certainly now it bears no relationship to what actually goes on. We have many, many more people who want to adopt the perfect healthy, white infant, than we have healthy, white infants available. Potential adopters frequently get upset when they discover the imbalance. Some people never accept it, and are heartbroken. But it has its good side. Children who would never have had families 10 or 20 years ago are now being placed with, I might add, great success for both the child and the family. You think about it. Call me if you decide that a nonwhite child is still a child that you could consider part of your family."

❑   ❑   ❑

Marge twisted around to get a better view of the other people in the room. "Mostly couples," she thought, "but it looks as if there might be a few other single women. Of course, maybe it's just that their husbands couldn't make it tonight. I always feel so conspicuous among all these husbands and wives. Oh, I guess they're starting now," Marge decided, as she saw two women walk to the front of the room and take seats in the two chairs facing the group.

"I'm Connie Glickman," one woman announced, "and this is Heidi Laughton. We're both adoption workers with the New York branch of the Baldwin Agency. As I'm sure you all know, because you got our introductory pamphlet, the meeting tonight is designed to tell you something about our agency, the kinds of children we have available for adoption, and the procedures we use in trying to find the right parent or parents for our children. This meeting is preliminary to everything that follows. It helps you to get acquainted with us and decide whether what we do is something you want. Not all of you will want to get involved. "Let's see," she said, scanning the audience, "there are about 30 people here tonight. Our experience has been that only about three or four of you will contact us again, and fewer than that will actually end up adopting a child from us. But I'm rushing ahead. While I set up the slide projector, so I can show you some pictures of children, Heidi will give you a brief history of the agency, and how we've changed during the last 51 years since our formation in 1932."

Marge was only half listening to the history. She couldn't wait to see the children. She knew most of what this woman was saying, anyway. She wasn't naive. She'd already done quite a bit of reading about adoption, about how it had changed, about what kinds of kids were available. This wasn't the first agency she'd contacted, either. Even in 1983, some of them didn't want to work with single adopters. It was only after several disappointments that she had heard about Baldwin and their philosophy. They were supposd to be on the frontier of adoption, not harboring preconceived notions about what kind of child could be adopted or what kind of person or persons might be able to provide a home for a child. They sounded like the kind of agency that she wanted, that she needed.

"OK," Heidi Laughton was concluding, "that's all I'm going to say for now. I'm sure you have lots of questions, and we'll give you a chance to ask them, but first, I know a lot of you are eager to see the children that are available for adoption, to see a child that might become your child. We brought about a dozen pictures tonight. We have many more children than that, but we didn't want to overwhelm you. Instead, we selected children who were representative of different types. As we describe each child to you, keep in mind that there are other children with similar characteristics whom we may have now or next week or next month." She looked to the side. "I'm ready for the lights now, Connie."

The first slide came on. It was a picture of three black children, about 6, 8, and maybe 12 or 13 years old. "They're awfully cute," thought Marge, "but there's no way I could control three kids." The next slide was of a boy who looked almost 6 feet tall. Heidi was describing him as a teenager with drug problems, abandoned by his parents because they couldn't handle him anymore. He needed a strong father figure. "I guess he's not for me, either," thought Marge.

"The next child is not actually available for adoption," reported Heidi. "We learned just this afternoon that he had been placed with a family. We decided to include him anyway, though, because we periodically have children like him for placement. But they go pretty quickly these days, so if this is the type of child you are interested in, you might have a substantial wait. The family who is adopting Ben waited about 18 months before he became available." The picture appeared; it was a blond-haired, blue-eyed smiling infant. Several oohs and ahs were heard in the audience. "Ben doesn't look all that different from the baby that everyone used to imagine as the ideal adoptive child. He is quite different, however. Despite his almost normal appearance, the prognosis for Ben's development *is not normal. Ben has Down syndrome—people used to call it Mongolism—which means that he is and always will be mentally retarded. He also has a heart defect, which will require corrective surgery when he gets a little bit older. Despite these problems, there are lots of people who want a child like Ben, in part because he is a baby. Now, the next child also has Down syndrome, but she is 7 years old. She is currently available for adoption."*

As soon as Tamara's picture was projected, Marge knew that she had found her daughter. Those long, thin, blond braids with the pretty, pink bows, that mischievous little smile, those somewhat oddly shaped but beautiful green eyes were all so appealing. She barely heard Heidi describe her as functioning like a 2- to 3-year-old, not yet fully toilet trained, and with barely intelligible speech. She would deal with all that. It didn't matter. She was in love.

❏   ❏   ❏

These three episodes are fictional, but they could easily have taken place at the times indicated in each story. That the events described are so different from each other is indicative of the changing practices in adoption, practices that have been influenced by strong social forces acting to alter dramatically the kinds of children who could be adopted, the ways in which those adoptions took place, and the characteristics of adoptive parents. This chapter provides a brief review of the history of adoption in the Western world, documenting these changes. The focus, however, is on contemporary adoptions, particularly on research, scanty though it is, that bears directly on the subject of the current study: adoption of children with handicaps.

ADOPTION THEN

Adoption is not a new practice nor is it limited to advanced societies. It has occurred in all historical periods and throughout the world (Payne-Price, 1981). References to it can be found in the Bible and in the writings of ancient Egyptians, Greeks, Romans, and other cultures (Leavy, 1954). However, adoption laws that resemble present-day legislation date from the latter half of the nineteenth century and the first half of the twentieth century. In the United States, Massachusetts in 1851 was the first state to enact modern adoption legislation. This legislation and other modern laws focused on adoption as a way of ensuring a relationship between a child and its parents. This focus was in contrast to the primary motivation in ancient adoption practice, which was providing an heir for the adopter.

With its 1851 law, Massachusetts was in the vanguard of adoption legislation. Some states and countries still did not regulate adoption for many decades thereafter. In Europe, the large number of orphaned children from World War I may have provided the impetus for adoption law passage. Sweden enacted its first Adoption Act in 1917 (Bohman, 1970), as did England, after many years of discussion, in 1926 (Kornitzer, 1952). Adoptions, however, took place without benefit of law for many decades prior to the official legislation. Indeed, the laws were seen by many as merely regularizing practice.

These early adoptions were different in several ways from the majority of adoptions that take place today. An important difference was the emphasis on providing a family with a perfect or near perfect child. Adoptive children were carefully selected according to criteria of health, age, family background, and other characteristics deemed crucial in predicting that the family would be satisfied with the child. For example, during a 3-year period the National Children Adoption Association in England reported being offered 7,000 children for adoption, but accepting only 2,000. Even of this group only 600 were actually placed in adoptive homes. The remaining 1,400 were put on a waiting list (Kornitzer, 1952).

Matching the child with the family was a common practice. As in the case of the Arnesons described at the beginning of this chapter, attempts were made to match on physical characteristics. Religion was also considered an important selection variable, as was intellectual functioning. This latter characteristic, however, was difficult to assess in the newborn, and it was commonplace to wait several months after the child's birth to make certain that he or she was normal. Many adoption agencies in the United States used infant exams, now known to be largely invalid for long-term prediction, both to screen out defective children who were considered unsuitable for placement and to selectively place other children according to intellectual potential (Wittenborn, 1957).

The perceived importance of placing only the children who had a definite prognosis for normal development cannot be overstated. Writings from the pre-1960 period emphasize this feature in no uncertain terms. For example, Kornitzer's 1952 book, considered to be the authoritative work on adoption of that era, is replete with statements like the following: "The great majority of social workers hold that no child should be offered who is not perfectly healthy, of normal intelligence and with a 'normal' background" (p. 49). Bohman (1970), writing of adoptive placements during this same period, reported that in Sweden, of 624 children originally registered for adoption, more than 10% had handicaps that made them presumably unadoptable. Interestingly, during a follow-up study 10 years later, Bohman discovered that almost half of these children had been adopted.

The adoption of supposedly unadoptable children thus took place even in this early period, although frequently against the advice of the experts. Some adoptive parents were not looking for the perfect child, the replacement for the one that they could not have biologically. Kornitzer (1952) stated that sometimes adopters who had a choice of several children chose the one who looked the neediest, the most forlorn, rather than the one who seemed the healthiest and most attractive. She reported on a couple who adopted eight children from institutions. One of them happened to be blind and therefore was considered to be unsuitable for adoption. To this family, however, blindness was not a deterrent.

And this family was not unique. In 1947, a social worker was able to write about the adoptions of more than 100 children originally placed in foster homes by the Jewish Child Care Association because their hereditary or developmental risks made them unadoptable (Wolkomir, 1947). The theme of this article was to demonstrate that such adoptions, although unusual, could be successful and should be considered more frequently.

Despite these glimmerings of a new view, the actual numbers of adoptions of less-than-perfect children comprised a very small percentage of the total number of adoptions. In addition, the children would not be considered particularly hard to place by today's standards. For example, the two case studies that Wolkomir presented are of a premature child and a child born to a schizophrenic mother. In contrast, casual mention is made of the occasional failure of placement when the child may be recognized as severely retarded and requiring institutionalization.

In summary, then, although mention was made of the adoption of children with handicaps in this early period, it was considered unusual and, by many social workers, undesirable. Desirable adoptees were white, healthy, preferably female, infants with good heredity and no prenatal or perinatal complications. Matching of child to parent was common on many characteristics and, although serving the needs of the child was viewed as important, it is not obvious that it was paramount. Clearly, adoption agencies also saw themselves as providing a service to the adoptive family. This emphasis began to change in the 1960s with the realization that former views of what was best for both children and families were rigid and perhaps quite wrong. Adoption began to be viewed more as furnishing a service to children in need (called Adoption II by Churchill, Carlson, & Nybell, 1979) than as providing one to childless couples.

ADOPTION NOW

What was responsible for the change in views and, ultimately, practice? A documented historical analysis is beyond the scope of this book and, indeed, would require a book in itself, probably written by a social historian. However, speculation based on adoption trends may be of interest.

In the United States, the first major deviation from adopting the perfect child came with the adoption of children of other races. This movement was given impetus by the Korean conflict of the 1950s and the large number of children who were the product of Korean women and American soldiers. Although some American fathers brought their children and the women who had borne them back to the United States, many did not. Large numbers of these children were also abandoned by their mothers, many of whom could not support them either economically or emotionally.

Pariahs in their own country, many of these children spent their lives in orphanages or wandering the streets (Buck, 1964). Personally moved by their circumstances and perhaps capitalizing on a national guilt, Harry Holt, private citizen, farmer, and businessman, began to act as an intermediary, travelling between Korea and the United States and bringing back Korean-American children for adoption by American families. Small at first in the 1950s, his agency grew into a major enterprise, responsible for the placement of many thousands of children over the years. Even now, more than three decades after the end of the fighting there, more children are adopted from Korea than from all other foreign countries combined. In 1984, the most recent year from which data are available, 8,327 children entered the United States as immigrant orphans, the status preliminary to an American adoption. Exactly 5,157, 62% of the total, were from Korea (National Committee for Adoption, 1985).

By the 1960s, Asian children were not the only children of other races being adopted by Caucasian families. Transracial adoption, the placement of black and racially mixed children in white homes, had become commonplace. As in Bob and Linda's case in the fictional account at the beginning of this chapter, many social workers were enthusiastic about this kind of adoption, frequently viewing it as the only chance for many mixed race or black children awaiting adoption to be reared in a family environment. By 1969, approximately one-third of the black children adopted were adopted by white families (National Committee for Adoption, 1985).

The civil rights movement, which probably provided a stimulus to transracial adoption, was also undoubtedly responsible for its decline. In 1972, the National Association of Black Social Workers formulated a position paper expressing opposition to the placement of black children in white families. It maintained that a white family could never provide the cultural heritage that was essential to a black child's developing a healthy identity (Berman, 1974). Implicit in the paper was the view that transracial adoption was another type of genocide designed to weaken the fabric of the black community.

This position sparked controversy that still exists in the adoption field today. Although transracial adoption still takes place, it began to decline in 1973 (National Committee for Adoption, 1985). Despite a number of studies (Altstein & Simon, 1981; Raynor, 1970) that find positive outcomes of transracial adoptions, many states now have regulations that restrict these placements. Unfortunately, one result is that large numbers of black children remain without permanent homes.

An example of the type of casualty that can result from this policy also brings us to the primary focus of this chapter: the adoption of children with handicaps. The example is of Robby, a black 3-year-old. He is also mentally retarded and suffers from cerebral palsy and hearing and vision defects. If he had not been black there would probably have been no problem when Jackie and James Haas, two special education teachers who worked with him professionally, became attached to him and began to pursue an adoption. He was free for adoption and his foster family encouraged it (Saperstein, July 24, 1984).

But the Haases were the wrong color. State adoption officials opposed their efforts and banned the weekend visits that had become a regular routine for Robby. It was necessary, they maintained, to preserve the child's cultural heritage and to search for black adoptive parents.

Although the cultural identity argument is not without merit, it is questionable whether it is the most important criterion in the case of a child with mental retardation who may never appreciate racial identity and who had formed a close relationship with two adults who, in addition to loving him, were professionals trained to work with his problems. They seemed uniquely qualified to be his parents.

Robby's story has a happy ending. The Haases' view prevailed, and he is now living with them permanently (Saperstein, August 4, 1984). Unfortunately, not all children with special needs, particularly minority children, are as lucky. Recent evidence demonstrates that the percentage of minority children in foster care has increased steadily during the last 40 years. In 1982, 47% of all children in foster care were minority children and 80% of these minority children were black (Gershenson, 1984). Furthermore, of the children with handicaps in foster care, more than twice as many white children as black children were in adoptive placement homes (Maza, 1983).

ADOPTING CHILDREN
WITH SPECIAL NEEDS

Robby is a child with special needs for two reasons. He is handicapped and a member of a minority race. In adoption vocabulary *special needs* replaces the older terms *hard to place* and *unadoptable*. The category includes children with handicaps, minority children, older children, and larger sibling groups. Representing a small fraction of all adoptions in the early era, by 1982 adoption of children with special needs constituted 27.6% of all unrelated (nonkin) adoptions in the United States (National Committee for Adoption, 1985).

It is generally accepted that a number of factors were responsible for this major change in a relatively short period of time. Improved contraceptive methods, liberalized abortion laws, and greater societal acceptance of single mothers rearing illegitimate children led to the decreased availability of healthy, white infants. Simultaneous with the decreased availability was an increased demand spurred by increases in infertility and more favorable attitudes toward adoption as a way of constituting a family (Berman, 1974; Children's Home Society of California, 1984).

By the early 1970s, adoption agencies had begun to recognize that the large majority of children that could be adopted fell into one or more of the categories now defined as special needs. Undoubtedly as an adaptive response to prevent their own extinction and as a realistic assessment of how to best serve the needs of their clients, agencies began to change their practices. Children were no longer considered unadoptable; one might just have to look for a different type of family or provide more extensive services to ensure that a placement would be successful.

In the case of children with handicaps, another major social trend—this one from the field of exceptionality itself—was influential in changing attitudes about adoption. Beginning in the 1960s, the views of individuals with handicaps as deviant and needing special treatment and protection, or as hopeless and needing nothing other than custodial care, began to change. Normalization, the right to live as normal a life as possible, was a movement that once promulgated (Nirje, 1969; Wolfsenberger, 1972) swept both Europe and the United States. *Normal life* did not mean life in an institution; it meant life in a family. Coupled with this new view was public recognition of some of the neglect and abuse that was widespread in institutions for people who were mentally retarded or mentally ill (Blatt & Kaplan, 1966; Rivera, 1972). Deinstitutionalization of residents became common and with it, the reduction of numbers in and the closing of many institutions.

It was no longer acceptable to recommend routinely that a baby with retardation be institutionalized. On the other hand, birthparents were still relinquishing children who were retarded, and older children, developmentally delayed perhaps in part from abuse and neglect, were being found and removed from families in greater numbers. These children were the new adoptees, replacing the healthy, white infants of former times.

As the types of children being adopted changed, so did the characteristics of those adopting. More single parents, like Marge described at the beginning of the chapter, were becoming adopters. Adoption by foster parents, considered somewhat taboo in the early era, began to be regarded more favorably, and qualities like high levels of education and economic status became less important than flexibility, patience, and familiarity with and positive attitudes toward handicapping conditions (Gallagher, 1968).

With the changes in "adoptable" children and the demand for families who would willingly rear a child with special needs, changes in agency practice were forthcoming. Whereas in the early era adoption through publicity or advertising the availability of a child was anathema (Kornitzer, 1952), it is now a frequent technique used to attract potential adoptive parents. The use of newspaper and television appeals is widespread, as is that of photobooks with pictures and short descriptions of waiting children. These techniques have been successful enough to allow the following conclusion by the authors of a survey concerning the adoption of children with developmental disabilities: "People have often thought that developmentally disabled children were hard to place and poor risks in adoption. However, this research shows that a large number of children of all ages and disabilities were placed for adoption with few disruptions" (Coyne & Brown, 1985, pp. 614–615).

The preceding sections provide a brief overview of the changes in adoption during the modern era. The research that occupies the remainder of this book could not have been done 20 years ago, because families were not adopting children with mental retardation in large enough numbers to make such research of either theoretical or practical interest. That has changed, but research concerning the types of families who adopt children who are retarded, their motivation for the adoptions, and the post-placement functioning of the families is still scarce. As late as 1977 it was still possible to write that essentially no information was available on the attitudes, policies, or practices of agencies regarding the adoption of children with mental retardation (Krisheff, 1977). By 1986, additional work had been published, although there is hardly a surfeit, and many questions remain to be addressed. In the next section, a review of existing relevant research is presented. The primary objective is to summarize what is known so that the findings of others can be compared with and contrasted to the present results as described in succeeding chapters of this book.

ADOPTION OF
CHILDREN WITH
MENTAL RETARDATION

There are two major difficulties in reviewing the research on families who have adopted children with retardation. First, there is not very much research to review. Adoption research, in general, is not scarce. In fact, it is published quite frequently and focuses on a wide range of issues. Studies vary from those that explore the adoptive family as one suffering role handicap (Kirk, 1964, 1981) to children's cognitive understanding of adoption (Brodzinsky, Pappas, Singer, & Braff, 1981), or to comparing adoptive and biological children in order to disentangle the relative contributions of genetic and environmental components to the development of various characteristics (Horn, 1983; Plomin & DeFries, 1983; Scarr & Weinberg, 1983). However, research that focuses on the families who adopt children with handicaps is a very small portion of the total adoption literature.

Secondly, research relevant to the issues of interest frequently studies a population somewhat different from the children who are the primary emphasis here. It is necessary to extricate information from larger studies of children with special needs (Nelson, 1985) or of children with medical difficulties (Wolkind & Kozaruk, 1983), for example.

Nonetheless, the following review focuses on two issues in the adoption of children who are retarded: (a) Who adopts them? and (b) What are the outcomes? Both of these questions are important ones for the present research. By examining the characteristics of families who choose to rear these children, insight into the important characteristics for all parents of children with retardation, birth or adoptive, should be gained. Additionally, the most fundamental question is whether adoptions of children with retardation are generally successful. If they are, as the thesis of this book presupposes, then the reality crises of rearing a child who is retarded must not be crucial in determining the adjustment of the family to the child. Instead, professionals should look to the existential crises and the preparedness of birth families for the entrance of a child with retardation into their lives.

Who Adopts Children With Mental Retardation?

To answer "almost anyone" to this question is not especially informative, although it does characterize the heterogeneity that has been found among those few studies that have described the people who choose to adopt children with handicaps. As one social worker who specializes in the placement of children with handicaps wrote, such families come "in many shapes and sizes" (Sinclair, 1985, p. 38). Despite this variability, however, there do seem to be some characteristics that appear in several studies. Familiarity with childrearing and/or handicapping conditions is the most salient of these characteristics.

One study described 11 families who had knowingly adopted or long-term fostered children with mental retardation. Five of the 11 families had fostered children before and 2 had children who were biologically handicapped. Eight of the families had biological children and were experienced childrearers, as many of these biological children were already adult (Gath, 1983).

Another study that examined the adoption of children with retardation as a subset of the adoption of children with medical problems reported similar findings. In the families of 12 children who were significantly developmentally delayed at the time of placement, familiarity with handicaps had been gained either through work or personal experience. Most of these families had specifically wanted to adopt a child who was handicapped (Wolkind & Kozaruk, 1983).

Spaulding for Children, an agency specializing in handling adoption of children with special needs, examined their records to compare 21 families who had adopted children who were retarded with 58 families who had adopted nonretarded children. They also found a tendency for the adopters of children with retardation to be more experienced childrearers than were the adopters of nonretarded children (DeLeon & Westerberg, 1980).

In an intensive interview study of 20 families who had adopted 23 children with mental handicaps, Macaskill found that 17 of the families had had previous experiences with children who were handicapped, experiences that had been uniformly positive. In addition, exactly half of the adoptive families had been foster parents at some point in their lives. Most of the families had birth children, with only four adopting families having been childless (cited in Bowden, 1984).

The most extensive study of special-needs adoptions to date corroborated the findings of these other studies. Nelson (1985) reported the results of a research project involving 177 families who adopted children with special needs. Although only a minority of these children were mentally retarded, the findings for this subset were not substantially different than those for the total sample. Most of the parents had at least one child prior to the target adoption and more than one-third of the respondents had previous experience, usually as foster parents, with special-needs children. Further, 93% of the families who adopted children with mental, physical, or emotional impairments had had an earlier experience of caring for a child with special needs.

The adopters of children with retardation were usually married couples and white. They tended to be slightly older than adoptive parents in general, with many mothers and fathers over 40 years of age (Franklin & Massarik, 1969a; Gath, 1983; Nelson, 1985). In addition, several studies reported that families adopting children with retardation were less likely to be well educated or of higher socioeconomic status than adopters of other children (DeLeon & Westerberg, 1980; Franklin & Massarik, 1969a; Nelson, 1985). Two studies mentioned the family- or child-centered orientation of the parents (Bowden, 1984; Nelson, 1985), and there was some suggestion that these families had stronger religious ties than most (DeLeon & Westerberg, 1980; Nelson, 1985).

In summary, then, the typical adopters of children with mental retardation can be expected to be experienced childrearers and familiar with handicaps, white and middle class but not in the professions, approaching middle age, and married and oriented toward the family. This description is based on a handful of studies, most with very small samples. Nonetheless, it does provide a portrait with which the findings of the present study can be compared.

What Are the Outcomes?

The answer to this question is simpler and can be summarized in one word: satisfaction. Of the six studies that examined outcomes of the adoptions, all found that the large majority of the parents were satisfied (Coyne & Brown, 1985; Franklin & Massarik, 1969b; Gath, 1983; Hockey, 1980; Nelson, 1985; Wolkind & Kozaruk, 1983). For example, Coyne and Brown (1985) reported an overall disruption rate (breakdown of placement prior to legal adoption) of 8.7%, with a rate for children 7 years of age or younger of only 3.3%. Nelson (1985) found that all but 3% of the adoptions were still intact between 1 and 4 years following legalization.

Even more compelling, however, than the lack of breakdown is the satisfaction that the parents reported. For example, in Wolkind and Kozaruk (1983) some specific questions that pertained to the success of the adoption were asked of the respondent parents. Raters were able to categorize the adoption outcomes as being at one of three success levels: highly successful, would definitely do it again; uncertain success, some regrets about doing it; and definite regrets, would not do it again. Of the 12 families who adopted retarded children in this study, 11 were scored in the first category and one was scored in the second. Thus, these families viewed the adoption of their children in a very positive way.

Similarly, Nelson (1985), using a 14-point index of parental satisfaction with the adoption, found that 73% of the adoptions had scores of 11 or higher and 93% had scores of 8 or higher. More than 25% of the families described the adoption in almost exclusively positive terms, yielding scores of 13 or 14. The mean outcome score for all 177 families was 11.1.

Both Franklin and Massarik (1969b) and Hockey (1980) reported comparable data for their samples, with the great majority of the adoptions rated as without major difficulties. Gath (1983), in describing her small sample of long-term fostered or adopted children with Down syndrome, concluded that, without exception, the parents found the adoption rewarding, "deriving considerable pleasure and self-respect" from their successes (p. 39).

SUMMARY AND CONCLUSIONS

Although there are only a few recent studies that have investigated the adoption of children with mental retardation, their findings uniformly indicate a high success rate. This outcome suggests that without the initial existential crisis to cope with, the reality problems of rearing a child who is retarded are quite manageable and can lead to rewards and satisfactions rather than stress and distress, to lifelong benefit rather than chronic sorrow. Of course, this conclusion must be qualified with the recognition that many of the adoptees were young children and many of the adoptions were quite new. Only investigations that examine the adjustment several decades later can speak to the issues of lifelong benefit and chronic sorrow.

The present project, to be described in detail in the remainder of this book, was designed to replicate and extend previous findings. It focuses exclusively on the adoption of children who are mentally retarded and it employs a larger sample of parents who are more intensively interviewed than in any previous study of the adoption of children with mental retardation. In addition to describing who adopts these children and why, it provides a detailed account of the experiences of the family following the adoption, of both the joys and the sorrows. In this way, it should add immeasurably to our understanding of the reality issues with which all families with children who are retarded must cope.

Chapter 4

Special Children, _____Special Families?

Geraldine and Donald Brook have been married for 7 years. They live in a three-bedroom house in a pleasant, middle-class neighborhood located in a northeastern London suburb. Their two birth daughters, Jennifer and Diane, are 3 and 7 years old. Everyone in the family is healthy and seemingly happy. But they feel a vague uneasiness. Several times during the past few years Geraldine and Donald have talked about the plight of needy children. They feel so lucky to be alive and vigorous and economically comfortable themselves. Donald, at 30, has a steady and secure job as a machinist. Geraldine, a nurse by training, has not worked outside the home since the birth of Jennifer. Nevertheless, they are able to maintain the middle-class lifestyle that they have assumed. But they want more. They want to share their family happiness with someone who wouldn't otherwise experience it. They have tried to express this need by doing foster care. They had fostered several children over a period of 3 years, but finally abandoned fostering because of dissatisfactions with the system. But they remain alert for an opportunity.

❏   ❏   ❏

Alice Welker is 50 years old. She lives in her own home in an urban neighborhood of a medium-sized British city. Having left school without passing any examinations, she has spent most of her life in jobs that do not require an advanced degree or special qualifications. Several of these jobs have involved working with children who have handicaps. More recently, however, she has worked as a clerk for a small firm. The job is not tedious or demanding and she can leave it behind when she goes home. It is from home and from her frequent church activities that she derives most of her fulfillment. She shares her home with two lodgers, a man and a woman who are living there under the auspices of social services because of mental health problems. Alice considers them *"family" and includes them in much of her decisionmaking and activities. These activities center primarily around her church and the friends she socializes with there three or four times a week.*

❑   ❑   ❑

Helen Lowell is 39 and her husband, Edward, is 50. They own their three-bedroom house with garden, along with one telephone, one television, and one car. Ed Lowell is college educated and holds a managerial position with a large metals firm. He enjoys his work as much as most, but does not live for it. His first marriage ended in divorce after only 5 years; the marriage with Helen, however, has already lasted 15 years. Helen stopped working as a secretary when their first child was born. As a result of a birth injury, this son, now 13, has cerebral palsy. Their second-born child, also a boy, had Down syndrome, and died following surgery to correct a congenital heart defect.

❑   ❑   ❑

Teresa and Nicholas Griffith were both born in the same English city. They met there, were married there, and still live near the neighborhoods in which they grew up. It's a pleasant community, and both of the Griffiths take pride in the home that they've owned almost the entire 9 years that they have been married. Although their house is not large, Teresa would like a big family. She is not certain where her ambition for motherhood comes from, though. She grew up with only one sister. Even though Teresa did some training in interior decorating after leaving school at 16, she does not work outside the home. Nicholas also left school at 16, but as a result of good job training is now a skilled carpenter. He moans about his work on occasion, but is actually quite content with it. Although he is a bit more wary of new ventures than is Teresa, Nicholas would also like to have children. He recalls fondly the good times he had with his young nephew, who lived in his house when Nicholas was a teenager.

❑   ❑   ❑

Each of these short descriptions is both typical and atypical of the 42 families who were participants in this research about adopting mentally retarded children. As do these four cases, the 42 families have many characteristics in common and do not, on the surface, seem particularly different from the average family that might live next door to any of us. On the other hand, there are some features that differentiate them from the typical British family. In this chapter, the similarities and the differences are examined and the families are compared with each other as well as with their peers in general. The lives of the adopters are explored from social, economic, religious, family, and community perspectives.

The purpose of this exploration is twofold. First, this book will provide intimacy with these families, familiarity with some of the most salient experiences of their lives. In order to understand the psychological meaning of those experiences for them, it is necessary to be acquainted with their backgrounds and with the fabric of their lives before and at the time of the adoption. Second, one of the more interesting issues that the current research addresses is the motivation for adopting a child who is handicapped, a child that few people freely choose and that some blatantly abandon. Although motivational issues are examined most directly in Chapter 5, the descriptions in this chapter will provide the bases, the groundwork for understanding motivation. As the lives of these families unfold, and as aspects of their family life, work, community, social relations, and religious orientation and participation are revealed, the features that define them as families who would choose to rear children with retardation will begin to take shape.

FAMILY LIFE

Families of Origin

Like the Griffiths, almost all of the mothers and fathers were British by birth, and were born in England rather than in other parts of Great Britain. Only five mothers and two fathers were born and brought up outside of England, and of these seven, four were born in other parts of the United Kingdom—two in Wales, one in Scotland, and one in Northern Ireland. Of the remaining three parents, two had come from the Republic of Ireland and one from Austria.

The large majority of the mothers and fathers were raised in nuclear families, living with their parents and siblings. For some mothers and fathers, however, major family disruptions occurred during their childhood years. Three mothers, 7% of the sample, had been separated from both parents and five mothers, 12% of the sample, had been separated from one parent. Similarly, two fathers, 5% of the sample, had been separated from both parents and six fathers, 16% of the sample, had been separated from one parent. These separations, the reasons for them, and their impact are explored in the next chapter, where they are considered as a factor motivating the adoption.

Most of the mothers and fathers grew up with other children in the family. Only 12% of the mothers and 14% of the fathers were only children.

Although a small number of mothers and fathers came from large families with at least four brothers or sisters (12% of mothers and 16% of fathers), most of the parents came from somewhat smaller families of origin. For example, 38% of the mothers and 30% of the fathers had only one sibling; 24% of the mothers and 16% of the fathers had two siblings; and 14% of the mothers and 24% of the fathers had three siblings.

Marital Status

Not all of the 42 families were families in the traditional meaning of the term; that is, they did not all consist of two or more people living together related by blood or legal ties. However, like the Brooks, the Lowells, and the Griffiths described at the beginning of this chapter, 88% of the adoptive parents were married couples at the time the child first entered the family. The remaining 12%, or 5 of the 42 adopters, were, like Alice Welker, unmarried women. One of these women was divorced and the other four had never been married. For 31 of the 37 married couples, the current marriage was their first. For the other six couples, either the wife only or both the husband and the wife had been married at least once before. The marital status of only one family changed from the time the child entered the family until the time of the interview. In this family, the husband had died. Table 4-1 presents a summary of marital information.

TABLE 4-1

Marital Status at Time of Adoption for 42 Adoptive Families

	Currently unmarried		Currently married	
	Never married	Previously married	Not previously married	Previously married
Mothers	4	1	31	6
Fathers	0	0	33	4

The data suggest a relatively stable family situation for these individuals. Because the present sample does not in any way constitute a representative cross-section of the British population, comparison figures have limited value in interpreting the data; however, according to British statistics, the divorce rate for all marriages in 1980–81 was one in three (*Social Trends, No. 15*, 1985). Of the 79 men and women who were adoptive parents in this research, only 14% had been divorced. Because most of the marriages had already survived the first 5 years, when divorce rates are highest, these families seem to have exhibited better than average marital stability. Their stability would seem even greater if compared with American couples, who divorce approximately 1.7 times more frequently than do their British counterparts (Department of International Economic and Social Affairs, 1985).

This stability is also reflected in the number of years that the couples had been married prior to the entrance of the first child with retardation into the family. The median duration of marriage was 9 years, with almost one-third of the couples having been married for 11 or more years and 75% of them, like the Brooks, the Lowells, and the Griffiths, married for at least 6 years. These figures are not surprising, given the age of the parents. The average age of the mothers was 35. Only 7 of the mothers (17%) were younger than 30 at the time the first adopted child entered the family, and 13 (31%) were 40 or older. Fathers were similarly mature, with an average age of 38 years and a range of 27–55 years.

Children

Given the average age of the men and women in this sample, it might be expected that most of them would have had children born to them. According to British census data, the average number of children per family in Great Britain in 1982 was 1.75 (*Britain 1985, An Official Handbook*, p. 19). If this statistic were applied straightforwardly, we would expect these 42 families to have 73.5 children. The actual number of children already born into these families before the entrance of the first target child was 57, 52 living children and 5 who had died. These 42 families had an average fertility rate of 1.36, substantially lower than the British national figure of 1.75 or the American figure of 1.80 (U.S. Bureau of the Census, 1986).

Of course, this comparison must be interpreted with great caution, because the present sample in no way constitutes one that is matched to the national average for variables such as social class, educational level, and length of marriage, all of which are related to fertility rates. In addition, and perhaps most importantly, a substantial portion of the women might still have been expected to bear children. Seventeen mothers, 40% of the sample, were less than 35 years old at the time of the interview. In fact, one mother was pregnant at the interview, 29 months after her adopted child had entered the family. Nonetheless, these families, for whatever reasons, had borne fewer children than average.

This observation is further documented both by the number of families without any children—full biological, step, or previously adopted—living with them at the time of target child entrance, as well as by the fertility of the adoptive women who were 35 or older at the time of the interview.

Seventeen families, 40% of the sample, were childless adopters. The 25 women who were 35 or older at the time of the interview had among them borne a total of 35 children for a fertility rate of 1.40, not substantially different from the 1.36 that was calculated for the sample as a whole.

These data are consistent with the stereotypical belief that people who would choose to adopt a child who is handicapped are people who find it difficult, for a variety of reasons, to have a child born to them. The validity of this belief is examined in depth in the next chapter, but for the present, further data on the number and origin of children living in the 42 adoptive families will be informative.

TABLE 4-2

Number and Origin of Children in Families at Time of Adoption

No. of children by origin	No. of families
Biological	
None	24
1	1
2	10
3+	7
Step	
None	38
1	2
2	1
3+	1
Adopted or long-term fostered	
None	35
1	3
2	4
3+	0

Table 4-2 summarizes the number and origin of children in the families at the time the first target child went to live with them. The 24 adopters with no full biological children were 19 married couples and the 5 single women. Of these 19 married couples, 3 had one or more stepchildren. In addition, 4 of the remaining 16 couples with no full biological or stepchildren were among the 7 families who had adopted or long-term fostered one or more children. Thus, only 12 (32%) of the married couples had no previous commitment to or experience in childrearing. Further, none of the single women had borne children, nor did any of them have either stepchildren, or nonhandicapped adoptive or long-term foster children. Thus, of the total sample of 42 adoptive families, 25 (60%) had reared or were rearing a nonhandicapped child, and 17 (40%) were not. In sum, although 24 of the adopters (57% of the sample) had no full biological children, the majority of the sample were experienced childrearers at the time of entry of the target child, the experience having been acquired in the rearing of stepchildren and previously adopted or long-term fostered nonhandicapped children.

The characteristics of the children already in the family were very diverse. Some of them were grown, out of the house, and starting their own families; others were still in early childhood. Although the large majority of the nontarget children already in the family were nonhandicapped, in eight families one or more children with handicaps had either been born to the adoptive parents or unknowingly adopted by them. In several instances these children were no longer living. These eight families are considered together in the next chapter, because their particular personal experience with handicapping conditions was clearly a factor leading them to the adoption of a child with mental retardation.

Other Household Members

Counting all household members, including the target child or children, the average number of people living in the 42 households was 4.95. Most of the household residents were nuclear family members. In only nine cases, or 21% of the sample, were there nonnuclear family members living with the adoptive family. In only one of these families was the person a member of the extended family: A maternal grandmother lived with that family during a portion of every year. In the other 8 families, the nonfamily residents were either adult boarders, as in the case of Alice Welker, or long- or short-term foster children.

Indeed, many of the families had had fostering experience prior to the time that the target child was placed. Sometimes this experience was minimal, but in other families it had extended over decades, with many dozens of children having been fostered. In the case of one family, in which the parents were in their fifties, pictures of former foster children papered the walls and dotted the tables. Portraits of girls and boys of every imaginable color and age were a testimony to this couple's years of effort. The mother estimated that she had fostered well over 100 children during a period of almost 30 years.

House and Neighborhood

Most of the adoptive families owned their own homes and lived in suburban or rural communities. Only 12 families, 29% of the sample, rented their house or apartment. Although only 12% of the families lived in inner city neighborhoods, most of the families did live close to a large city. Indeed, all but eight of the families lived within a 125-mile radius of London.

As might be expected for nonurban home owners, houses were of moderate to large size. All but two of the residences had six or more rooms, and 24 of the homes had nine or more rooms. Similarly, 95% of the homes had their own gardens. This portrait seems not to differ substantially from that described as typical of today's British families: "Many families now live in houses grouped in small terraces, or semi-detached, usually of two storeys with gardens, and providing two main ground-floor living rooms, a kitchen, from two to four bedrooms, a bathroom, and one or two lavatories" (*Britain 1985*, p. 23).

Also like the typical British family, these 42 families had most of the household furnishings considered usual. More than 95% owned a telephone and 93% owned a television. The comparable percentages for Great Britain as a whole in 1982 were 76% and 97%, respectively (*Britain 1985*, p. 25). The families in the present sample were more likely to own a car than the average British household; more than 88% of the 42 households owned at least one car and 26% owned two or more cars. These figures are in comparison with the national data of 61% with at least one car and 15% with two or more (*Britain 1985*, pp. 24–25).

These families are also quite similar to the American norm. For example, in 1986, 92% of American families owned a telephone and 98% owned a television. In 1985, 78% of U.S. households owned at least one motor vehicle; the average number of vehicles per household was 1.8 (U.S. Bureau of the Census, 1986).

Thus far, the composite picture of these families is one of relatively comfortable and ordinary existence. The data suggest that conclusion, and my impression as I entered their homes as an interviewer and viewed a slice of their lives corroborated those data. The landscapes of these people's lives were not dramatic. They were engaged in the routines of domesticity that characterize the existences of most individuals in a developed country in the contemporary world. Indeed, without the fact of their adoptions it is not likely that they would be noticed more than their next-door neighbors or the family across the street. With further examination, features of their lives will be added, but the landscape will remain substantially the same, undramatic unless the details are looked at very closely.

One of the landscape features is that of work and economic status. It is a major determinant of life experience and life decisions and a critical factor to explore in examining both motivation for adoption and outcome of the placement of the adopted children.

WORK AND ECONOMIC
STATUS

Family Socioeconomic Status

Socioeconomic status was measured by the standard instrument used in Great Britain, the Registrar General's index of occupations (*Classification of Occupations*, 1970). This index is quite similar to those commonly used in the United States and assigns each job to one of six categories differentiated by skill and status factors. Registrar General categories 1 and 2 (RG 1, RG 2) are called *professional* and *intermediate* categories, respectively. Professionals such as university teachers, physicians, and attorneys have RG 1 status. Social work, nursing, and primary school teaching are classified as RG 2, as are most managerial and senior administrative occupations. The RG 3 category is subdivided into two levels—3 *nonmanual* (RG 3NM) and 3 *manual* (RG 3M). Examples of RG 3NM occupations are secretary, police officer, and salesperson. Manually skilled jobs such as carpenter, welder, and beautician are classified as RG 3M. Semi-skilled jobs such as those found in many factories, on public transport, and in hospitals are considered to be RG 4, while unskilled jobs such as dishwasher, domestic, truck driver, and farmhand are classified as RG 5.

For the present study, coding of the father's occupation was used except in the five instances where the adopter was an unmarried woman, in which case her occupation was used. All of the fathers were employed except one, who was temporarily off work because of a disability. He was classified according to the job he had been in for the several years prior to the disability.

TABLE 4-3

Percentage of Adoptive Families in Various
Socieoconomic Status Groups

Registrar General Category	1	2	3NM	3M	4	5
Percent (%)	12	43	14	19	12	0

As Table 4-3 displays, the majority of adopters (55%) were in RG 1 or 2. These data replicate those found in other studies of adoptive families and indicate that the sample is clearly more professional than the British or American population in general. In 1981, only 25% of all British workers were classified as occupying RG 1 or 2 jobs, in contrast to 55% in the present study (*Social Trends,* 1985, p. 22). In 1985, 24% of American workers were in the managerial and professional classes that would be comparable to RG 1 and 2 (U.S. Bureau of the Census, 1986).

However, the sample is also less skewed toward RG 1 than is the general adoptive population of developed countries. Only 5 of the 42 families (12%) were in RG 1 at the time of placement, whereas other adoption studies report higher percentages. Raynor (1980), for example, classified 22% of her adoptive families in the highest social class, and Jaffee and Fanshel (1970) studied an adoptive sample where 38% were in the highest social class. Similarly, in Bohman's (1970) Swedish study, which used the British RG system, 27% of fathers were in RG 1. These interesting differences will be discussed in the next chapter, which examines why these families adopted children with mental retardation, and in Chapter 6, which explores the process by which a particular child came to be placed in a particular family.

Diversity was seen not only in terms of the socioeconomic status of the jobs. The men and the women in the sample were also engaged in a wide variety of occupations. They were teachers, social workers, ministers, factory workers, engineers, nurses, and business people at the executive, managerial, sales, secretarial, and entrepreneurial levels. There were two fathers with medical degrees and several skilled craftsmen. Places of work included farms, schools, shoe factories, paper mills, post offices, libraries, mines, hospitals, trains, and many other sites. Despite this diversity, however, there was a common thread that seemed to weave these individuals into an integrated fabric. Many of the jobs of the individuals, particularly of the women, were characterized as being in the caring professions. Thirty of the 42 mothers, 71% of the sample, had worked or were working at occupations that involved taking care of, treating, or teaching others. Twelve of these women were either nurses or nurses' aides, and another 10 were either teachers or teachers' aides. Despite the lack of precise comparison data, it seems safe to conclude that these women do not represent a cross-section of even their socioeconomic group. This common feature in their background seems clearly attributable to other than chance factors. It is discussed more fully in the section on adoption motivation.

Educational Background

As would be expected, given the occupational status of the adopters, educational level was also high. In Great Britain, a three-tier classification system is most appropriate to categorize educational status: leaving school without passing any examinations; certification by one of several examination systems; and college or university education. This system is comparable to an American division into no high school diploma; high school graduation; and college study. Using this tripartite system, 74% of the mothers had passed at least some school examinations and 62% had some college or university training. The fathers were similarly well educated, with 73% of them having at least passed school examinations and 57% having some college or university training. Whereas 24% of the mothers had completed at least one college or university degree, 32% of the fathers had at least one such degree. These data are similar to those found by Nelson (1985) in an American sample of families adopting children with special needs. In her sample, more than half the parents had attended college and 75% had graduated from high school.

Work Life at Time of Placement

All of the 37 fathers were working at the time the adoptive child was placed in the family. Thirty-six fathers were engaged in full-time work and one father worked parttime. As already described, these men held a variety of jobs. Regardless of the nature of the job, however, most of the fathers described their work as generally satisfying. No father indicated that he was less satisfied than average with his work and more than half of the fathers thought that they were more satisfied than average.

Despite this generally high level of satisfaction, some fathers did voice complaints. These expressions of dissatisfaction varied in their focus. Some fathers felt that their work situation was too stressful and pressured; other fathers were frustrated with a system that they thought was either inefficient or unfair or led to poor products. There were several complaints about low wages and job insecurity, work hours, and a variety of other difficulties specific to the workplace. In addition, a few fathers, although they rated themselves as at least average in work satisfaction, explained that they derived more satisfaction from other activities in their lives. One father mentioned his religious involvement, and several volunteered that they would rather be at home with their families. Typical of this small group was the man who had been working in wholesale clothing sales for 10 years, who said, "I'd rather buy a house, fill it with children, and run a children's home."

By the time of the interview the majority of the mothers were not working outside of the home. Exactly two-thirds of the mothers, 28 of 42, described themselves as homemakers with no paid jobs. Of the other 14 mothers, 57% worked full time and 43% worked part time. Many of the nonworking mothers, however, had worked before the adoption of the target child. Ten mothers, 36% of the homemakers at the time of the interview, had worked either full or part time prior to the entrance of the first retarded child into the family. Thus, only 43% of the mothers were full-time homemakers before adopting or fostering the target child.

SOCIAL RELATIONS

Although the families were involved with work, with homemaking, and with childrearing, they were also engaged in numerous activities with others both within and outside the home. Contact with relatives, friends, and neighbors was frequent, except for those families who lived quite distant from their relations. More than 50% of the families had at least weekly contact with relatives outside the nuclear family and 14% said that they had daily contact.

Contact with friends and neighbors was even more frequent. Almost 50% of the families reported that they socialized with friends and neighbors at least once a day and 81% of the sample said that social interactions of this sort took place at least once a week. This socialization went beyond the mere exchange of greeting that might take place in the neighborhood postal office. It frequently involved shared family activities of an informal nature, but also included formally structured clubs, organizations, and neighborhood groups. For those families with younger, preschool children, social relationships frequently centered around mothers getting together with other mothers with similarly aged children for cooperative playgroups or just for an afternoon's outing. These relationships sometimes were intimate and sometimes were formed for the sake of convenience. The intimate relationships with both relatives and friends were frequently important in the parents' decision to adopt a child with mental retardation. Sometimes these intimate relatives and friends served as a strong support group in that decisionmaking; sometimes they did not.

Again, these data corroborate impressions formed during the interviews with the families. Although there were individual exceptions, as a group the mothers and fathers seemed remarkably friendly and quite used to coping with multiple ongoing tasks. During the course of the interview, it was not at all uncommon for interruptions to occur. These interruptions involved childcare, telephone conversations, household tasks, and daily arrangements. Other people sometimes dropped in unexpectedly. These families were actively and eagerly involved in the process of living. They were engaged in many activities and seemed to enjoy their busyness. Taking 2 or 3 hours out of the day or evening for the interview did not seem to be an imposition, but just one more of many activities to which they devoted themselves.

RELIGIOUS AFFILIATION
AND PARTICIPATION

Religious Affiliation

The established church in England is the Church of England. Unlike the American tradition of separation of church and state, the English relationship between church and state is one of mutuality. The Church of England, in addition to being the official religious group, is also the affiliation of the majority of English people, with an estimated 60% of the population being at least nominal members of the Church (*Britain 1985*, p. 181). This national figure of 60% was reflected in the current sample: 60% of the mothers and 61% of the fathers were affiliated with the Church of England. Other Protestant denominations accounted for 19% of the church affiliations of both mothers and fathers. Approximately 14% of the mothers and 11% of the fathers were Roman Catholic. The remaining 7% of the mothers and 9% of the fathers said that they had no religious affiliation. Despite the fact that non-Christian religions represent a growing number of Great Britain's religious communities, no adoptive mother or father in the present sample was affiliated with a non-Christian church.

These data are, again, quite similar to those that Nelson (1985) reported for Americans. More than 90% of her sample said that they had a religious affiliation and almost all of the parents with affiliations were either Protestant (68%) or Catholic (27%).

Religious Participation

Although more than 90% of the mothers and fathers stated that they were church affiliated, not all of the affiliations were pursued with the same degree of vigor. More than half of both mothers and fathers had little involvement with their church. Regarding church attendance, 55% of the mothers and 57% of the fathers went to services infrequently, many never going or going only for the occasional religious festival like Easter or Christmas or for family or personal events such as a christening or a wedding. The remaining 45% of the mothers and 43% of the fathers attended some church activity at least once a week.

In addition to frequency of church attendance, parents were asked whether they considered themselves more, less, or about the same as the average Briton in terms of religious devotion. The results of this question are congruent with those from church attendance frequency, suggesting that the religious affiliation of many of the families was nominal. For mothers, 62% considered themselves to be either the same or less devoted to their religion than the average Briton. The comparable figure for fathers was 67%.

Despite the inescapable conclusion that the majority of the sample was not actively involved in formal religion, there was a significant minority of families for whom religion was an important aspect of daily living. For example, 15 mothers and 13 fathers saw themselves as more religious than the average British citizen and reported that they participated in some church activity at least once a week. Their involvement with and commitment to their religion was obvious during the interview; they mentioned it often and definitively in discussing many of the aspects of their children's adoptions. Because it played a major if not a central role in the lives of these families, it is discussed in greater depth in subsequent chapters.

SUMMARY

The Brooks, Lowells, Griffiths, and Alice Welker considered together typify the adoptive parents in this sample of 42. Most of the parents were married couples like the Brooks, Lowells, and Griffiths, but there were five currently unmarried women like Alice Welker. Somewhat more than half of the adoptive parents were already rearing children when the first target child with retardation was placed with them, but like Alice Welker and the Griffiths, a substantial minority had no biological children and had not previously adopted a nonhandicapped child. Almost all of the mothers and fathers were English born and bred and many, like the Griffiths, were living quite close to the places where they had spent many of their childhood years.

Like all four of the cases described, the sample as a whole was economically comfortable, with most of the parents owning their own home and the usual personal property that comes with being middle class in a developed nation in the 1980s. Donald Brook as a machinist, Alice Welker as an office clerk, Edward Lowell as a business manager, and Nicholas Griffith as a carpenter represent a fairly accurate cross-section of the occupations of the group as a whole. Moreover, Geraldine Brook's training as a nurse and Alice Welker's experience of working with handicapped children are also typical of the backgrounds of many of the 42 mothers. In addition, like Geraldine, Helen, and Teresa, many of the women were not working even prior to the entrance of the first-adopted child with retardation.

A significant minority of the sample was actively involved in religious observance, as Alice Welker was. Frequently this involvement, as in Alice's case, represented the bulk of the social activities of the individual or the family. However, for the majority of the 42 families, religious affiliation seemed to be a nominal association. Rather than being structured around the church, the socal lines of these families revolved around family, neighborhood, and friendship networks. Social activities were frequent and usually informal, often involving the children as well as the adults.

In conclusion, then, these families seem ordinary rather than extraordinary. Yet by definition they each did at least one extraordinary thing in their lives: They voluntarily committed themselves to rearing at least one child who is retarded. The portrait painted thus far contains few clues as to what characteristics or events might have led to this commitment. Is it something they are or something that happened to them? In order to answer that question it is necessary to delve a bit deeper to attempt to understand the motivation for the adoption. In the next two chapters, the evolution of the commitment is traced from its origin, sometimes long in the past, to the point at which it resulted in the actual process of agency contact and review, and in a real child to consider.

Chapter 5

The Decision
to Adopt

Geraldine and Donald had been thinking about having another child, but they already had two birth children and they felt that it was not right to bring more children into the world when there were so many who were so needy already here. They loved children, though, and realized that they had a good family life, one that they could share. Foster care seemed like the answer. They tried it for 3 years, but after a succession of children, the children's relatives, and agency representatives, they changed their minds. Donald Brook thought that the children were wonderful; it was just everybody else involved in the fostering that he didn't especially like. He was particularly graphic in his description of the various relatives that had dropped over one afternoon without warning, wanting to see one of the Brooks' foster daughters. So the Brooks stopped fostering. But they did not stop wanting another child to become a part of their family; they did not stop wanting to share what they had with someone who had much less. As Geraldine said, "We got each other; we got a home; we got a dog, a cat. . . . We can offer ourselves."

❑   ❑   ❑

Alice Welker remembers when she first started thinking about raising a child with a handicap. About 15 years earlier she had worked for 3 years as a housemother in a residential school for 10- to 14-year-old girls with physical handicaps. She had decided then that if she were ever in a position to do so, she would want to adopt a girl like that. For many reasons, however, the idea lay dormant. Alice described intervening events that had made it impossible to realistically consider such an adoption for a long time. She had had other obligations until recently; she had cared for her sick mother until her death a few years before, and she had devoted a lot of her energies to helping a friend who had been mentally ill but who seemed to have recovered and now could function quite independently. Alice also described the practical difficulties. She couldn't afford it until she had saved money, bought a house, and paid off her mortgage. And then, too, she mentioned that it was not until quite recently that single women were able to adopt.

Lawrence was only five years old when the doctors convinced the Lowells that the surgery needed to correct his congenital heart defect was both necessary and desirable. They had been told about the risks, about Lawrence's chances of not surviving, but they had never quite believed it. So, of course, they were devastated when he died 3 weeks following the operation. Their older son, Geoffrey, also retarded, was heartbroken, too. Although there was a 5-year age difference between them, they had gotten on quite well together; they both loved playing with LEGO. They could spend hours together, building fantastic towers and castles, spaceships and monsters to fly them.

Therefore, it was not long after Lawrence's death that the Lowells began to think about another child. A birth child was out of the question because Helen had had a tubal ligation after Lawrence's birth. Helen had been continuously nauseated by birth control pills, and after two handicapped children they decided not to risk another pregnancy. Thus, adoption seemed like an obvious alternative. Actually, a pediatrician friend had made the suggestion, and they did not wait long to pursue it. The Lowells attended their first information meeting about adoption only a year after Lawrence's death.

Although the Griffiths initially wanted four children, after trying for 3 years they still didn't have any. That's when they first thought about adopting. They contacted their local social services agency, but after being thoroughly studied, they were turned down. They were told that the waiting list was long and that very few children were available. Discouraged, the Griffiths nevertheless tried other places. It was the same story everywhere. The lists were full. There were no children available. Then, Teresa got pregnant. They were very excited, having waiting all these years, and thus doubly disappointed when she miscarried. Another pregnancy and another miscarriage and 5 years went by before the Griffiths decided to try fostering. Initially, they were turned down as foster parents, but they persevered and were eventually accepted, fostering several children for 2 years. They still wanted their own, though. Teresa didn't like the gaps in between the foster children.

The house seemed dead when they were gone. "It's a nice atmosphere when there's a bit of bedlam," Teresa explained.

❑   ❑   ❑

The four cases described are prototypical of the similarities and differences among the 42 families who adopted children with retardation. Although each family or parent was unique, there were also common elements among families that will allow summary and generalization when considering the question of motivation, of why these families decided to adopt a child with a handicap, in many cases a severe handicap, a child considered by social workers as hard to place and by society at large as undesirable.

But before considering the motivations of these 42 specific families, it would be fruitful to explore briefly why adults, in general, want children at all. Despite the publicity surrounding the increasing numbers of couples opting for a childfree marriage, it is clear that most of them still do want children. Estimates are that more than 95% of adults report that they intend to raise children (Ross & Kahan, 1983). Although there is a strong species imperative for continued reproduction, individual motivations for parenthood are neither unitary nor unchanging over the course of the individual's lifetime or in different historical eras. Indeed, it is only fairly recently that men and women have needed to scrutinize these motivations, because it is only recently that choice has predominated over chance in reproductive decisionmaking (Miller, 1983).

In former eras, children were viewed as an economic advantage, but contemporary analyses suggest that economic motives for having children have largely disappeared in developed countries (Bigner, Jacobsen, Miller, & Turner, 1982). In addition, although men and women used to consider duty to society as a strong motive for childbearing and childrearing, it is not mentioned as frequently in current surveys (Adams, 1951; Callan & Gallois, 1983). However, traditional motives such as continuing the family name, religious duties, and carrying on family traditions are still considered important by some people. In addition, respondents report motives such as achieving adult status; satisfaction in watching children grow and develop; creation of a deeper bond between husband and wife; satisfaction of affectional needs; attainment of companionship and security in later life; and stimulation, novelty, and fun (Bradt, 1980; Callan & Gallois, 1983; Fawcett, 1978; Hoffman, 1978; Hoffman & Hoffman, 1973; Houser, Berkman, & Beckman, 1984).

Many of the 42 families described in this book had motivations that were not dissimilar to some of the ones just listed. However, some of the families also had special experiences, and their desires to adopt children with handicaps frequently derived from needs, beliefs, and strengths that were somewhat unusual. This chapter explores both the usual and the unusual in an effort to understand an action that frequently amazes and sometimes disturbs not only the layperson but also many professionals who work daily with people who are handicapped.

THE INITIAL IDEA TO ADOPT

Most of the 42 families did not arrive quickly or easily at the decision to adopt a child with a handicap. Although Alice Welker was unusual in that few of the parents waited 15 years before they actualized their idea of adopting, she was typical in that approximately half of both the mothers and fathers originally thought of adopting a child at least 6 years prior to the time the first target child was placed with them. Indeed, 14% of both the mothers and fathers said that they had been thinking of adopting for more than 10 years and three mothers and two fathers claimed that there was not a time that they could remember when they had not thought that they would adopt a child—it was something that they had always planned to do. In contrast, only 10% of the families had first started thinking of adopting within 1 year of when the placement was actually made.

Frank and Carol Garner were in this small group of 10%. One night they saw a television appeal for adopting a child with retardation. A close friend of the family had just given birth to a daughter who had Down syndrome, and the Garners had become involved in some lengthy and heated discussions with other friends and family members about the morality of abortion and individual responsibility to other individuals. They had expressed their views about how important it was for all society members to assume responsibility for all other society members. This conversation, coming so close to the television appeal, stimulated them to thinking that they should adopt a needy child. The birth of their friends' daughter focused them specifically on a child with Down syndrome. They acted quickly, and in less than a year Penelope, an 11-month-old girl who had Down syndrome, was placed with them.

In the case of the Cookseys, it was also a personal circumstance that prompted their thinking about adoption. Warren and Rochelle's birth daughter who had Down syndrome was now 14 years old. Their other three nonhandicapped sons and daughters were grown and no longer living at home. Their large house, previously filled with people, seemed somewhat empty. During the course of a routine medical examination, their family doctor mentioned to Rochelle that he worked with people who were mentally handicapped at a local state hospital. He said that it was a pity that so many had to live there rather than with a loving family. Rochelle immediately thought of their big house, their now only child—the daughter with Down syndrome—and their years of experience in raising a child with a mental handicap. After discussion with Warren, they contacted their local authorities. It was only months later that Sarah was placed with them.

Whose Idea?

For the 37 married couples, the initial idea for the adoption was sometimes the wife's, sometimes the husband's, and sometimes a joint decision, or at least arrived at so simultaneously and through general discussion that the respondents were unable to specify whose idea it was originally. The Shelfords and the Hiltons were two couples representative of the approximately 25% whose initial thought of adopting a child with a handicap was joint. Both Sylvia and Ned Shelford worked in special education and thus came into a great deal of contact with people who were mentally handicapped. It was not long after they were married that they started talking about adopting one of their own. They knew that they both found children with Down syndrome appealing, and so they focused their efforts on them. When they saw a boy who had Down syndrome advertised in the local newspaper, they decided to make inquiries. Although they did not adopt that particular child, about a year later 13-month-old Jessica came to live with them.

The Hiltons also jointly decided to investigate adopting a child, but their motivation for doing so was somewhat different. They both wanted a family and were very disappointed when infertility prevented them from having children by birth. Quite naturally, they thought of having children via adoption. Originally, they thought of a normal, healthy baby, and it was only after extensive consultation with adoption agencies that they came to the idea of adopting a child with a handicap.

Spouse Response

Regardless of whether the husband or the wife originated the idea to adopt, most of the spouses responded enthusiastically to the idea when it was first proposed. Of the 22 husbands whose wives were the initiators of the idea to adopt, 68% responded with enthusiasm right away. For example, Isabel Gross talked about how she had always been interested in adoption and how she had always felt compassion for children. She felt that she had a lot to give and, although their two birth children kept her busy, she knew she could do more. When she broached the possibility of a special needs adoption to her husband, Fred, he responded positively. They went ahead and wrote to the British Agencies for Adoption and Fostering and were soon put in touch with a local agency that eventually placed 9-year-old Roy with them.

In the case of the Kimbles, it was also the mother who initiated the discussion of adoption. They had been trying to conceive for more than 5 years with no success. One day Sonia mentioned adoption to Peter, who had no reservations and thought it was a good idea. Sonia had originally wanted a child who was young and nonhandicapped, but they soon found out that there were few of those available. They decided instead to initiate a social contact with a child, whereby they would visit back and forth regularly but the child would remain in the children's home. It was through this program that they met Jane, who was placed with them permanently several years later.

Although usually the husband was enthusiastic when his wife broached the idea, in four families he was initially neutral and in three families he was initially negative. For example, the Campbells could not have any biological children and so considered adoption. Betty Campbell worked at a local children's home and had met a lot of children with handicaps there. When she suggested that they adopt a child like that, Victor Campbell was "dead against it." However, when he went to work with Betty a few times, he began to get involved with the children. One little girl was very affectionate, constantly holding his hand, and he became quite attached to her. Gradually, his general attitude changed, and after extensive discussion between them the Campbells did make the decision to apply to adopt a child with a handicap.

In only three families did the respondents report that the husband was the family member to initially think of the adoption. In two of these families the wife was very quickly enthusiastic about the possibility of adoption. In the third family the wife was initially negative, not about adoption in general but about the particular type of child that her husband had wanted to foster or adopt. But because he had always gone along with her ideas and plans, she decided that she owed him the same. They did, indeed, proceed, and the mother described becoming enthusiastic quite quickly.

Precipitating Events

A variety of events and stimuli seemed to precipitate the original idea and its consideration. As seen in the examples above, sometimes adoption was an obvious outgrowth of an inability to start a family in the usual biological way. Sometimes, an immediate precipitating stimulus such as a conversation with someone or information presented on television or in the newspaper impelled action for a family that was already receptive to the idea. In fact, 11 of the 42 families, or 26%, said that a television program or television or newspaper advertisement was the stimulus that initially prompted them to explore adoption. In a number of families, as described in a later section, there was such a long history, experience, and familiarity with adoption and fostering in general that it was difficult to separate what had become a way of life and a mode of thinking from a particular decision made at a particular time.

ADOPTING A CHILD
WITH A HANDICAP

Not all of the families in this study thought about adopting a child with mental retardation, or even a child with a handicap, when they first started thinking about adoption. A substantial minority (40%) reported that when they first considered adopting a child, they thought about a so-called normal child, one without any handicaps. Some of these families admitted that they had some vague idea that the children who were available for adoption tended to have problems, but they did not translate this idea into the reality of adopting a child with a handicap until much later in the adoption process. For example, Brenda Romford, 39 years old and single, wanted a child. She had no intention of marrying in the near future and had rejected the idea of becoming pregnant as an unmarried woman. So adoption seemed like the only alternative open to her. She said, in explaining how she first started thinking about adoption:

> It was another way round, not the ideal, but I always think you've got to look round things and take the best option, not necessarily the ideal, but the best that's available.

Brenda would have liked to adopt a nonhandicapped child, but she became aware that it was unlikely, given the scarcity of such children available for adoption and her less than ideal circumstances of being a single parent. She said:

> All the time I was aware that there's less and less 'more normal' children available, certainly to a person in my position who's not the married couple with the one or two kiddies or just the married couple. . . . It puts me at a considerable disadvantage; so my sights were somewhat lowered as I went along. And, of course, I see what's advertised in a lot of these magazines and pamphlets. . . . They are, on the whole, they are kiddies with problems, aren't they?

Brenda, after four years of inquiries and contacts with more than half a dozen agencies, adopted Stephen, a 10-year-old boy with Down syndrome.

Yvette and Sheldon Bixton also wanted to adopt a child without handicaps, a child who would be like the one that they seemed unable to conceive. When they started making inquiries about normal, healthy white babies, they were essentially told to forget about that possibility. They didn't forget, but they did begin to consider alternatives in terms of race, age, and normality. They started looking for a child with the least severe handicap, perhaps a handicap that was correctable, like a minor vision or hearing loss or a minimal physical disability. About 4 years after they had started making inquiries, they saw an advertisement for 6-month-old Kevin, a boy with Down syndrome. He looked appealing and he was young enough so that it was "like having a clean slate," said Yvette. Kevin was placed with them only 2 months later. Two years after that, Mary, another child with Down syndrome came to live with them.

Although 40% of the families first thought about adopting a nonhandicapped child, the majority of families, the remaining 60%, thought about adopting a child that was handicapped, or at least a child that was especially needy, at the same time that they thought about adoption at all. The Brooks and Alice Welker are good examples of this majority. Geraldine and Donald loved children, felt that they had a lot to offer, had done fostering, and were receptive to any information that might help them to realize their vague but strongly felt humanitarian desires. Then one afternoon Geraldine saw a television advertisement, sponsored by an adoption agency, for a child who needed a home. Geraldine said that her response to that advertisement was immediate, strong, and emotional. "She looked so lost. I wanted to help that little girl."

Alice Welker's situation has been described already. Having worked 15 years earlier with children who were handicapped, she decided then that this was the kind of child she wanted to help raise. This decision was made in the context of generally loving children and of living the sort of life devoted to caring for others who needed her help—a mother who was sick, a friend who was emotionally disturbed, adults who lived in her home and were somewhat dependent on her for emotional support—these were all people who at some point in her life she had nurtured willingly and well. Adopting a child who was handicapped seemed not substantially different in the kind and even degree of commitment involved.

Experience with Handicaps

Some families wanted to adopt a child who was handicapped because they already had or had once had a child with a handicap living with them. Of the five families who had borne children with handicaps, all initially thought about adopting a child with a handicap when they first thought about adoption. The Kents are an excellent example of this type of family. Nancy and Lawrence had given birth to four children, a son and a daughter who were normal and healthy, and two sons who had suffered from a progressively and severely debilitating, genetically caused form of cerebral palsy. Both sons had died of complications arising from the cerebral palsy. After mourning the second son's death, the Kents began to feel the loneliness and emptiness resulting from his absence. Their remaining two children were teenagers and no longer needed the sort of care that the Kents were used to providing for their sons who were handicapped. Nancy Kent explained that she did not want to replace her dead sons; she just wanted something to keep her occupied. She described how they had spent 10 years looking after their two sons and now there was nothing to do. She tried going out to work, but she realized that it was not really what she wanted. Nancy and Lawrence also realized that they knew a lot about looking after children with handicaps, that as a result of their extensive experience they had a lot to offer such a child. It was only 18 months after their second son's death that 3-year-old Brian, a lovable boy with Down syndrome, came to live with them.

In addition to the five families who had given birth to children with noncorrectable and rather severe handicaps such as Down syndrome and spina bifida, an additional two families had adopted children who were seemingly nonhandicapped at the time of presentation and placement, but who were later found to have handicaps. Although these two families did not initially think of adopting a child with a handicap, when they began to consider the adoption of the target child or children they were already familiar with handicapping conditions and were quite receptive to adopting another child with one or more handicaps.

Giving birth to or previously adopting a child with a handicap was one way in which these 42 families had gained extensive experience with handicap. There were other ways also. As mentioned in Chapter 4, many of the parents, particularly the mothers, had gained experience with handicapping conditions as nurses, teachers, or foster mothers. Exactly twice as many mothers, 22, as fathers, 11, had worked with children or adults who were handicapped. In addition, 17% of the mothers and 22% of the fathers had some extensive personal experience with handicaps. These personal experiences included, of course, the families who had birth children with handicaps. Other personal experiences with handicaps included the birth of a child to a close relative or friend or growing up with a child in the home, as in the case of one adoptive mother who was a "second generation" adoptive parent. Her own parents had fostered children while she was a child, and one of those children had had Down syndrome.

Similarly, Karen Norton's experience with handicaps went back to her own childhood and continued throughout her growing-up and adult years.

When she was only 5 years old, a neighbor gave birth to a child with Down syndrome, and she remembered being very interested in her. Karen elaborated:

> Handicapped children made an impression on me when I was young. I can remember going to see the *Wizard of Oz*, but I don't remember the Wizard of Oz, I remember seeing a child in calipers [braces] . . . [it's] something that's always been on my mind, I think.

In regard to her later work in institutions for people with retardation, Karen described some of her reactions to the practices there:

> I was horrified by the subnormality hospitals and fought against the routines of children being tied onto toilets for hours and hours on end and being fed on toilets and awful things.

For Karen, giving a home to a child with a handicap was a way of preventing those sorts of abuses.

Of the 42 families, it was only in 6, 14% of the sample, that neither parent had previous experience with handicaps. These six families were the exception and indeed five of them did not initially think about adopting a child with a handicap when they thought about adoption. It was only after they began to explore the field of adoption, learning what kinds of children were generally available, that adopting a child with a handicap became a viable possibility for them.

Knowing the Child

The sixth family in which neither parent had experience with handicaps prior to the placement of the child is a special case that warrants description. Audrey and Thomas Mueller had been foster parents for about 8 years when Evelyn first came to them on a short-term fostering basis. In addition to their three children by birth, they had looked after several dozen foster children over the years. Most of them had been infants and none of them were handicapped, according to the Muellers. However, when Evelyn came to live with them at only 2 months of age, she had already been diagnosed as spastic, with no possibility of ever walking. Her degree of mental handicap was unknown, but the prognosis was that it was probable and could be severe. Originally, Evelyn was to be with them for only 3 months, until the mother was able "to get on her feet again." However, the 3 months extended into a year, and when Evelyn's birth mother suggested that the

Muellers keep her permanently, they were attached enough to Evelyn to agree readily. Thus, although the Muellers had not had experience with handicaps prior to Evelyn's initial placement, they had had that experience by the time they actually considered adopting her. As Thomas Mueller said, "We couldn't think of us without her as time went by. She was a part of us."

The Muellers were not the only adopters who knew the child prior to the adoption and whose bonding with the child was perhaps the primary motive for the adoption. In all, there were five adoptive families in which the child was already known to the family prior to the decision to adopt. In two instances the child was being fostered by the family, initially on a short-term basis as with the Muellers.

In two other cases, the child became known to the mother through her work. For example, Peggy Floyd first met Betsy when Betsy was only 4 years old, living in the children's home in which Peggy worked. Peggy started taking Betsy home for weekends, feeling sorry for her because she never had any visitors. The whole family, including the Floyds' three birth children, became attached to Betsy and they made inquiries about fostering her. The assigned social worker, however, was against the move, and Betsy was moved to another children's home, with all contact between her and the Floyds broken. Twelve years later, Peggy saw Betsy's photograph in an article about children with mental handicaps who needed foster homes. She and her husband cried when they read that she had had 11 different moves and places of residence in about as many years. Although they were still disturbed about their earlier disappointment in trying to secure Betsy's placement with them, they immediately made inquiries about fostering her. This time they were approved rather quickly.

In two other families, the couples decided to adopt primarily because of infertility, but were not accepted by the agencies to which they made applications. As a result they tried alternative ways of caring for children. The Kimbles, described earlier in this chapter, are one of these families. After being discouraged about adoption, in part because of their age, they initiated a social contact with a child. Their bond with the child grew and they later decided to long-term foster her.

Experience with Adoption/Fostering

As mentioned above, most of the families had either personal or work experience with handicap. Another characteristic of many of the 42 families, although not a majority, was their previous experience with adoption or fostering. In 31% of the families the wife, the husband, or both were experienced with either adoption, fostering, or both. Three mothers had been adopted themselves, and one mother and one father had grown up with adopted siblings. These individuals expressed that adoption seemed like a way of life to them. Ten of the families, 42%, had previous experience as adoptive or foster parents—in most cases, as foster parents. Some of these families had been fostering during almost their entire marriage and, as briefly mentioned in Chapter 4, had fostered many dozens of children.

Combining the variables of previous experience with handicaps and previous experience with adoption or fostering yields a characteristic that is representative of almost all of the 42 families in this sample. There were only three families in which neither the husband nor the wife had had previous experience with either handicap, adoption, or fostering prior to considering the adoption of the handicapped child. Interestingly, it is one of these families that suffered the worst outcome of placement. Indeed, the adoption disrupted and less than a year after placement the child returned to the children's home in which he had been living. This case will be discussed in much greater detail in Chapter 9, in which the problems that the families experienced with the placements are examined.

In summary thus far, these families seem to be unusual in their degree of familiarity and experience with handicap, adoption, and fostering; although comparative data are not available, it seems safe to conclude that a totally random sample of 42 women and 37 men would not have the degree of familiarity that this sample had. Although informative, this characteristic is not in and of itself explanatory. After all, there are many nurses, special educators, physicians, physical therapists, and other men and women who work with people who are handicapped who would never seriously consider fostering or adopting one. Indeed, probably the majority of individuals involved in these professions and occupations have no desire to bring their work home with them.

Similarly, of the mothers and fathers who have given birth to a child with a handicap, how many go on to adopt another one? Again, the data are not available to answer that question conclusively, but surely it is a very small number. Thus, although these families' experiences with handicaps, adoption, or fostering seem to be an almost necessary condition of their willingness and often even eagerness to adopt a child who is retarded, it is clearly not a sufficient condition. Other factors usually accompanied this experience and familiarity, frequently providing additional impetus for the adoption. In the next sections, additional factors that seemed to motivate the adoption for many families are examined.

Wanting a Family

A simple motive for adopting a child, even a child who is handicapped, is that an individual or a couple might want a family or a larger family.

TABLE 5-1

Relation Between Children in the Family and Adopting to Increase Family Size

	Children already in family		
Wanted larger family	None	Some	Totals
No	6	9	15
Yes	9	18	27
Totals	15	27	42

Indeed, 27 respondents, 64% of the sample, mentioned this reason as a primary one for the adoption. As can be seen in Table 5-1, some of these families already had children and some did not. A nonsignificant X^2 suggested that there was no relationship between adopting a child because of wanting more children and whether or not there were already children in the family.

Although this result may seem counterintuitive, two factors help to explain it. First, for nine families the children in the family were either stepchildren or previously adopted or long-term fostered children rather than children born to both the mother and father. Several parents of stepchildren indicated that they wanted children that they could rear together from the beginning. Second, several families had children who were grown and either ready to leave home or already out of the home. These families expressed the desire for more children in order to continue their parenting role. Thus, families in both of these categories would have said that they wanted to increase their family size even though they already had children in the family.

Wanting to increase family size was unrelated to the presence of children already in the family. However, it was related to whether a family initially sought a child with a handicap. Table 5-2 presents the crosstabulation of these two variables. This table shows that families who primarily

TABLE 5-2

Relation Between Wanting a Child with a Handicap and
Adopting to Increase Family Size

	Initially sought child with a handicap		
Wanted larger family	No	Yes	Totals
No	1	14	15
Yes	16	11	27
Totals	17	25	42

adopted because they wanted to increase family size were not as likely to initially seek a child with a handicap as were families who did not mention increasing family size as a motive. A χ^2 analysis of these frequencies shows them to be significantly different from each other ($\chi^2 = 8.99$, $df = 1$, $p < .01$).

Commitment to Religious Ideals

A substantial minority of the adopters specifically mentioned religious values and principles in the context of why they would choose to adopt a child that many other families would be unwilling to raise. Ten respondents, 24% of the sample, directly mentioned religion in the context of one of the questions in the interview that probed for motivating factors. In addition, by considering responses to other items in the interview, three more adopters were assessed by raters to have had a commitment to religious ideals as an important motivating factor. Thus, 13 adoptive families, 31% of the sample, possessed religious principles and practices that were important in motivating them and committing them to the adoption of a child who was handicapped.

TABLE 5-3

Relation Between Religious Commitment and Adoption Motivation

	Religious Views Important?			
	Mothers (N = 42)		Fathers (N = 37)	
	Yes	No	Yes	No
Church Attendance				
< Weekly	0	23	0	21
≥ Weekly	13	6	12	4
Self-rated Religious Devotion				
Average or less	1	25	1	22
More than average	12	4	11	3

These adopters were substantially different from the rest of the sample in terms of their religious practices and their self-perceptions of religious commitment. As Table 5-3 shows, all of the 13 mothers and 12 fathers in this group reported that they participated in church activities at least once a week. These data are in marked contrast to the other 29 mothers and 25 fathers, who as a group attended church much less frequently. Only 21% of the mothers and 16% of the fathers in this less religiously committed group attended church with that frequency. Similarly, when asked to rate themselves as to degree of religious devotion, all but one of the mothers and one of the fathers rated themselves as more devoted than the average Briton. Again in contrast, in the less committed group only 14% of the mothers and 12% of the fathers rated themselves as that devoted.

Laura and Jonathan Atkinson represent one of the clearest examples of the importance of religious commitment in the motivation and support for the decision to adopt. Laura had done volunteer work with people with handicaps before her marriage and the birth of their two children. She said that she had always felt strongly about people with handicaps. "They needed a voice, because they hadn't one of their own," she commented. When she received a leaflet from one of the adoption societies describing some of the children with handicaps who were available, it immediately seemed like the right thing for them to do. When she broached the idea to Jonathan, his initial response was discouraging. "It seemed like a mad idea, at first," he volunteered in a description of his reaction.

But he began to contemplate it. Part of that contemplation was conversation with others, getting more information about mental handicaps. Another part of that contemplation was prayer. Both Jonathan and Laura mentioned the importance of their Christian beliefs as a determinant of their decision to adopt. Jonathan stated, "We had to be prepared to take whatever the Lord would give us." Despite the support of his religious beliefs, the decision was not an easy one for him. He worried about disrupting the tranquility of the home environment, about disturbing the peace. But he reasoned:

> I think we were challenged because I felt that's not the life I want, anyway. If the Lord has called us to work amongst people, then we can't, when we get home, say, well I'm sorry, mate, but I'm home.

Both Laura and Jonathan had doubts about what it would be like when the child grew up, about whether they'd always have a "child" living with them. Despite these doubts, however, Laura said, "We felt quite strongly that because of our faith that this would be the right thing for us to do."

Jonathan described the final conflict before making the decision. He had prayed and finally felt at peace with doing it. The next day, the church reading from Matthew 25 included the statement "Inasmuch as you've done this to the least of my brethren, you've done it to me." Jonathan felt that it was a message for him, reinforcing the decision to take on the task of helping one who needed it, despite that person's characteristics or seeming value to society.

Not all of the families who were coded as having been motivated by religious convictions were as obviously committed as the Atkinsons. For example, the Ellsworths never specifically mentioned religious beliefs as a factor that motivated them to adopt 3-year-old Daniel, a child with mental and physical handicaps. They maintained throughout their interview that their primary motivation was to have children together. Because this was a second marriage for both of them and they were in their forties, it seemed unlikely that they would have those children biologically, so they had turned to adoption. Nonetheless, they both attended church almost daily, saw themselves as very religious, and frequently responded to other questions by making reference to their religious beliefs. In this instance, although the Ellsworths themselves did not attribute their adoption of Daniel to any sort of religious commitment, that commitment seemed to give them the strength and support that they needed to cope with the rearing of a child who needed a great deal of medical and psychological support.

Commitment to Humanist Ideals

Many of the respondents who were not deeply religious nevertheless expressed many of the same values as did the religious Christian individuals in the sample. For them, the general motive of helping a child who desperately needed help was paramount in deciding to adopt a child with a handicap. More than half of the respondents, 22 of 42, mentioned that an important reason for the adoption was to help children in need. Ten of these families were also rated as deeply committed to religious principles, but the other 12 did not express strong religious convictions. They did, however, express values consistent with a humanitarian ethic. Geraldine and Donald Brook, already described in this chapter, are fairly typical of these 12 families who wanted to help children in need but did not express this value in the context of religious beliefs. Indeed, Geraldine, a Roman Catholic, considered herself only average in the degree of her religious devotion and went to church "maybe once a fortnight." Donald, raised in the Church of England, attended church services for religious festivals only and considered himself less religious than the average Briton.

Although their humanitarian motives were clear to the raters, the Brooks did not always directly admit them. Whereas Geraldine explicitly stated that they wanted more children, but they did not want to have any more birth children when there were so many needy children already in the world, Donald hastened to reassure the interviewer that they weren't "do-gooders"—they were really selfish. He explained:

> It's not social conscience or anything like that which people do tend to accuse you of . . . we just like kids. When it comes to kids, we're just big softies.

Linda and Vincent Johnson also talked about wanting to help children in need, but not in the context of religious values. Both nominally in the

Church of England, they said they never attended services and did not consider themselves particularly religious. Linda, however, had a very strong desire to help needy children. Even with four children born to them, all still quite young, they decided to adopt or foster an additional child or children. Linda attributed the strength of her commitment to help needy children to her own childhood difficulties. She described:

> . . . I had a very unhappy childhood. Although I lived with my natural parents, my father's health is, and always has been, very poor. My brother, who's younger than me, was a very sick child, and consequently they didn't really need me. You know, I was basically in the way most of the time. And quite frankly, I was knocked around considerably. In fact, in this day and age I would have probably been in care myself. I think, because I feel that I never really had a childhood, I've always felt that I ought to do something.

Linda continued to explain her emotional ties to children in need:

> I mean, I can't ever say I was never loved, because I was loved, but they just couldn't cope. They had so many stresses . . . they had so many problems, healthwise and financially, that they tended to have somebody to take it out on, and I was in the middle and it tended to be me, and I mean I've been knocked from one end of the room to the other, you know, and I think, mentally scarred, and I just feel that I have a lot in common with children who feel they're not wanted . . . you tend to feel that there's something different with you, you know, there's something wrong, and so therefore I feel . . . that I've got to do something to help them . . . I know what it's like to feel not wanted and it's the most appalling feeling for a child. I've got this great need in me to save a life—or save the world.

Personal and Emotional Experiences

Linda Johnson's motivation to help children in need obviously derived from a personal and emotional experience that she traced back to her own childhood. In precisely one-third of the families, 14 of the 42, either the husband or wife or both mentioned some salient experiences that had emotionally affected them in the direction of making them receptive to adopting a child with a handicap. In addition to Linda Johnson's story, Dorothy Oppler's is representative of this substantial minority. Born illegitimate, she was surrendered into care at birth, and adopted when she was

2 years old. This adoptive placement lasted until she was 10, when she was removed from her adoptive family because of the discovery by school officials that she was being both physically battered and sexually abused. She spent the rest of her childhood in care in a children's home. Dorothy had no doubt that this experience was significant in her decision to adopt. She felt that she was damaged by it, but that it enabled her to have a rapport with children who had had similar dreadful experiences.

Childhood Separations

Several other adoptive mothers and fathers also had had extended separations from their families during their childhood years. Three mothers and two fathers were separated from both parents, and five mothers and six fathers were separated from one parent during childhood. These separations were caused by a variety of circumstances, including the death of a parent, parents being unable to cope and putting the child into care, and work- or war-related separations. Most, but not all, of the adoptive parents attributed their desire to adopt a child with special needs at least in part to their childhood experiences of separation, as Linda Johnson did.

Peggy Floyd was one of the few who did not. Although she was separated from her father by his death and was later separated several times from her mother when the latter put her into care because she could not cope, Peggy did not think that these separations influenced her decision to adopt and foster. She described herself as a very placid child who had not been much bothered by the separations. She did admit, though, that she probably had more insight into children in care than she would have had without her childhood experiences.

A MODEL OF THE
ADOPTION DECISION

Thus far, a number of variables that seem to be related to the decision to adopt a child with handicaps have been examined. These variables include wanting a family and being unable to form one by bearing a child, commitment to a set of religious and/or humanitarian ideals, experience with handicap, experience with adoption or fostering, already knowing and having formed an attachment to a particular child, and personal/emotional experiences during childhood that seemed to provide a heightened sensitivity to the plight of children in need.

This study was not designed to assess the relative importance of each of these variables, nor indeed to determine whether any of them was either necessary or sufficient. However, some of the variables characterized such a large segment of the sample of 42 families that it does seem safe to speculate that if they were not actually necessary, they were at least strongly predisposing to the decision to adopt. For this reason, it seems instructive to suggest a model for how an adoption decision is made and what factors are important in that decision. Figure 5-1 presents such a model. On the left-hand side of the figure is a list of the predisposing factors that have been described in some detail in this chapter. This list is not meant to be all inclusive, nor does it allow the assessment at this point of the relative importance of these various factors. Rather, it should be regarded as heuristic, subject to a great deal of additional exploration and investigation. Although it would be surprising if any of these factors were to be deleted after further data gathering, surely additional factors might be added.

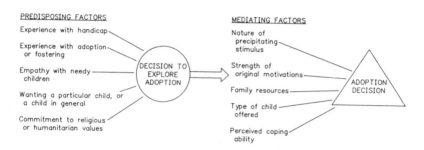

FIGURE 5-1.   Deciding to adopt a child who is handicapped. Predisposing and mediating factors are not necessarily exhaustive.

The predisposing factors illustrated in Figure 5–1 all lead to the decision to explore adoption. The process of that exploration will be examined in detail in the next chapter. For purposes of this model, however, it is crucial to recognize that for some families the outcome of that process is the decision to adopt a child who is handicapped, whereas for other families, indeed the large majority, the outcome is a decision *not* to adopt a child who is handicapped. On the right-hand side of Figure 5-1 is a list of variables that undoubtedly influence the final decision whether or not to adopt a specific child. For example, for many families in this study, the precipitating stimulus was in the form of an advertisement or a media appeal. Adoption agencies report that they frequently receive hundreds of inquiries after such an appeal. Only a very small number, however, actually result in the adoption of a child who is handicapped. On the other hand, if the original precipitating stimulus was more generic to the life of the family, such as the death of a son or daughter who was handicapped, then the exploration of adoption might be much more likely to result in a decision to adopt.

The importance of the strength of the original motivations seems rather obvious. Some individuals may have a vaguely conceived and perceived notion of wanting to help a child, or the world in general. Others, like Karen Norton, whose experience of and empathy with children in need went back to her earliest memories, possess deeply felt and long-held convictions that seem merely to await the right time to be translated into action.

This "right time" is clearly critical in determining the final decision to adopt. Alice Welker, for example, waited for 15 years before she was able to actualize her motivation; her resources did not allow her to make that commitment sooner. Other adopters reported similarly long periods between their first exploration and the time when they actually had a child placed with them. Frequently, it was a function of family resources and circumstances that caused the delay. Sometimes, however, it was a function of the adoption agencies themselves, the conclusions they came to, and the type of child that they offered the family. As described in the next chapter, some families ended up adopting a child with characteristics very different from the ones that they had originally imagined and stipulated. Many families to whom this happened probably dropped out of the process.

Finally, the parents' perceived coping ability most certainly interacted with one or more of these other variables to determine adoption outcome. When asked why they were willing to raise a child with a handicapping condition like that of their adopted child, 29% of the respondents said that they felt that they could cope, that they could handle the problems and difficulties. Brenda Romford's reply to this question makes her self-confidence and self-assurance quite clear:

> Must be mad, mustn't I? No, sometimes I do think I'm mad. I'm sure, put it this way, I'm sure I've got the capabilities. I'm perfectly competent in that respect, and I've got the patience, . . . and I'm sure I can push him to his full potential.

Many of the other mothers and fathers replied in a similar manner, emphasizing one or more characteristics that they possessed, such as patience, calmness, determination, or professional skills and knowledge, that would make it particularly easy for them to cope. These self-assessments frequently influenced their perception of how difficult it would be to raise the child. Indeed, a number of families said that their child didn't seem "all that different" from a normal child. With that perception, adopting a child who is handicapped would seem to differ little from adopting any other child. The amazement of others at the supposed burden adopters are assuming seems inappropriate, a misconstrual of the family environment and belief system.

As already implied, the depicted model is not meant to be either definitive or immutable. Rather, it is intended to summarize the findings from this research regarding motivations for adopting a child who is handicapped as well as offer some tentative descriptions of how those motivations operate in the process of decisionmaking. Additional research specifically designed to investigate more fully one or more of these factors will allow the model to change and expand. Families who have explored adoption but have decided not to adopt are especially important subjects of study. A comparison of families who do and families who do not make the final decision in favor of adoption should lead to more definitive conclusions concerning which predisposing factors and adoption decision variables are more or less important, which may be necessary, and which merely sufficient.

Chapter 6

Choosing
the Child

    Yvette and Sheldon Bixton were approaching their thirtieth birthdays. They had been married for 5 years and had been unsuccessfully trying to conceive a child for most of that time. Vaguely, they began to consider adoption as an alternative to secure the healthy, nonhandicapped baby that they had assumed they would have by birth. By generally being alert to news about adoption, they quickly learned that there were not many "nice, healthy, normal babies about." They talked about alternatives—an older child, a mixed-race child. They decided against an older child almost immediately. With a baby, "it's like having a clean slate," said Yvette. They talked longer about a child of mixed race, but finally decided that the child would never be accepted in the very conservative neighborhood in which they lived.

    After 4 years of discussion and a job-related move that made them postpone action for some months, Yvette saw an advertisement for Kevin, a baby with Down syndrome. They had never before considered a child with a mental handicap, but they realized that this was probably the only kind of baby that was going to be available. They both had work experience in the field of disability, so the characteristics were familiar to them. They decided to apply for Kevin, and within 2 months he was placed with them.

    A year later, after Kevin's adoption was legalized, the Bixtons began to discuss a second child. Still thinking about a normal, healthy baby, they started making the rounds of agencies. After exploring more than a half dozen and getting the same response of "Sorry" from all of them, they saw Mary's picture in a photo-book of children waiting for adoptive homes. She was a baby and had the same handicap as Kevin. They applied for her, and within months she was placed with them.

❏   ❏   ❏

The Lowells began to think about adoption within a year after the death of their son, born with Down syndrome. Although their initial thinking was about a "needy" child rather than a child with handicaps specifically, when they learned of the types of children available, they quickly decided that a child with retardation would be a perfect placement for them. After all, they had the experience and they also had Geoffrey, their other birth child, born with both physical and mental handicaps. Marty, diagnosed at birth as having a chromosomal translocation, was placed with them directly from the hospital, only several months after they had made application. A year later, 2-month-old Melanie, with Down syndrome, came to live with them. It was all done very quickly and expeditiously, in part because the Lowells insisted on getting the children as soon as possible.

❑   ❑   ❑

It was through her work as a special education teacher that Rochelle Packard first met Charles, a 6-year-old boy with a severe physical handicap and mild mental retardation. Charles was in a children's home, but had occasional contact with his biological father. When Rochelle changed jobs, she decided to maintain a relationship with Charles, and she became a social auntie, having him visit weekends and holidays. Their attachment to each other continued to grow and about a year later Rochelle decided to try to confirm her commitment to Charles by taking him on a long-term fostering basis. She was rejected, at first, by an agency that thought her attachment and emotional involvement with him was unhealthy. But she persisted; she found a social worker who was sympathetic, and when no other family emerged who was willing to take him on, Charles went to live with Rochelle on a permanent basis.

About a year after Charles had moved in, Rochelle decided that she wanted to do more and that it would be a positive experience for Charles to have a companion. Thomas, only a year younger than Charles but severely mentally handicapped, came to live with them soon thereafter. Rochelle wasn't sure that taking a child with severe retardation was the right decision, but she had been persuaded that her original intention of another boy with physical handicaps was foolish. Two wheelchairs were more than she could handle, people told her.

❑   ❑   ❑

Frances and Kenneth Travert did not marry until they were in their forties. Past the age when they were likely to have birth children, they thought almost immediately of adoption. They went to their local agency, were approved, and then began the search for the right child. They made inquiries about two sisters who were advertised in an adoption information book, but they had already been placed. The agency that had made the placement, however, had a sibling group of four that they were trying to keep together and place with one family. The Traverts' initial reaction was one of apprehension. Going from no children to four, all teenagers, seemed as if it would be more of a challenge than they could handle. They continued to talk about it, however, and finally made a tentative decision. It was then that they found out that Peter, one of the two boys, was mentally handicapped. At that point, however, they did not consider changing their decision. It was probably the last chance that these children were going to have, and the Traverts were determined to give it to them.

❏   ❏   ❏

The stories of these four families indicate the substantial variability in the way a particular child came to live with a particular family. In some cases, the child was markedly different from the original ideal that family members had conceptualized when they first began thinking about adoption; in other cases the child was quite similar to that ideal. In some instances, the period of time from the beginning of adoption exploration to child placement was very long; in others, it was quite short. In some cases, the child was already known to the family; in most families, the child was an unknown. This chapter discusses these and other aspects of choosing the child, an obviously important process in the totality of the adoptive placement. Regardless of motives and context, people in general like to believe that they have freedom of choice in making decisions. They like to believe that they have control over outcome. In the context of adoptive placement, choice and control is exercised primarily in the decision of whom to adopt, the decision of choosing the child.

ORIGINAL IDEAL

As described in Chapter 5, a large minority of adopters, 40%, did not initially think of a child with handicaps when they first thought about adoption. For many of these 40%, including the Bixtons, their first image was of a healthy, normal, white baby. Clearly, then, there was a substantial difference between the child whom they eventually adopted and what they had at first envisioned as the child that they wanted. Even with the 60% of families who wanted a child with handicaps from the outset, the child who was eventually placed with them was not necessarily similar to the child that they had first imagined. For example, when deciding to long-term foster a second child, Rochelle Packard distinctly thought of another child with physical handicaps. Charles, the first child placed with her, although mildly mentally handicapped, was, in Rochelle's view, primarily physically handicapped. Thus, when she thought of another child, in part motivated by the desire for a companion for Charles, she thought of a child like Charles. Thomas, the second child to be placed, was severely mentally retarded, but not physically handicapped.

Laura and Jonathan Atkinson had also initially wanted a child with handicaps. Indeed, they had told their social worker that they wanted a child with severe handicaps, one that nobody else would take. They definitely did not want a blue-eyed, blond-haired baby with Down syndrome who seemed, in looks and behavior, almost normal. Andrew, only 7 months old at placement, was very close in appearance to that blue-eyed, blond-haired, normal-looking child that they had specifically said that they did not want!

Rochelle Packard and Laura Atkinson are typical of approximately 56% of the placements in which a mother had a preconceived image of the child that the child did not match. The data for fathers are quite comparable, with 58% of the fathers having initial images that did not match the child who was eventually placed with them. Given this lack of correspondence between the target child and the maternal and paternal images, it is not surprising that for 48% of the target children, the parents had some reservations about the child when he or she was initially suggested for placement. Indeed, for 15% of the children, the initial parental response was very negative. This initial negative response, however, seemed to have no predictive value for placement outcome, as described in Chapters 8 and 9.

RESTRICTIONS

In addition to having definite images of what the child should be, most of the families had ideas of what the child should not be. Fewer than 10% of the respondents reported that they would take virtually any child who was offered. All of the other families imposed some restrictions in terms of age, sex, race, type of handicap, and severity of handicapping condition. Thus, although many of these families were willing to adopt or foster a very hard to place child, they were not willing to adopt or foster any child.

Age Restrictions

Only 14% of the mothers and 24% of the fathers had no restriction regarding the age of the child that they would be willing to adopt. The most common restriction, stated by approximately one-third of both mothers and fathers, was a child as young as possible. The following comments from different respondents are fairly typical of the subgroup who wanted a very young child:

". . . The younger you have them, the more chance you have of bringing them up your way rather than someone else's."

"Like everyone else we wanted a normal baby in arms, but there's a shortage."

"We would have liked to have it as young as possible, yes. You know, in the streets where we lived we had some teenage children who came in sometimes . . . and I got on quite well with them, but I . . . would really have felt awkward with a 15-year-old boy . . ."

"We thought as young as possible. Our oldest child is very much the older brother of the family, and we didn't want to go above him, or even between our boys, because they're quite close."

As illustrated by the quotations, there seemed to be two dominant reasons for families imposing an age restriction on the potential adoptee. Many of the families expressed the belief that the younger the child, the more likely they could have an impact on him or her, raising the child according to their own style. This rationale is identical to ones that have been expressed by adoptive parents in general, whether or not the child is handicapped (Kornitzer, 1952, p. 30). The reasoning is usually expressed as some variant of "if the child is young, it's more similar to having given birth; you can mold it better." Occasionally, a respondent supplied the rationale in a somewhat more negative fashion, suggesting that with an older child it was more likely that previous events in the child's life would cause difficult behavior or emotional problems.

As in the last quotation above, sometimes families expressed a desire for a young child because of the age of existing children in the family. Again, it has been long considered good adoption practice not to disturb a child's ordinal position in the family. The eldest should remain the eldest, and younger children should not have new older siblings (Kornitzer, 1952, p. 151). Clearly, some families had assumed this view and restricted themselves to adopting a child younger than the youngest child already in the family.

In addition to wanting a child as young as possible, it was quite common for families to put a general age limit on the child they were willing to adopt. Approximately one-third of the respondents gave quite a large age range that would be acceptable, but specified that they would not adopt a child older than a particular age. This upper age limit varied from family to family, but the large majority of families were not willing to take on a teenager. Their reasons were similar to the ones already described for the respondents who wanted a child as young as possible. They felt that a teenager was already almost fully formed and might have difficult and unchangeable behaviors. An additional reason mentioned by some respondents is that a teenager would not be with the family for very long, but would be ready to move into some other residential setting in just a few years. Given the trend for out-of-family residential placements in some variant of a group home (Bruininks, Hauber, & Kudla, 1980), an age restriction for this reason indicated a realistic awareness of current treatment modes for adults who are mentally retarded.

Although most adopters wanted a young child, some age restrictions were specifically for an older child. The Cookseys, for example, had a birth child with retardation who was a teenager at the time they decided to explore giving a home to another child with mental retardation. They clearly wanted someone who was very close in age to the child already in the family. In addition, Rochelle Cooksey, over 50 and having raised four children, said (not unreasonably):

> I've had enough of running after children you've got to watch continuously . . . I wanted somebody with a certain amount of responsibility.

Sex Restrictions

Fewer mothers and fathers expressed restrictions regarding the child's sex than the child's age. Slightly less than one-third of the parents had a preference for adopting a girl or a boy. The preferences were not markedly different in favor of one sex or the other; while seven of the families who expressed a preference preferred a girl, five preferred a boy. This lack of difference contrasts with the usual preference for girls that historically has been present among families who are applying to adopt nonhandicapped children (Bohman, 1970, p. 186; Kornitzer, 1952, p. 169). Of course, contemporaneously, many applicants are aware of the shortage of children and have undoubtedly suppressed some preferences they might have had if many children had been readily available.

The families in the present sample who preferred either a boy or a girl sometimes had definable and expressible reasons for this preference and sometimes did not. For those families who did have reasons that they could verbalize, the sex of existing children in the family was usually a factor. The Cookseys, for example, definitely wanted a girl because they thought she'd be more likely to get on better and have more in common with their daughter, who is retarded. Another family already had three boys, and wanted a girl for the experience of rearing a daughter. Only one mother stated that she preferred a child of one sex over another because she thought that a child of that sex would be easier to raise. She said:

> . . . We thought that a boy would probably be easier, going through puberty. We thought he wouldn't be quite as much worry as a girl. A girl has got to be difficult enough anyway, and I thought that a handicapped girl would be more difficult.

Although she did not directly say it, and the interviewer did not go on to explore this area, it is not difficult to infer that this mother may be worrying about emerging sexuality in adolescence and the possibility of pregnancy for a girl.

All but one of the families who expressed a preference for one sex or the other adopted a child of that preferred sex. In the family that got a child of the other sex, the preference seemed to be weak, ill-defined, and not based on any particular family circumstance. Valerie and Paul Underwood, with three daughters born to them, had originally wanted another girl. However, when Alex was suggested to them, they did not hesitate because he was a boy. In addition, a few years later, when they decided to adopt another child with a handicap, they had changed their preference to a boy.

Race Restrictions

Although all but two of the families adopted children of Caucasian origin, only 18% of the families admitted to a race restriction. All of these families except one presented the restriction in terms of the welfare of the child. The following comments from respondents are typical:

> "This is a very white district. It would be unfair for the child."
> "We knew the grandparents wouldn't accept a colored child, and that's important."

"We didn't think it was suitable to . . . colored children, not that we have any prejudices along those lines, but they really would stick out in this sort of an area."

In the one family where the restriction was not couched in terms of the welfare of the child, the mother said that she would not mind a racially different child and in fact had even suggested it, but her husband was against it, "putting his foot down."

In addition to the relatively large number of families who said they would be willing to accept a racially different child, two families actively sought a child of this type. One family originally began to explore adoption with a Vietnamese child in mind, and the other family specifically wanted a colored (African, Indian, etc.) child. This last family did, in fact, adopt racially different children.

Type of Handicap Restriction

Almost all of the families who adopted a child not already known to them prior to initiating adoption exploration stated that they had some restriction regarding type of handicap. Only four families did not mention a type of handicap restriction. These restrictions were quite idiosyncratic to particular families and varied greatly among families. Perhaps the most striking between-family variability was the restriction regarding adoption of a child with Down syndrome. Some families wanted no handicap other than Down syndrome, whereas other families refused to consider a child with Down syndrome. The statements below illustrate these different attitudes. The first three are from families who stated that they would adopt only a child with Down syndrome:

"My husband and I have always worked with handicapped children, especially Down's. We felt that when the time was right we would want to foster or adopt one."

"We know a lot of Down's syndrome people and what they are like, and you know, we just fell in love with Down's syndrome. . . . They seemed so lovable."

"When you don't know the reason for the handicap, it's hard to know what they'll grow up to be like. There's more certainty with Down's syndrome."

In contrast, Florence Vance had adopted Nicole, a child whose retardation was moderate at the time of adoption, but because of her background of neglect and deprivation might improve with an improved environment.

Florence said that she would not want to adopt a child with Down syndrome, and elaborated:

> With Nicole there's a lot of unknowns, and although that might make for insecurities, it also makes for hope, and although people who have Down's children or work with Down's children would say that you can't write a child off—there is a lot of hope, there's a lot of potential—it seemed to me to be a very sort of definite commitment to a child who was going to be permanently handicapped.

Thus, Florence Vance felt that an uncertain prognosis was, in this instance, better than a more definite prognosis.

Other families did not want to live with the uncertainty of a vague prognosis or of limited life expectancy. Several respondents specifically mentioned that they did not want a child with a known defect that might result in early death. They felt that it would be difficult to live with the knowledge that tragedy might befall them at any moment. Several of these respondents had already experienced the death of a child and expressed the sentiment that they did not want to live through such an experience again. For example, the Lowells, whose biological child with Down syndrome died following surgery to correct a heart defect, specified that they would not accept a child with heart problems.

Although some families stated that they could accept a child with mental or physical handicaps, other families stipulated that the child could not be physically handicapped. Several parents talked about weak backs and the inability to lift a child once he or she was older and larger. Some mothers and fathers specifically mentioned their houses and the architectural barriers that would make it impossible to care for a child who was nonambulatory. Other respondents talked about the difficulties of fitting a child with physical handicaps into the family's lifestyle. For example, the Youngs, an active family with two nonhandicapped birth children, had this to say:

> . . . there was a lot of physically handicapped children on holiday, and we began to realize that it wouldn't be right, because we could see the parents struggling to get the children down on the beach, and you know, and we felt with our children . . . being very active . . . that if we had a physically handicapped child in our family, it would probably feel outclassed. If we had a mentally handicapped child, they would be able to feel more part of us and do what we do, even though it would be slower.

In addition to families specifying a type of mental or physical handicap that they did or did not want, 12 families volunteered that they would not accept a child with severe behavioral or emotional problems. This restriction was frequently put in the context of such a child creating too many difficulties for other children in the family. Sometimes the parents frankly admitted that there were some behaviors with which they did not think they could cope. Behaviors such as violence and hyperactivity were mentioned, as were emotional problems that would render the child unresponsive to love and affection.

Severity of Handicap Restriction

Even when parents did not specify a restriction with respect to type of handicapping condition, they frequently offered the qualification that they would not adopt a child with a very severe handicap. A large majority of the families, 83%, expressed this restriction. Sometimes the restriction was described in terms of a specific severe handicap, and sometimes the respondents stated that they would not be willing to accept a child with any type of severe handicapping condition. The following comments are illustrative of this prevailing attitude:

"I think I would have had difficulty in accepting a child who is, say, doubly incontinent—not because of the incontinence, but because of the inconvenience that goes with it. And there was another type of chap that we came across, he was so badly brain damaged that he wasn't even able to recognize even the people he was closest to. I think that would have been very difficult to accept. I suppose in a way it's being selfish, you like a little bit back from the child, you know, if you give them so much."

"I think a severe physical handicap would be one that we wouldn't really like to cope with, or one that would be nasty to look at; I'm very squeamish. Or anything like a child you couldn't really communicate to. We felt we weren't equipped for nursing."

"We were open for a blind or deaf child, or for certain medical handicaps. We wouldn't have accepted anything that would have presented problems too difficult for us to handle in a realistic way . . . we couldn't cope with a severely mentally handicapped child, for example, a mongol child."

"Possibly a child who is really a vegetable. I think I might have a great deal of difficulty coping with that."

Many of these families who set restrictions on the severity of the handicapping condition nevertheless frequently accepted children with quite severe handicaps. For example, the final quotation above is from Linda Johnson, who adopted Nicholas, a child with severe mental retardation and autism who exhibited many psychotic behaviors when he first came into the family.

In summary, although the 42 families all adopted children who were diagnosed as mentally handicapped, these families differed considerably in the type of child they had originally imagined as well as in how closely the children who were placed with them matched that image. They also differed in what restrictions they placed upon the characteristics of the child and in how steadfastly they held to those restrictions. In the next section, the way in which the target child was actually presented to the families is explored, as well as the family responses that resulted in a positive placement decision.

PLACEMENT PROCESS

Rapidity

Although some families or individuals in the sample thought about adoption long before a child was placed with them, the time between a family's actual initial inquiries to an adoption agency and the target child's entrance into the home was usually quite brief. The interview data did not allow precise scoring of this variable for all of the sample families, but a few anecdotal cases are illustrative. Alice Welker, for example, had been thinking about adoption for approximately 15 years, but she did not actually make any inquiries until about a year before Elizabeth was placed with her. She initially contacted her local authority, the British equivalent to a state or local department of social services in the United States. They conducted interviews and three different children were considered by them for placement with Alice. For various reasons, none of these children were actually placed with her, and after several months the local authority referred her to another agency that specialized in children who were hard to place. Elizabeth was the first child considered with the second agency, and was in Alice's home within months.

Similarly, the Lowells experienced fairly rapid placement of both of their adopted children once they made the initial inquiry. They adopted from the only agency that they contacted and the first placement was made in less than a year after their initial inquiry. Indeed, Marty came to live with them when he was only a week old, placement being made directly from the hospital in which he was born.

Frequently, the rapidity of placement was related to the types of children the family said it was willing to accept and the relative availability of children with those characteristics. The Hiltons, for example, unable to have biological children, originally thought of adopting a nonhandicapped baby. They applied to six different agencies over a period of about 4 years before Adam, a baby with Down syndrome, was placed with them. It seems that once they became more flexible about the type of child they were willing to accept, placement occurred rather rapidly. However, the Hiltons did not see Adam as being substantially different from a normal child, from the child that they had originally imagined 4 years earlier. As Thelma Hilton explained in describing her reaction to a child with Down syndrome:

> They didn't seem too bad, no worse really than a normal child except they just need more attention, of course, and you got to work with them harder.

Mr. Hilton affirmed his wife's remarks:

> Well, they are normal children when you look at it. The only thing is they're just lower learning. This is the way I see it.

Thus, the perceptions of potential adopters regarding a child's handicapping characteristics may be markedly different from the perceptions of agency workers or others. In the case of the Hiltons, it is possible that they could have accepted a child with a handicap several years earlier if one had been offered to them.

Occasionally, placement was slower than the family desired, even when the family wanted a child with a handicap. This pace was, in part, a function of what kind of restrictions the family held. For example, adoption agency workers report that there has been a definite trend in the last decade for easier and easier placement of children with Down syndrome, especially if they are babies and have no associated congenital defects. In fact, one agency that specializes in working with the most hard-to-place children limits the number of children with Down syndrome that it will work with because these children are now much easier to place than many others. This trend was confirmed by several families who reported having to wait quite a while before a child with Down syndrome became available. For example, Karen Norton said that she "rang around" the local authorities for a child with Down syndrome and found that there weren't any. "They seem to be in demand," she added.

This reduced availability may be related to more prospective adopters being willing to accept a child with Down syndrome. It may also be a function of changing attitudes about mental retardation in general. As discussed in Chapter 2, professionals may be less likely than in previous times to recommend abandoning a child with handicaps when it is born, and more likely to encourage the birth family to rear the child in the home environment. Increased services contribute to the ease of homerearing, and it is likely that fewer babies with Down syndrome are being given up by their birth families.

Agency Role

All of the 42 families in the present sample adopted their children through agencies, either a local authority or a voluntary (private) adoption society. Sometimes the agency that studied and approved the family also worked with the child and sometimes the child was under the auspices of a different agency. Some families made their contact with the British Agencies for Adoption and Fostering (BAAF), a central clearinghouse whose function is to bring together families who want to adopt and waiting children who need homes, regardless of the geographical distance between the two.

The adoption situation is quite similar in the United States. Public agencies, adoption units of local or state departments of social services, and private agencies all handle adoptions, including the adoption of children who are handicapped. Private agencies that specialize in the placement of children with special needs, such as Spaulding for Children with branch offices all around the country, are involved in many of the adoptions of children who are retarded. The Council on Adoptable Children (COAC), supported by government grants and private funds, like BAAF in Great Britain is a national clearinghouse that serves as a resource on children available for adoption for agencies all over the country.

Even though all the families in the current sample adopted through agencies, the parents' views of the role of the agency or agencies with which they worked were variable. Whereas some families felt that the agency was relatively unimportant other than in offering the child and performing the paperwork necessary for processing the application, other families were laudatory in describing the social workers' helpfulness during the period of child selection. They frequently emphasized how much information, support, and guidance the agency workers provided, and how sometimes these workers helped them reach a decision that they might have been unable to reach on their own. Even the 48% of families who said that the agency's role was relatively unimportant in their making the decision to adopt the target child sometimes praised individual workers for postadoption support, an area to be explored in Chapter 8. Almost no families reported negative attitudes about the adoption agencies in their work with families in choosing the child. In fact, the following quotation is the most negative comment made in this regard:

> I think we would have adopted, if we could, without them. They were unimportant. I knew we'd be all right as parents. It was just convincing everybody else.

The Role of Nonagency People in Making the Decision

In making the decision to adopt a child who is handicapped in general or a specific child who is handicapped, many parents consulted or at least discussed their intentions with relatives, friends, or professionals who were not involved in the placement of the child. Sometimes the parents were looking for guidance and support in coming to a decision and sometimes they seemed merely to be explaining their decision to significant others. The attitudes they encountered from nonagency persons were sometimes helpful and encouraging and sometimes destructive and discouraging. Almost half of the sample, 48%, said that they had talked with at least one person who had discouraged them from adopting a child with handicaps. For example, Dorothy Oppler, a single adopter, said that several close friends had warned her against the adoption—they said she would waste her life. Although Dorothy was disturbed by their reactions, she felt that she had to make her own decisions. "It's my life," she maintained.

Similarly, Isabel Gross reported that some of the family's friends were negative, literally waiting for them to collapse. She thought that that attitude made her and her husband even more determined to do it because they wanted to prove these people wrong.

Several respondents described comments from friends that, although on the surface did not seem discouraging, had the effect of being so. These comments were of the "Oh, aren't you wonderful; I couldn't do it" variety. The adopters said that when other people expressed that feeling, it made them realize that these people saw them as taking on some tremendous burden, and that sometimes made them doubtful about their decision.

In addition to experiencing discouraging attitudes from friends, 29% of the adoptive families were discouraged by relatives. The following quotations are illustrative of the way in which respondents described these attitudes:

> "My husband's parents were totally against it. Absolutely against it, right up until the moment they saw Kevin."

"My father was dead against it. . . . People expect a screwed-up baby who couldn't move."

"Lawrence's grandfather tried to discourage us. He said he knew you could get babies."

"My parents were absolutely devastated. They could hardly bear the idea."

"Some of the relatives said that they didn't know why, especially when we came with a Down's child. They said every time you were expecting a child you were praying that everything goes well, and then you go and do something like that."

Despite these negative attitudes, these families obviously went ahead with the adoptions. In part, this decision was related their being able to discount the importance of the negative attitudes. Frequently, respondents commented that they did not take the remarks too seriously, because these people did not really know what they were talking about. In the case of negative reactions from the adopters' own parents, respondents often said that their parents were just trying to be cautious and protective. Pervasive among the adopters was the belief that you have to live your own life and not pay too much attention to what other people think.

Many families were also able to discount the discouraging attitudes because other friends, relatives, and professionals were encouraging. Almost all of the families who reported that some people were discouraging also described the reactions of others who were very supportive. For example, it was not unusual for one set of parents to be discouraging and the other set to be encouraging. Similarly, whereas some friends were negative, others were positive. One mother divided her friends into the Christians, who were supportive, and the non-Christians, who were waiting for the family to disintegrate under the burden.

Nonagency professionals who were consulted also varied in their attitudes. If a family consulted an outside professional, it was usually a medical person, a clergyman, or a teacher. Some of them were quite cautious, painting what many parents described as an unnecessarily bleak picture of the family's future life; others were very enthusiastic, encouraging the adopters in their decision, offering information to them in the present, and promising aid in the future. This variability was also typical of the reactions of professionals after the child was placed in the home and is described in some detail in Chapters 8 and 9.

MEETING THE CHILD

Thus far in this chapter various aspects of the decision to adopt a child who is mentally handicapped have been described. Most parents had an image of the child that they wished to adopt, and most mentioned restrictions, characteristics that would be unacceptable. Many parents engaged in extensive introspection and discussion with others prior to making their decisions. Ultimately, however, regardless of the attitudes of others and of their own ideals, parents frequently made the decision to adopt a specific child based on a reaction akin to falling in love. This emotion was activated sometimes by seeing a photo of the child and sometimes by meeting the child. These reactions occurred frequently, but there were instances in which they did not occur and the family went ahead with the adoption nonetheless.

Initial Description

In slightly more than half of the adoptions, the parents first heard about the child as a result of an advertisement or by examining a photo book of children available for adoption. Photo books are quite commonly used in placing children with special needs both in Great Britain and in the United States. They offer prospective parents a catalogue of the types of children who are currently available, and they also provide them with a concrete image that parents report is very valuable. They may also facilitate the "falling in love" process. Even a child with quite severe handicaps can look very appealing in a photograph and can arouse a strong desire to nurture. This feeling of nurturance becomes very difficult to deny in a later, perhaps more intellectual, decisionmaking process.

The families who did not initially learn about their child from an advertisement or photobook were told about him or her by a social worker. These initial descriptions were usually quite brief, including, of course, age, sex, and details about handicapping conditions, but sometimes not much else. They were used as a screening device to assess whether the parents were interested. When interest was expressed, more information was supplied.

Families were generally pleased with the way in which agencies presented the children, with the exception of several families who thought that the child was portrayed too negatively. These families said that the social worker talked only about what the child could not do, rather than what the child was capable of doing. If the perceptions of these families are accurate, the workers' behaviors are also understandable in the context of the placement. Clearly, it is the responsibility of the agency workers to make certain that adoptive parents are fully aware of the child's level of functioning and limitations. It is possible that in fulfilling this responsibility, they created an overly pessimistic view of what to expect. Better that than false expectations, they might reply.

Initial Meeting

It was usually at the first meeting that the falling in love took place. The story told by Donald and Geraldine Brook is quite typical of the many poignant descriptions given by adoptive parents of their reactions to seeing the child for the first time. The Brooks were described at the beginnings of Chapters 4 and 5. With two biological children, they had decided they wanted a larger family, but that it was unfair to have more by birth because there were already so many needy children waiting for the kind of loving home life that they could provide. They became directly involved when Geraldine responded to a television advertisement. "He looked so lost; I wanted to help that little boy," she said.

Although an adoptive family had already been selected for that child, they began to work with the agency toward placement. When a baby with Down syndrome was suggested to them they were open, but they didn't know much about Down syndrome. They were taken to see Annette at her foster home against Donald's better judgment. He thought it was emotional blackmail. "Once you'd seen her," he said, "it's hard to forget." Geraldine affirmed his position:

I just fell in love with her. She touched my face and she smiled. . . . When she smiled at me, that was it; I was lost.

Donald added:

You've got that bond, once you've seen her. You couldn't walk away.

Nevertheless, they did walk away—but not very far, nor for very long. The agency wanted a decision by the next morning, and after staying up all night discussing it, the Brooks decided that they didn't know enough to make a commitment. "You can't let your heart rule your head," Donald explained. They telephoned the next day with a refusal. Geraldine continued with the story:

When we said no, we thought it was finished, but I couldn't get her out of my mind. Neither could he, but we never said anything to each other.

Both of them began independently to talk to friends about it. Everyone seemed to know someone who had a child with Down syndrome, and everyone seemed to have positive reactions. They took some books out of the library and began to read. The more they read, the more positive they became. About a week later, Donald's mother, who had listened to each of them, said:

> Well, you are both saying the same thing; you want to do it. Why don't you say yes?

And they did say yes, phoning the agency with their changed decision. Annette was still available and was placed with them not long thereafter. Almost 2 years later, at the interview, they expressed no regrets about Annette's adoption and were obviously still very much in love with her.

The Underwoods reported an experience similar to that of the Brooks. Initially negative about a child with Down syndrome when it was suggested by their agency, they began to read a bit and made efforts to meet children with Down syndrome and their parents. Through this process of familiarizing themselves, they became positive, so when Alex was suggested to them they wanted to see him as soon as possible. Valerie was worried about her reaction, though. "What if I see him and can't love him?" she thought. They did go to meet him, bringing their three birth children along. Valerie described her first reaction:

> He looked awful weedy, and very pimply, and really had arms like wool, you know, very floppy . . . and I just saw him and I knew he was ours.

She continued:

> We were allowed to take him out in the car, and while we came out a wasp came and stung him near the eyes and we just all stood around that pram and we cried, really.

Thus, in the case of the Underwoods, the falling in love seems to have occurred in spite of a first meeting in which the child looked quite unattractive. Other parents also described how an initial appearance suggesting that the child was pathetic, and in need of care, was instrumental in their strong emotional reactions.

The men and women in this sample are in no way unique in this regard. For example, in former times adoptive parents might go to an orphanage and choose the child they wanted from among several. They did not always select the child who presented the best appearance. Frequently, they would choose the one who seemed to need the most care (Kornitzer, 1952, p. 117).

In the present sample, choosing a needy child was not always a result of falling in love, either. Sometimes the child aroused pity or a sense of challenge in the prospective adopters. The Johnsons represent such a case. Linda Johnson described the first meeting with Nicholas as follows:

> When we first met him he was in the children's home. He'd got hold of a pot of vaseline in the night and he'd smothered himself with it, and they'd bathed him sort of six times, and they were unable to get it out of his hair. He had this enormous black eye where he'd fallen and caught his face against a radiator; he was pathetically thin, really white . . . and it made his features seem huge . . . he really looked a mess, and he was wearing a dreadful jumper which was all eaten away, because at that stage he used to eat, or chew his clothes. . . . He was screaming the entire time, and we took him out for 10 minutes; we took him to the park, and it was very difficult. He just kept trying to pull away and then he was trying to kick. . . . Basically, to look at him, he was really like the living dead, because his eyes were so blank, but there was something there that you felt you could work on, do you know what I mean? So we decided then that we would take a chance.

It wasn't always the case that parents experienced an immediate bond or rapport with the child or much of any positive response, even one of determined commitment as described by Linda Johnson. Indeed, some parents reported quite negative initial reactions. The Atkinsons, for example, said that on first meeting him, Andrew looked very ugly to them, not beautiful at all. He had hardly any hair, and his forehead seemed huge. They couldn't understand how his foster parents thought him beautiful. "We were shocked at his physical appearance," Jonathan Atkinson said. Whereas this appearance did not lead them to reject Andrew, neither did it arouse parental feelings that made them more eager to nurture him.

SUMMARY AND CONCLUSIONS

There was substantial variability among the 42 adoptive families in all of the circumstances relating to choosing the child. For some families, the child or children actually placed with them were very similar to their original images; in other families, the children were quite unlike those images. For some families, placement was very rapid once they had made an initial inquiry; for others, the placement process was prolonged. Some adopters contacted many agencies before a placement was made, and other adopters worked with the first and only agency they contacted.

While they were involved in the process of deciding to adopt a child with a handicap, some adopters got support and encouragement from relatives, friends, and other individuals, whereas other adopters encountered mostly discouraging and negative responses from others. Finally, for some families the initial meeting with the child was a time of joy, signaling affirmation and the strengthening of their commitment. For other families, this first meeting was a shock, a confrontation with the reality of the child and his or her less-than-perfect characteristics. Undoubtedly, the differences in these reactions may reside, in part, in the differences among the adopters themselves who, although similar in that they have all adopted children who are retarded, are also very different in many characteristics, as described in Chapters 4 and 5. Another locus of difference, however, is the children. Although the children all share retardation as a common feature, they are also very different in many characteristics. In the next chapter, the focus is on the children—who they are, where they had been, and why they were available for adoption or fostering.

Chapter 7
The Children

Annette was born at only 7 months' gestation, weighing 3 lbs., 9 oz. It was not an exceptionally low birthweight given her prematurity and the fact that she was a twin. Annette and her twin brother were, of course, fraternal twins, and therefore not expected to be any more similar than average siblings. Indeed, in this case they might be expected to be quite dissimilar, because Annette was born with Down syndrome and her twin was not.

The Down syndrome was diagnosed immediately and Annette's birth parents, particularly her father, reacted strongly and negatively. Well educated themselves, they saw no place for a child with mental retardation in their lives. Annette's father was adamant about not acknowledging the child. "Come home with two children and no husband or one child and a husband," he told his wife while she was still in the hospital.

Annette stayed in the hospital for 2 months and then went to a foster family. But her birth parents had not totally abandoned their responsibility to her. They took her from the foster family and tried caring for her. They realized quite soon, however, that it was not going to work, and they made arrangements for her to return to her foster family. She remained in that home until she went to the Brook family for adoptive placement when she was just a little over a year old.

During her 8 months of living with her adoptive family, Annette had made excellent developmental progress. At 13 months she was unable to sit unsupported or hold objects in both hands simultaneously. At 21 months she was feeding herself with hand and spoon, walking with minimal help, taking occasional steps on her own, and climbing stairs. Although she did not yet exhibit expressive language, she understood simple words and commands. The Brooks were very pleased with her progress.

❏   ❏   ❏

Daniel had just celebrated his first birthday when he became acutely ill. Following admission to the hospital, diagnosis was a

brain tumor that had to be surgically removed for him to survive.
The operation successfully removed the tumor, but in the process
destruction of visual cortex brain tissue left him blind. In addition,
mental retardation and medical difficulties arising from pituitary
gland dysfunction were diagnosed as a result of the tumor and
surgery.

It was more than Daniel's mother could cope with. She had
separated from her husband when Daniel first entered the hospital,
and she knew that she wouldn't be able to handle on her own a
child who was blind and retarded with severe medical problems.
So, after more than a year in the hospital, Daniel was released to
a foster family on a short-term care basis. After 6 months, that
placement ended and Daniel went to a residential children's
nursery. It was there that the Ellsworths first met him about a year
later.

At age 5, when he had been with the Ellsworths for almost a
year, Daniel was active and mobile. Although still walking with a
toddler-like gait, neither this awkwardness nor his blindness
seemed to inhibit his movement. He roamed around his environment quite freely, hands outstretched—perhaps to avoid injury,
perhaps to aid in object exploration. Although still lacking
expressive language, Daniel vocalized quite a bit and seemed to
understand many of the commands given by his parents. When
he began a stereotyped head nodding, a firm "stop" from his
mother or father resulted in immediate cessation of the behavior.

❏   ❏   ❏

Roy was not a first child, but his birth was not easy, physically
or psychologically. Born by Caesarian section, he returned home
to a family in which the parents had newly separated. Roy seemed
to be the primary victim of the family's difficulties and was admitted
to the hospital when he was only 9 weeks old. He was malnourished, dehydrated, and covered with bruises signaling
extensive injury to many parts of the body, including the head.
There seemed to be little doubt that this was an instance of neglect
and abuse, and Roy was removed from the care of his parents
because of it.

Roy remained in the hospital for several months, regaining his
health. By this time, however, the diagnoses of physical and mental
handicaps were definite, most likely the result of nonaccidental
injury. Rather than return him to the same abusive environment,
officials transferred Roy to a residential nursery for the next year
and thereafter to a children's home that specialized in the care of

children with handicaps. Nonambulatory and with very primitive speech, he was severely mentally and physically handicapped when at age 7 he first met Isabel and Fred Gross, soon to become his adoptive parents.

❑   ❑   ❑

Diane was 10 years old when she went to live with Nora and Stephen Zigler. Going to a new place was not a novelty for her, though. Since she had left her home of birth at age 2, she had moved to foster homes, to hospitals, and to children's homes more than 30 times. Actually, her loss of parenting figures began immediately after birth. Her mother, who was mentally retarded, abandoned Diane, in part because she was ordered to leave the home by Diane's father.

Not obviously handicapped at birth, by age 5 Diane was clearly mentally retarded, visually impaired, and spastic. Although the etiologies of the handicaps were not definitively known, meningitis and subsequent brain damage, self-administered pills and poison, and nonaccidental injury committed by the father were all assumed to be contributory factors.

After Diane went to live with the Ziglers, her medical and health problems worsened. She began to have frequent epileptic seizures that were diagnosed several years later as symptoms of a progressively degenerative and incurable brain disease. Because of her severe problems and the lack of appropriate school facilities locally, the Ziglers placed Diane in a special residential school. She lived there during the school year, returning to her adoptive home for holidays.

❑   ❑   ❑

The stories of Annette, Daniel, Roy, and Diane represent the variability in the characteristics of the 56 children who were adopted or long-term fostered by the 42 families in the present sample. It might be expected, of course, that the children would be of different ages, of both sexes, and with different handicapping conditions. Their previous histories, however, are also remarkably variable. Some, like Annette, were released for adoption or fostering as babies primarily because of the reluctance or refusal of the birth parents to rear a child with mental retardation. Others, like Roy and Diane, had early home environments that undoubtedly contributed to their handicaps and possibly even caused them. In this chapter, the characteristics of the 56 children are presented. Their previous history is emphasized— where they had been and what had happened to them prior to their placement in their adoptive homes. The implications of these histories for the children's growth and development are also examined, and a brief review of the evidence for the importance of stable, nurturing environments in producing optimal developmental progress is presented.

INTRINSIC CHILD
CHARACTERISTICS

Age

On average the children were 54 months of age when they first went to live with their adoptive families. This mean, however, masks a wide range of 0–198 months. Some children went to their adoptive families almost immediately after birth, directly from the hospital with no intervening placements, whereas other children were already adolescents when they went to live with their adoptive or long-term foster families. Despite this variability in age, the majority of children were infants or toddlers when they first were placed for adoption. Table 7-1 presents the distribution of children according to gender and age at the time of their placement. This table shows that 30 children were 24 months or younger when they went to live with their adoptive families; only 10 children were 10 or older at placement. At the time of the interview, the children were an average of 25.2 months older ($SD = 27.2$).

TABLE 7-1

Age and Sex Distribution of Children at Placement

Age	Sex	
	Male	*Female*
Birth–6 months	9	6
7–12 months	5	5
13–24 months	3	2
25–60 months	3	3
61–120 months	6	4
Over 120 months	3	7
Totals	29	27

The relative youth of this sample bodes well for successful adjustment to family life. As discussed in Chapter 6, most families wanted a younger child and very few wanted a teenager. In the general adoption literature, adopting an older child is considered to be risky (Bohman, 1970, p. 25), despite research evidence that does not consistently support the pitfalls of such placements (Raynor, 1980, p. 9). Undoubtedly, the writings of child psychologists who emphasize the importance of early experience in determining the course of both emotional and cognitive development reinforce the negative view (Bowlby, 1951; Spitz, 1946). Chapters 8 and 9 examine both positive and negative adjustment outcomes and the relationship between age and difficulty or ease of family adjustment to the child who is retarded.

Gender

As Table 7-1 indicates, the sample of 56 children was quite balanced between the two sexes with 27 girls and 29 boys. This balance may reflect the lack of preference that the adoptive parents held with regard to the potential adoptee's gender. As reported in Chapter 6, less than a third of the families expressed a preference for a child of one sex or the other, and those that did were rather equally divided between preferring a girl or a boy.

How typical this rather evenly balanced gender distribution might be of children with handicaps who are available for adoption is at this point an unknown. More boys are diagnosed as retarded than girls (Jones, 1979; MacMillan, 1982), and there is some evidence that the negative impact of a retarded child on the birth family is greater if the child is a boy (Farber, 1959). Fathers, particularly, are described as preferring male children and being more disappointed if a male child does not possess the characteristics that will allow him to carry on the family name and achieve success in life (Price-Bonham & Addison, 1978). However, the evidence for this impact is quite meager; furthermore, there are no systematic data available concerning the characteristics of children with handicaps who are available for adoption, so it is not known whether the number of boys and girls is approximately equal. In the absence of this comparative information, it is impossible to do anything other than note that balance exists in the present sample.

Handicapping Condition

The large majority of the 56 children were definitively diagnosed as mentally retarded because of organic handicapping conditions. Indeed, there were only two children who were functioning at a subnormal level and who did not have some identifiable impairment that could be presumed to be responsible for that functioning. More than half of the 56 children, 33, or 59%, had Down syndrome, a chromosomal abnormality in which there is extra material in the 21st pair of chromosomes. Down syndrome almost invariably results in mental retardation and is associated with the presence of a number of distinctive physical features. A characteristic small nose, eyes with an upward slant and a fold of skin at the inner corner, a flat back skull, a small mouth from which the tongue tends to protrude, and hair that is fine, sparse, and straight in Caucasians are some of the features indicative of this disorder. In addition to these readily visible characteristics, children born with Down syndrome are also quite likely to have congenital abnormalities of the heart and intestine, increasing their risk of a shortened lifespan. Children with Down syndrome are usually readily recognizable, and diagnosis at birth is now common.

In addition to possessing many physical features in common, Down syndrome children have a reputation for being loving, affectionate, and temperamentally easy. Although the scientific evidence for this belief is actually quite minimal (Belmont, 1971; MacMillan, 1982), the reputation persists and may explain why they were so much in demand as adoptive children. In fact, many of the adoptive parents voiced the belief that a child with Down syndrome would be easy and rewarding to rear, and indicated that this belief was a factor in their desire to adopt one.

Four children had other identifiable chromosomal or genetic abnormalities that were judged to be responsible for their mental retardation. One child was diagnosed as having Prader-Willi syndrome, a disorder believed to result from an irregularity in chromosome 15. Usual features of this disorder include central nervous system dysfunction, small stature, floppiness in infancy, and obesity accompanied by food obsession and chronic overeating (Nardella, Sulzbacher & Worthington-Roberts, 1983).

Another child had Cornelia de Lange syndrome. This disorder usually results in severe mental retardation. Various craniofacial anomalies are present, as are short stature and microcephaly. Etiology of the disorder is unknown, although a chromosomal abnormality is currently suspected (Grossman, 1983; Jervis, 1975).

One girl had Turner syndrome. Caused by a missing X chromosome, this syndrome is associated more with severe defects in space-form perception than with overall mental retardation, although this particular girl was severely mentally retarded. Because of the missing X chromosome, many normally female sex characteristics are lacking. In fact, when intellectual development is not markedly disturbed, diagnosis frequently is not made until adolescence, when the presenting symptoms are short stature and lack of sexual development.

Finally, one child had a very unusual chromosomal abnormality that involved a translocation; part of one chromosome had broken off and attached to another chromosome. Prognosis for this child, only 18 months old at the interview, was very guarded because so few instances had occurred. At the time of the interview, she was functioning in the moderate to mild range of mental retardation.

In addition to the 37 children accounted for in the categories described above, 12 children had diagnosed organic impairments that are frequently, although by no means uniformly, associated with mental retardation. Cerebral palsy was the most common of these organic impairments. Cerebral palsy is a physical impairment that is the result of damage to the motor control centers of the brain. It can assume any degree of severity from nothing more than a general awkwardness to profound disability with almost no control over the gross and fine motor movements of arms, legs, mouth and jaw, and other parts of the body. Although the majority of the affected population functions in the normal range of intelligence, it is also likely that damage to the motor centers of the brain will be accompanied by damage to the areas of the brain responsible for mental functioning, thus producing below average intelligence.

Cerebral palsy may be the result of a genetic disorder or of prenatal, perinatal, or postnatal injury. Of the six children who had cerebral palsy, one's condition was known to be genetically caused, two were attributed to postnatal injury or disease, two were of unknown prenatal or perinatal origin, and one was of unknown etiology and had not been diagnosed until the child was 5 years old.

In addition to cerebral palsy, other organic involvement included hydrocephaly (enlarged head size because of improper drainage of cerebrospinal fluid); microcephaly (abnormally small skull and presumably brain size); spina bifida (neurological damage caused by the failure of the bony spine to develop and properly fuse); and other brain damage caused by disease or injury.

Although IQ data were not generally available for the children, most were functioning at a moderately retarded level or below. There were, however, six adoptees who were classified as *educationally subnormal*, a level usually regarded as equivalent to mild retardation. In four of these children, there was indication of organic involvement by the presence of associated defects such as epilepsy. Two children, however, had no organic symptoms, but did have environmental histories that would suggest that their retardation was related to psychosocial disadvantage. Their profiles reflected substantial deprivation and neglect, and one child had a birth mother who was classified as mildly retarded.

HISTORY PRIOR TO PLACEMENT

Just as there was a great deal of variability in the age at which children were placed and in the nature of their handicapping conditions, so there was variability in where they had been and in what had happened to them prior to their entry into their adoptive homes. In this section, characteristics of the children's families of origin are examined, as are the number and kinds of placements that they had experienced before their adoption and the reasons that they were available for adoption.

Background information about the children was gathered from three different sources: adoptive families, social workers from the agencies involved in the placement, and directly from agency files. For the younger children who had come into care very soon after birth, records tended to be more complete than for older children, whose histories were often long and complex. For the older children there was sometimes a hiatus of several years in the agency files, nothing being known about the child during that period of time. Nonetheless, this section does provide a global picture of the children's experiences prior to their adoptive placement.

Birth Families

For 11 of the 56 children (20%), information on the birth families was either nonexistent or too sketchy to allow any sort of description or classification. For the other 45 children, the families were classified into two categories: stable and unstable. A family was classified as stable if there was an indication of steady employment by at least one parent, if the birth mother and father were married to each other at the time of the child's birth, and if there was no history of abuse or neglect, criminality, drug or alcohol addiction, mental illness, or mental retardation for either of the parents. Using these criteria, 24 (53%) of the classifiable families were considered stable and 21 (47%) were considered unstable.

Annette, described at the beginning of this chapter, came from a birth family classified as stable. Her biological parents were well educated and there was no apparent reason for their rejection of her other than her handicap. Indeed, Annette's birth mother seemed willing to try raising her, but received little support from her husband. Despite their decision to give her up for adoption, they did not abandon their responsibility to her. They remained involved enough to ensure that she was placed in a good foster home.

Annette's situation is in contrast to Roy's, also described at the beginning of the chapter. There seemed to be little doubt that Roy's birth father was abusive toward him. His father was prosecuted, convicted, and went to prison for his abusive behavior. There was also evidence that Roy's birth mother participated in the abuse, although criminal charges were never brought against her. In addition, at the time of Roy's birth, his parents were having marital problems and were no longer living together. The mother, not a British citizen, left the country for lengthy periods of time, only haphazardly arranging for the care of her other two children.

Roy's story, and the abuse and neglect he received in his family of origin, was not unique. In 18% of the sample of 56 children, there was suspected or proven child abuse or neglect. These children, not surprisingly, tended to be older when they were placed with their adoptive parents than were children who suffered no abuse or neglect. The mean age of the children with histories of abuse or neglect was 115 months at placement, in contrast to a mean age of 41 months for the children with no suspected abuse or neglect. These older children with poor environmental histories might be expected to present more problems to their families and manifest greater adjustment difficulties in their adoptive homes. The present data do not allow a valid test of this expectation because the children who were abused differed in many ways from the children who were not abused. However, in Chapters 8 and 9, when postadoptive family adjustment is examined, so also is evidence confirming or disputing adjustment differences between the two types of children.

Previous Residences

The variability in the previous histories of the adopted children extended to the number and type of places that the children had lived in prior to placement in their adoptive homes. Some children were placed in their adoptive homes directly from the hospital in which they were born, whereas others experienced a round-robin of residences before they arrived at the place that was to become a permanent home. The record number of placements was 33, held by a girl who in the 10 years before her adoptive placement had lived in a variety of foster homes and children's homes as well as in the hospital and with her birth father.

This appalling background, however, was not typical for the 56 children. As Table 7-2 displays, the majority (34 children, or 61%) went to their adoptive homes either directly from the hospital in which they were born or with only one intervening placement. Quite typically, a child was born, diagnosed as mentally retarded, rejected by the birth parents, and taken into care. Occasionally, there was an adoptive family waiting and the infant went immediately to it. More commonly, however, the child was put into a short-term foster care home while an adoptive family was sought for him or her.

TABLE 7-2

Institutional Placement and Number of Residences Prior to Adoptive Placement

	Number of previous residences							
	0–1		2–3		4+		Totals	
Institutional Placement	Freq.[a]	%	Freq.	%	Freq.	%	Freq.	%
Yes	4	7	16	29	5	9	25	45
No	30	54	1	2	0	0	31	55
Totals	34	61	17	30	5	9	56	100

[a] Freq. = frequency of children.

For the other 22 children, 39% of the sample, there were more intervening placements. However, even here most of the children were in only two or three residences before they went to their adoptive homes. Only five children, 9% of the sample, experienced more than three different residential placements before going to live in their adoptive homes.

Of course, unless the environments are inimical ones, the fewer placements the better. Many researchers have explored the effects of frequent changes of caretakers and failure to establish bonds with caretaking figures since Bowlby's (1951) classic report to the World Health Organization (Bowlby, 1969; Rutter, 1979). Indeed, it is this research that has been instrumental in changing adoption practices to placement of the child in a permanent home at as young an age as possible. This prevailing view typifies the belief and general practice in the placement of children who are retarded, as well. It is no doubt responsible for the relatively rapid placement at rather young ages of the majority of the present sample.

Institutional Care

Of course, not all placements are equal in terms of the impact on the child. Institutions or children's homes where there is no guarantee of a one-to-one relationship between child and caretaker are generally regarded as inferior to homerearing in producing optimal emotional and intellectual development. As can be seen in Table 7-2, a substantial minority of the 56 children (25, or 45%) had spent at least some time in an institutional setting. The more residences a child had had, the more likely that he or she had been in an institution. Only 4 of 34 children with 0 or 1 intervening placement had been in an institution, whereas all 5 children with 4 or more placements had been in institutions.

Length of Time in Care

The number and type of residential placements are important considerations for growth and development, but so also is the length of time that a child spends in care and without a permanent home. Table 7-3 displays the frequency and percentage of children who spent varying amounts of time in care. The majority of the children were in care for a month or less, although almost a third (32%) were without a permanent home for more than 3 years, with the majority of this group (61%) in care for more than 5 years.

The three variables of length of time in care, number of previous placements, and institutional placement formed the basis of a 3-point rating scale designed to describe the quality of the preadoptive environment.

TABLE 7-3

Length of Time in Care Before Permanent Placement

Time	Frequency	Percent
≤ 1 month	31	55
> 1 month to 1 year	3	5
> 1 year to 3 years	4	7
> 3 years to 5 years	7	13
> 5 years to 10 years	8	14
> 10 years	3	5
Total	56	99 [a]

[a] Rounding error.

Children received 1 point for being in care for more than a year, for having more than one placement between birth and adoption, and for ever having been in an institution. The results of this rating showed a bimodal distribution. For the most part, children had either experienced very poor preadoptive environments, receiving a 3 on the scale (36%), or they had had relatively good environmental histories, receiving a 0 (54%). Preadoptive history is considered in relationship to postplacement adjustment in Chapter 9.

Adoption Availability

Based on information obtained from agencies as well as adoptive parents, an assessment was made for each child as to why that child had been available for adoption. Raters judged whether the child had been available because of the handicap and the inability or unwillingness of the birth parents to cope with the problem or whether other factors were primary. The results of this analysis are presented in Table 7-4 for children who were either (a) 24 months of age or younger at time of placement or (b) older

TABLE 7-4

Age and Reason for Adoption Availability

Age	Reason for adoption availability		
	Handicap	Uncertain	Definite other
≤ 24 months	24	6	0
> 24 months	11	5	10
Totals	35	11	10

than 24 months. As can be seen from this table, younger children were far more likely to be available for adoption because of their handicaps than were older children. In fact, none of the younger children was scored as definitely available for a reason other than a handicap $\chi^2(df=2) = 14.97$, $p < .001$).

Annette's story, told at the beginning of this chapter, is quite typical of those 35 children who were very clearly rejected because of their handicaps. Indeed, in her case, because she was a twin and her nonhandicapped twin was not rejected, the cause of her rejection seems particularly obvious. In all of these cases, however, there was little doubt that the primary reason for adoption availability was birth parent rejection as a result of the diagnosed handicap.

In Roy's case, however, the situation was quite different. He was removed without voluntary consent from his family because of the abuse and neglect he had suffered there. Whether this abuse caused his mental and physical handicaps or whether a preexisting handicap was a factor contributing to the abuse was not known. The latter is certainly possible, and there is research evidence that children who are handicapped or otherwise "difficult" are more likely to be abuse victims (Belsky, 1980; Frodi, 1981; Meier & Sloan, 1984). Regardless of the direction of this relationship, however, Roy was one of nine children who became available for adoption because of involuntary removal from the family.

For 11 of the 56 children, either the information was too scanty or complex factors made it impossible to assess a definite reason for adoption availability. Evelyn, adopted by the Muellers, was one of these complicated cases. She was born to a young and unmarried mother, whose boyfriend left her when she was pregnant with Evelyn. Depressed even before Evelyn's birth, the mother voluntarily surrendered Evelyn because she felt that she just couldn't cope. Her inability to cope may have been partly because of Evelyn's handicap, but may also have been a result of her own situation, which was economically and psychologically unstable; she might not have been able to cope with a nonhandicapped child, either.

SUMMARY

As is apparent from the descriptions of the children's characteristics, the sample was heterogeneous. The children differed from each other in age, gender, handicapping condition, number and kind of previous placements, type of birth family, and reason for adoption availability. There were newborns and teenagers, girls and boys, children who were severely mentally and physically handicapped with other associated abnormalities, and others who were mildly retarded with no other apparent problems.

There were children who were placed directly into their adoptive homes after birth and others who were in dozens of residences, including institutions. There were children who were born to parents who were well educated and affluent, and others who came from families barely surviving on the fringes of society. And some children were clearly available for adoption only because of their handicap, whereas for others the handicap was incidental to their adoption availability.

This variability has both disadvantages and advantages. Because the sample is heterogeneous and because there are so few children of any one kind represented, it will not be possible to draw conclusions about certain child characteristics and ultimate adjustment. For example, a comparison of older with younger children with Down syndrome will not be possible because there would be too few children in each of these categories. A major advantage of the heterogeneity, however, is that it will make the findings and conclusions derived from them more generalizable to the adoptive population with mental retardation as a whole. Although there are no census data available on children who are labeled and adopted as retarded, the current sample is probably representative. In most cases, adoption agencies identified all of the children that they had placed within the preceding 4 years who were retarded and referred them to this study. Because only one family who was referred declined to participate, the sample of 56 children can be presumed to be quite representative of the population as a whole.

This representativeness is important in assessing the conclusions that will result from the next two chapters. These chapters are perhaps the most important of the book, because they focus on the outcome of the adoption, on the adjustment, both short term and longer term, to having a child who is mentally retarded in the family. The results relating to adjustment clearly have important implications for the future feasibility of adoption as a strategy of choice in providing optimal environments for children with handicaps. It is only by evaluating adjustment after placement that professionals can determine success or failure of the adoption and formulate techniques and programs for ensuring the former and avoiding the latter.

Chapter 8

Impact of the Adoption
I. Emphasizing the Positive

From the Innises, who had adopted Frank more than a year earlier:

Mother: I think he's made us more patient. I think we take a lot more time with Frank . . . in many ways I think it's brought us closer together.
Father: Yes.
M: Not for the reason that our marriage was on the rocks, but for the fact that we had our own interests. Just being two of us, we could get away with going off and doing our own thing and the other one would cope without the other . . .
F: [Now] we all do the same thing.
M: Yes, we have to talk to each other and see if, where, when, and how.

❑　　　❑　　　❑

From Sonia Kimble, describing the positive impact of their adoption of almost 3 years:

Well, the fact that I've got a child, because I consider her my own now. I don't think about the fact that she's fostered really. She's considered our daughter and although she calls us "Aunt" and "Uncle" rather than "Mother" and "Father," we don't mind that. And I think it's just nice to be a family rather than just the two of us.

❑　　　❑　　　❑

From the Floyds, who have been fostering Caroline for 2 years and Betsy for 1 year, describing the benefits for their other children:

M: They all benefit in strengthening their own character, I think, really.
F: Well, I think it's given them a lot more reason for living. It's made them appreciate what they had, what they could have

been *without all their life. I think it's given them a lot more value in life.*

M: And it's only really since we've had foster children that our children have realized that everybody doesn't have a home and everybody doesn't have a daily newspaper. When little things like this would come up, they'd say, "Well, everybody has that," and it's surprising because it's not something you sit down when you're working out yourself a holiday, and say, "Well, some people won't be having a holiday this year." Maybe it's something that doesn't come up and it's only since we've been fostering that that situation has come up.

❑   ❑   ❑

From Linda Johnson, describing positive changes since she and her husband began fostering Nicholas more than 2 years before:

It's brought us much closer together, as a couple and as a family. From the children's point of view, they no longer mock handicapped people; they have far better insight. Vincent and myself, I think we're far more tolerant, not only of people like Nicholas, but of each other, than we perhaps were beforehand.

In answer to a question about happiness:

I think we get an awful lot of pleasure out of watching Nicholas, and I know the things he's learned to do are only small things, but for Nicholas they are really very enormous things. Like, for example, the first time he blew [a toy instrument] and produced a noise, I mean my kids were actually up to the moon, and I mean they really were, oh, so excited, so they take an enormous amount of pleasure in what Nicholas does. And I think they take an awful lot of pride in what he does as well. They feel as if they're part of it, they've helped him.

❑   ❑   ❑

From Isabel Gross who, with her husband, Fred, adopted Roy 2 years before the interview, in response to questions about whether the adoption has made them better people and added meaning to their lives:

We've had to face things in ourselves that aren't nice. Our anger and frustration and impatience at his not trying. We've had to come to terms with feelings within us and it shows us what we're really like. . . . We've learned to say "sorry" to each other and to Roy. . . . It's deepened how we think of ourselves; it's deepened our faith.

❏   ❏   ❏

From Grace Morgan who, with her husband Dennis, had adopted Heather more than 2 years before the interview, in response to questions about becoming a better person and life having more meaning:

I've got very much more confidence around children . . . I think I can appreciate other little ones more now that we know more about children . . . my husband spends a lot of time with her, playing with her, which has changed our lives. It's given our lives more meaning. . . . My husband's more content now we've got a family . . . he gets a lot of response from Heather. It's a big exciting time when Daddy comes home at teatime and, well, I know Dennis really enjoys that because Heather is up at the window with a big smile, and if she isn't there, if she's asleep one day, it's "Where is she?" He looks forward to coming home to that.

❏   ❏   ❏

From Valerie Underwood who, with her husband Paul, had adopted Alex 4 years and Eliot 1 year before the interview:

We just feel we know more what life is all about because of them, and I always think it made us more tolerant to those people who don't find it as easy to cope with their own children. It really made it very clear to us that life is about living and not about just getting and consuming and trying to reach something in a material way.

Valerie continued, in response to a question about whether family members have become more flexible since the adoption:

You know, things just don't seem to matter so much . . . we laugh a lot more. I mean, often, when, for example, Alex does something stupid, or he upsets some things, or he makes a mess, there's always a choice. You can really get uptight about it, or you can try and see the funny side. And we see much more the funny side than we used to.

❏   ❏   ❏

From Patricia Weston who, with her husband Maurice, had adopted Doris a year earlier:

We're just happier. We didn't think we could become happier.
And how she's done that, we can't quite put our finger on it.
We just seem to be a lot more aware of each other.

❑   ❑   ❑

The overwhelming majority of the adoptive families experienced positive outcomes from the adoption. Although reality crises did occur, and the occasional family or family member even underwent an existential crisis of sorts, the preceding quotations typify the reactions of most of the adoptive families. This chapter examines those reactions, demonstrating the overall positive impact using a variety of measures. The most general and global results that relate to postplacement adjustment are presented first. These results derive from the semi-structured interview, the Holroyd QRS, and the Farber questionnaire, all described in Chapter 1. Following the description of the more general results, outcomes relating to specific adjustment areas, including effects on the marital relationship, on siblings, and on social relations outside the family, are explored. Most of these data come from the interviews.

GLOBAL ASSESSMENTS
OF THE PLACEMENT

Interview Responses: General Assessments

Although the semi-structured interview contained several dozen questions relating to postplacement family functioning, some assessments of the placement were more global than others. In particular, two different questions, asked toward the conclusion of the interview, required the respondent to make very general assessments of the adoption. These questions were as follows: All things considered, has (child's name) adoption worked out: Better than you expected, about as well as you expected, or less well? (Appendix A, Q. 135); and Thinking back over your entire experience with (child's name), and all the good times and the bad times—if you had to do it over again, do you think you'd adopt (child's name), would you not adopt him (her), or are you unsure? (Appendix A, Q. 142).

Each of these questions was coded on a 3-point scale, with 3 being the best outcome category and 1 being the worst. The scores were summed to yield a single composite scale, which could vary from a low of 2 to a high of 6. Thus, a respondent who said that the adoption had worked out better than expected (3) and that she would do it again (3) received the maximum

TABLE 8-1

Scores for Two Global Assessments of the Adoption

	Response Score	Frequency	%
Expectations?	3	35	62
(Q. 135)	2	14	25
	1	6	11
	Don't know[a]	1	2
Do it again?	3	48	86
(Q. 142)	2	6	11
	1	2	3
	Don't know	—	—
Composite score[b]	6	33	59
	5	16	28
	4	2	4
	3	3	5
	2	2	4

Note. Questions are from the semi-structured interview. Responses are scored 1, 2, and 3, with 3 representing the best outcome.
[a] For the composite scoring, this mother was assigned a 2.
[b] Responses to questions 135 and 142 summed, with 6 representing the most positive outcome.

score of 6. In contrast, a respondent who replied that the adoption had worked out less well than expected (1) and that she would not adopt the child again (1) received the minimum score of 2. Table 8-1 presents the frequencies and percentages of responses to each of the categories for each of the questions, as well as the composite values.

As can be seen from this table, most of the mothers thought that the placement was better than expected and the large majority, 86%, said that they would do it again. Only two mothers received the lowest combined score of 2, indicating that the placement had been worse than expected and that, given the chance to remake their decision to adopt, they would not do it again. These two placements will be described in detail in the next chapter, which focuses on negative outcomes.

Of the 16 mothers who received combined scores of 5, 13 said that the adoption had worked out as well as expected and they would definitely do it again; one said that she could not answer the question about expectations because she really had had none, but that she was certain that they would adopt this child again. These outcomes seemed little different from the adoptions that received combined scores of 6. For example, some of these mothers said that they had expected it to work out well, it had worked out well, and therefore, it was just as they had expected. Thus, combining these 14 scores of 5 with the 33 scores of 6 yields 47 of the 56 adoptions, or 84%, that can be classified as definitely successful. The following comments, made when respondents were asked if they would adopt this child again, typify this success:

—He's so much part of the family now that we can't imagine life without him.
—If we felt that we had sufficient time and money we'd have another.
—We would take her on. Don't ask me why we enjoy it. We just feel as if she fits a little slot that needed fitting with her. She's a missing piece of the jigsaw which is still spreading.
—We've already talked about doing it again. As soon as this adoption goes through we'd like to go and do it again. We'd like to get a girl this time.

Like this last respondent, several families expressed their positive feelings about the target child in their enthusiasm about adopting another child with a handicap. It was not unlikely that this enthusiasm translated into later action. In this sample of 42 families, 12 (29%) had more than one adopted or fostered handicapped child living with them.

The success rate, stated above as 84%, is even higher if one separates the first-adopted target child from later-adopted target children. Respondents seemed more ambivalent about second-adopted children, with only 58% of the respondents certain that they would do the adoption again, in contrast to 93% of respondents for the first-adopted children. Other measures of outcome will also examine first- and second-adopted children separately to determine whether this intimation of difference is repeated.

In addition to the two global assessments of the adoption yielding the composite score described above, the interview contained a series of five questions (Appendix A, Q. 83–87) that required the respondent to classify the placement as either very positive or negative, somewhat positive or negative, or not at all positive or negative, and to decide whether the positive impact outweighed the negative or vice versa. Based on the responses to these questions, a 7-point scale was created, ranging from the most negative impact of -3 to the most positive impact of $+3$. Mothers who said that the impact had been very negative and that there was no positive effect at all received a score of -3; similarly, mothers who responded that the impact was very positive with no negative impact received a score of $+3$. Other responses fell between these extremes, with replies of equivalent positive and negative impact receiving scores of 0.

TABLE 8-2

Maternal Assessment of Adoption Impact

Impact Score[a]	First-adopted child		Second-adopted child		Combined	
	Frequency	%	Frequency	%	Frequency	%
−3	1	2	0	0	1	2
−2	1	2	0	0	1	2
−1	1	2	0	0	1	2
0	4	10	2	17	6	11
+1	7	17	3	25	10	19
+2	14	33	2	17	16	30
+3	14	33	5	42	19	35

Note. Responses to questions 83–87 of the semi-structured interview. The mean impact scores for first and second adopted children and the combined scores were 1.69, 1.83, and 1.72 respectively.
[a] A score of −3 represents the most negative impact; +3 represents the most positive impact.

Table 8-2 displays the frequencies and percentages as well as the means for the first- and second-adopted children, separately and combined. The data from this measure corroborate the result from the previous assessment. Mothers considered the large majority of adoptions, 83%, to have had more positive than negative effects. The mean score for all 54 first and second adoptions was 1.72, with only a small difference between the mean of 1.69 for first-adopted children and the mean of 1.83 for second-adopted children. Note that for this measure, there is no indication that second adoptions were regarded more negatively than first adoptions. In addition, although the scores are not presented in Table 8-2, the third and fourth adoptions in one family were rated +2 and +3, respectively.

The three adoptions that mothers assessed to have had more negative than positive impact were also judged problematic by the other global assessment, the composite score. These three adoptions, which received scores of −3, −2, and −1, received scores of 2, 2, and 3, respectively, on the 2- to 6-point scale. Again, these three cases, along with others, will be described in the next chapter.

The six adoptions that received a 0 on the present scale, indicating equal positive and negative impact, received composite scores ranging from 3 to 6. Four of these adoptions scored 5 or 6, with all of the mothers indicating that they would adopt the child again. Thus, these adoptions do not seem problematic. A more detailed description of one of them will prove the point.

Harriet and Evan Quinton had adopted Laura, a child with Down syndrome who was functioning in the moderately retarded range. She was in primary school and working up to her ability level, according to teacher reports. The Quintons also had two birth children, both boys older than Laura. Harriet Quinton viewed the adoption as very easy and uneventful, with Laura quickly fitting into the routine of the household. She said that there had been neither an overall positive impact nor an overall negative impact on the family. Thus, she scored a 0 on the impact scale. However, she also responded that the adoption had worked out better than expected and that she would definitely adopt Laura if she had it to do over again.

Harriet's responses to specific interview questions generally confirmed the lack of change in the family as a result of Laura's entry. However, she did admit that family members had become more flexible, that her sons had matured because of the experience, but that one son had had some shoft-term negative reactions to being displaced by Laura. Thus, all in all, the impression of this adoption is that it was successful, with minimal impact or change in a family that was already functioning quite smoothly.

In conclusion, then, these global interview assessments taken together indicate positive outcomes for 51 of the 56 adoptions, or 91%. For the other five adoptions, the mothers did not think that the positive impact outweighed the negative; also these adoptions received composite scores of 4 or lower. These five adoptions are examined at length in Chapter 9. In the present chapter, however, additional measures that verify the positive outcomes for most of the families are examined.

Interview Responses: Specific Assessments

Further indications of the very positive outlook that parents had on their adopted children come from their answers to a series of quite specific interview questions. In these questions (Appendix A, Q. 137–141) they were asked to rate the child along a number of different dimensions of functioning. As in the global questions, responses were usually positive rather than negative. For example, 54% of the respondents thought that the first-adopted child was less difficult to raise than they had expected, whereas only 17% thought that the child had been more difficult to raise than expected.

This pattern is repeated in the answers to the other questions. For the first-adopted child, 72% felt that it had taken less time than expected for the child to become part of the family; only 10% thought it had taken more time. Just over half (51%) of the respondents thought that the first-adopted child's intellectual abilities were better than expected and 57% felt this way about the child's physical abilities. In addition, 62% of the mothers said that the child's ability to form relationships with others was better than they had anticipated it would be, and only 7% admitted that the child was not as good at forming relationships as expected.

The data for second-adopted children are somewhat less positive overall. For example, 67% of the mothers thought that this child was more difficult to raise than expected, in contrast to only 17% for the first-adopted child. Only 25% of the mothers of second-adopted children responded that the child's intellectual abilities were better than they had anticipated, in comparison with 51% for first-adopted children. Indeed, in none of the questions that probed specific postplacement functioning categories did mothers score second-adopted children as high as first-adopted children. Thus, along with the earlier data examined, these results suggest more problematic adjustment for second-adopted children in comparison with first-adopted children.

Holroyd Questionnaire on Resources and Stress (QRS)

The QRS was introduced in Chapter 1, and all of its 285 true/false questions appear in Appendix B. The QRS was left with parents to complete and return by mail. Most, but not all, mothers and fathers completed and returned it. Completed questionnaires were received from 39 mothers for 49 adopted children and from 33 fathers for 41 adopted children, representing a return rate of 93% for mothers and 92% for fathers.

The QRS is divided into 15 different subscales that are organized into three different categories: parent problems, family functioning, and child problems. Each of the subscales contains between 6 and 32 items that the respondent must answer either as *true* or *false*. On some items an answer of *true* is more indicative of stress, whereas on other items stress is indicated by an answer of *false*. For example, an answer of *true* to the item *I have no time to give the other members of the family* would earn 1 point on Excess Time Demands subscale, whereas an answer of *false* to the item *Our family agrees on important matters* would earn 1 point on the Lack of Family Integration subscale. Thus, the higher the score on the subscale, the more difficulties the respondent perceived in that dimension. A high score on scale 2, Excess Time Demands, for example, means that the respondent thought that the target child required a lot of time. In contrast, a low score on scale 8, Lack of Family Integration, means that the respondent perceived the family as doing a lot together and as being well integrated.

Because the QRS is not yet normed with percentile rankings, responses on it have little meaning when viewed in isolation. Therefore, for comparison purposes, in Table 8-3 the maternal means for the 39 first-adopted children in the current sample are presented, along with means from both

TABLE 8-3

Comparison of Groups on Holroyd Questionnaire on Resources and Stress (QRS)

Category/QRS subscale	Group 1 Mean	Group 2 Mean	Group 3 Mean	t-test values for Groups 3-1	1-2
Parent problems					
Poor health/mood	1.49	2.05	4.95	7.52**	−0.98
Excess time demands	4.41	3.67	5.53	2.33*	1.02
Negative attitudes	5.38	4.24	10.98	7.54**	1.42
Overprotection/dependency	4.00	3.14	6.17	4.62**	1.39
Lack of social support	4.05	2.52	4.45	1.67	4.25**
Overcommitment/martyrdom	2.85	2.24	3.50	4.64**	2.03*
Pessimism	3.59	2.71	3.53	−0.14	1.81
Family functioning					
Lack of family integration	2.59	2.86	5.23	4.89**	−0.45
Limits on family opportunity	0.59	0.43	1.80	4.84**	0.63
Financial problems	3.18	2.57	5.49	5.02**	1.07
Child problems					
Physical incapacitation	3.90	1.00	2.81	−2.48*	6.17**
Lack of activities	1.18	0.52	2.47	4.96**	2.49*
Occupational limitations	3.28	1.05	3.43	0.58	6.19**
Social obtrusiveness	1.80	0.48	2.41	2.82**	5.37**
Difficult personality	13.10	3.38	15.33	2.59*	10.23**

Note. Group 1: Glidden's 39 adopted children with mental retardation, mean age 4.7 years. Group 2: Holroyd's 21 control children, mean age 10.4 years. Group 3: Holroyd's developmentally disabled sample of 143, mean age 9.8.
* $p < .05$.   ** $p < .01$

nonhandicapped and handicapped samples studied by Holroyd (1985). The handicapped group is a somewhat heterogeneous mixture of 143 subjects with developmental disabilities, including children who had Down syndrome, children with autism, children who were retarded and behaviorally disordered, as well as others. The nonhandicapped group consists of 21 children with a mean age of 10.4 years.

Although the adopted children in the current research differ on a number of characteristics such as age, culture, and social class from the children in these groups that Holroyd studied, it is still informative to examine the patterns of results for the different groups. As can be seen in Table 8-3, the adopted children score significantly lower, indicating more successful functioning on 12 of the 15 subscales, than do the children in the Holroyd developmentally disabled sample. In fact, they do not differ significantly from the normal controls on many of the subscales that involve psychological and attitudinal variables, such as Poor Health/Mood, Negative Attitudes, and Lack of Family Integration. This close resemblance to the normal controls is especially noteworthy given that the children themselves are markedly different from the normal controls, with their scores on all five of the scales relating to child problems being significantly higher. Indeed, the adopted children score higher on the physical incapacitation scale than even the children in the Holroyd developmentally disabled sample do, probably because they are younger.

Another interesting comparison involves a subset of the 39 first-adopted children, 23 with Down syndrome, and a sample of biological children with Down syndrome studied by Holroyd. The QRS data for these two samples are shown in Table 8-4. The differences here are not so striking as they were in Table 8-3. However, the adopted children, although significantly more physically incapacitated than the biological children, have mothers who have fewer problems, as reflected by four of the seven Parent Problems scales and one of the three Family Functioning scales. The differences in Poor Health/Mood, Negative Attitudes, and Overcommitment/Martyrdom seem particularly indicative of existential concerns rather than reality con-

TABLE 8-4

A Comparison of Adoptive and Biological Mothers of Children with Down Syndrome on the Holroyd QRS

Category/QRS subscale	Glidden adopted Down syndrome Group[a] Mean	SD	Biological Down syndrome Group[b] Mean	SD	t-test values
Parent problems					
Poor health/mood	.65	1.53	3.5	2.4	4.60**
Excess time demands	3.83	1.92	4.7	2.9	1.15
Negative attitudes	3.91	1.86	8.6	4.1	4.79**
Overprotection/dependency	3.26	1.86	5.0	2.4	2.64*
Lack of social support	3.91	1.16	4.3	1.2	1.08
Overcommitment/martyrdom	2.65	.83	3.4	1.5	2.03*
Pessimism	2.96	1.82	3.4	2.2	0.71
Family functioning					
Lack of family integration	1.87	1.46	3.1	2.6	1.98
Limits on family opportunity	.39	.94	1.0	1.7	1.45
Financial problems	2.91	1.68	5.0	2.7	2.70**
Child problems					
Physical incapacitation	4.30	1.99	2.1	1.8	-3.86**
Lack of activities	.96	.64	1.2	1.7	0.42
Occupational limitations	2.74	1.32	3.3	0.8	1.70
Social obtrusiveness	1.39	1.03	2.2	1.4	2.19*
Difficult personality	13.09	4.95	12.7	4.7	-0.26

[a] $N = 23$.   Mean age = 2.25 years.
[b] Holyoyd (1985). $N = 22$.   Estimated mean age = 7.9 years.
* $p < .05$.   ** $p < .01$.

cerns, and lend credence to the hypothesis that the different ways in which the child might enter the family have an impact on later functioning.

Of course, again, caution must be exercised in interpreting these differences because the children and families differed in both known ways—for example, child age, country/culture—as well, undoubtedly, as in many unknown ways. Child age may be an especially important variable that influences current adjustment and reality crises. A 2-year-old child with Down syndrome may not seem much different from a nonhandicapped 2-year-old; teenagers who are retarded, however, frequently present an entirely different set of reality crises and, indeed, even existential crises as parents must confront issues of emerging sexuality, adult living and working, and planning for a future when they can no longer be the primary caretakers. In fact, several of the adoptive parents expressed these concerns and indicated that they were worried about whether they would be able to cope.

Because the current sample was a young one, younger than the comparison samples were, the better adjustment of the adoptive families must be viewed as only heuristic and as calling for additional research. This research should compare adoptive and birth families, matching on important child and family characteristics, such as child age, family size, socioeconomic status, education, and so on. This issue is discussed again and more fully in Chapter 10.

Data for the fathers on the QRS generally corroborate those for the mothers. On only 2 of the 15 scales did t tests reveal significant differences between fathers and mothers. Mothers, more than fathers, felt that the child made excess demands on their time ($t = 3.15$, $df = 32$, $p<.01$). On the other hand, fathers more than mothers had negative attitudes toward the child ($t = 3.30$, $df = 32$, $p < .01$).

Because mothers were the primary caretakers of the children, it is not surprising that they felt the impact of excess time demands more than the fathers did; their perceptions may be a straightforward interpretation of the reality. It is not as easy to explain the negative paternal attitude. It may be the result of less attachment on the part of the fathers as a result of less involvement in the childrearing. However, the finding needs to be replicated and further explored before conclusions and interpretations are accepted.

Farber Questionnaire

The results of responses to the Farber questionnaire also show remarkably little difficulty in coping with the problems of rearing a child who is retarded. As displayed in Appendix C, this questionnaire consists of 10

TABLE 8-5

**Adoptive Parents' Responses to Farber Questionnaire
for First-Adopted Children**

		Mothers			Fathers	
Item[a]	N	Mean	% Negative Response	N	Mean	% Negative Response
Patient	42	.50	5	35	.43	2
Friends	41	.32	0	35	.17	0
Worry	42	−.02	19	35	.06	5
Nervous	42	.17	5	35	.17	2
Angry	41	.17	7	35	.17	10
Happy	41	.66	2	35	.63	0
Global change[b]	42	1.10	0	35	1.17	0
Marital	37	.40	0	34	.44	0

Note. The Farber Questionnaire is presented in Appendix C.
[a]Scored on a 3-point negative–neutral–positive (−1, 0, +1) scale, except as noted.   [b] Scored on a 4-point negative-to-positive (−1 to +2).

items, 7 of which can be scored on a positive-neutral-negative 3-point scale. For example, for item 1 a respondent received a +1 for checking the response *more patient*, a 0 for checking *about as patient*, and a −1 for checking *less patient*. Because the value of change for items 2 and 4, concerning planning for the future and religion, are not clear, they are discussed not in this section, but rather later in this chapter, along with the consideration of more specific outcomes.

Table 8-5 presents the mean ratings for both mothers and fathers for each of the seven items that was scored on this 3-point scale and for the one item that was scored on a 4-point scale (described below). For the 3-point items, a mean of 0 indicates equivalent degrees of positive and negative change, whereas a mean greater than 0 is interpreted as more positive change and a mean less than 0 as more negative change. Most notable about the data displayed in Table 8-5 is that of 16 means only one has a negative value, and even that score, −0.02 for the question about worry for mothers, is very close to 0.00. Thus, both mothers and fathers saw themselves as either not changing very much or changing for the better as a result of the child's placement.

This conclusion is further substantiated by the percentage of respondents reporting no negative changes for a specific item. This information is also displayed in Table 8-5. On three questions—making friends, global change, and marital relationship—not one mother or father reported a negative change. On a fourth question, happiness, no fathers and only one mother reported a negative change. And finally, on most of the other questions, very little negative change was reported. The question about worry, whose mean for mothers was the only one below 0, also showed the highest percentage of negative change. Eight mothers, 19%, said that they worried more after the adoptive child was placed with them.

The question about global change is a bit more difficult to interpret than the others are, because it had four response choices rather than three. Respondents could check *change for the worse* (− 1); *no change* (0); *some ways better, some ways worse* (+ 1); and *change for the better* (+ 2). Therefore, it is important to look at the percentages for different response categories for this question. Most parents reported overall change for the better, with 45% of mothers and 60% of fathers checking this response. Approximately one-third of the parents reported no change, with 31% of mothers and 34% of fathers making that choice. The fewest parents reported mixed change, 24% of mothers and only 6% of fathers. And, of course, as Table 8-5 shows, no fathers or mothers said that they had only changed for the worse.

Summary

In summary, then, the results of the global interview assessments, the Holroyd QRS, and the Farber questionnaire all lead to the same conclusion: Adopting a child who is retarded leads to a generally positive result for almost all families. This positive outcome is in contrast to more negative outcomes for families with biological children who are retarded, as the review in Chapter 2 concluded and as the QRS comparisons in this chapter indicated. This latter conclusion, however, must be very tentative. The literature reviewed in Chapter 1 was in some cases more than 10 years old and was rarely based on the same methodology as is the current study. The comparison data using the QRS are more legitimate, because the same dependent measure is being examined. However, as already discussed, because the comparison groups used were not equated with the current sample on many important variables, any conclusions based on them must also be suspect.

Probably the most reasonable statement that can be made at this time is that adopting a child who is retarded does not seem to be fraught with the same sorts of problems and crises that characterize a family into which a child with mental retardation is born or otherwise precipitously introduced. The importance of the way the child is perceived as a determining factor in the experience of crisis may be paramount (Hill, 1949; McCubbin & Patterson, 1983; Wikler, 1986). A more precise understanding of the variables that control these perceptions and more definitive and specific statements must await additional research with appropriate control conditions.

In addition to examining the overall impact of the adoption, it is important to consider effects in individual adjustment areas. There were many interview questions that probed for very specific changes. The next section describes some of these specific effects, primarily using the interview data for mothers and, when available, for fathers, but also comparing responses to the interview with both QRS and Farber responses when they overlap.

SPECIFIC POSTPLACEMENT
CHANGES

Parental Happiness

Two interview questions asked the respondent whether any family members were either happier or unhappier as a result of the target child placement (Appendix A, questions 88 and 89). The responses to these questions are presented in Table 8-6 for mothers and fathers for first- and second-placed children. Both for mothers and fathers and for first- and second-placed children, these results confirm the findings from the other measures examined thus far. That is, the outcomes are positive. More specifically, only one mother and one father are reported to be unhappier as a result of the first-placed child, and only two mothers and two fathers are reportedly unhappier as a result of the second-placed child. (*Note:* Most interview data come from mothers' responses. Therefore, *paternal* happiness almost always represents the wife's perception of her husband's happiness.)

The following comments made in response to these questions underscore the overall positive impact:

—The whole family's happier. Life's a lot of fun with Jeremy around. He's a happy child.
—We're all more of a family. You know, it's difficult to describe, but definitely we are more together . . . we're much more warm because of that.
—All of us. We got what we wanted. It makes you happy when you get what you want.
—There was a quiet joy about Kevin's coming.
—Yes, I'm happier. I think we all are really. The boys idolize her. They do literally fight over her sometimes. And Daddy's got the little girl he's always wanted.
—She's a little bright spot in all our lives. We wouldn't be without her now.

TABLE 8-6

Happiness Ratings After First and Second Adoptions

| | Child 1 | | | | Child 2 | | | |
| | Mother N = 42 | | Father N = 37 | | Mother N = 12 | | Father N = 10 | |
Response	Freq.	%	Freq.	%	Freq.	%	Freq.	%
Unhappier	1	2.4	1	2.7	2	16.7	2	20.0
No change	12	28.6	8	21.6	3	25.0	3	30.0
Happier/unhappier	1	2.4	0	0.0	2	16.7	1	10.0
Happier	27	64.3	28	75.7	5	41.7	4	40.0
Don't know	1	2.4	0	0.0	0	0.0	0	0.0

The second result to note from Table 8-6 is the apparent difference between first-placed and second-placed children. More than two-thirds of the parents report that they are happier as a result of the first child's placement; the comparable figure for second children is approximately 40%. Here again is the suggestion that later placements may be more problematic than first placements.

Other Parental Existential Changes

In addition to parental happiness, the interview contained questions about whether life had more meaning, whether any family members had become better people, and whether family members had become more flexible as a result of the placement. No parents reported that life had become less meaningful for them as a result of the adoption. In contrast, more than two-thirds of mothers and fathers were scored as having more meaning in their lives following the child's placement, with approximately one-third reporting no change on this variable. The following responses typify comments made when answering this portion of the interview:

—Yes, it's given us a sense of purpose.
—It's two kids that you hope you've given the best in life.
—It puts landmarks on life. Someone to think for and plan for all the time.
—Every woman has an instinct towards a child which I've never fulfilled. Suddenly you have this child in your care and you're responsible for it.
—We really love our girls, but we love our boys in a way that hurts much more, because they are much more vulnerable. . . . We feel we know more about what life is all about because of them.
—It's deepened how we think of ourselves; it's deepened our faith.

Supporting this last parental comment are the answers to the Farber questionnaire item about religion, also indicating a strengthening of religious commitment for some parents. Five mothers, 12%, thought that they had become more religious since the child's placement, and only one mother responded that she had become less religious. Similarly, five fathers, 14% of the sample, responded that they had become more religious, with only one father indicating a loss of religious meaning.

It seemed difficult for some respondents to admit that they had become better people as a result of the placement. They frequently responded with embarrassment to that question. Nonetheless, based on their reports, slightly more than 60% of mothers and 50% of fathers felt that they had done so. Comments made in this regard were:

—I've become more tolerant, I think. More understanding.
—We've got other people to think of, so we've become less selfish.
—I'm more sympathetic with the parents of the children I teach.

Finally, one woman talked at length about the compassion she had gained as a result of the adoption:

To live with Susan, I think for me, is to look at a reality that there is a terrific amount of suffering in the world, that this little child has had more than her fair share of it. That helps me to keep really in touch not with the material side of life, but really with the heart of the universe, almost. . . . That keeps us together, that holds us together; I'm in touch with her suffering.

Approximately two-thirds of respondents reported greater flexibility for either one or both parents as a result of the adoptions. The following comments were typical of those recorded:

—I'm less concerned about cleaning, less meticulous. I live at a different pace.
—I used to be very rigid in schedule. Now I'm more likely to accept what comes.
—I'm probably more adaptable than I was. I've had to adapt my social life around Cindy, but I have no great problems thinking of her first.
—We've all learned to take life as it comes, each day as it comes, I'd say.

This final remark, an indication of living more in a day-to-day orientation, relates to one of the questions on the Farber questionnaire that was not described in the section on global assessments because it was not clear which response was desirable. This question referred to whether the respondent planned more for the future or lived more day to day. For mothers, a more day-to-day orientation seems to have resulted from the adoption: 43% of the mothers checked this response category, in contrast to only 21% saying that they planned more for the future. The results for fathers, however, are diferent. Only 9% of the fathers responded that they lived more from day to day, while 23% said that they planned more for the future. However, most fathers (69%) checked the *no change* category.

Whether this more day-to-day orientation is good or bad is difficult to ascertain. Obviously, a balance is needed between living life in the present and living in the future. The present study did not determine whether these mothers and fathers had achieved that balance. What was clear, however, is that many of the mothers felt that it was good to live more day to day. They saw it as a sign of greater flexibility, of the recognition that it was often difficult to plan very far ahead because the prognosis for the child was frequently so uncertain. They perceived this day-to-day orientation neither as an indication that they had given up hope nor as a sign that they were refusing to acknowledge that in many ways they had to plan more for this child than for a nonhandicapped child. Indeed, many respondents talked about the plans they had for education, training, medical procedures, and so forth that would benefit the child and help to guarantee optimal development.

In summary, the responses to questions about specific existential changes corroborate the analyses of the global assessment. Most parents experienced positive outcomes, seeing their lives as more meaningful and perceiving themselves as having become better people, living their lives in a more flexible and adaptable way. In the next sections, items relating to marital and sibling functioning are examined to determine whether the positive impact extends to these relationships.

Marital Relationships

Four interview questions asked specifically about the marital relationship in terms of closeness, arguments, and sex life (Appendix A, Q. 117–120). Of the 36 married mothers, 20 (56%) responded that they felt closer to their husbands as a result of the first adoption and 15 (42%) said that there was no change in the degree of closeness. Only one mother reported a loss of closeness after the placement. This degree of closeness was achieved in spite of (because of?) spending less time together, which 39% of respondents said had occurred. Wives who reported that they felt closer to their husbands frequently made the following types of comments:

—Yes, we're closer. I think because with a child like Nicholas you really need to be able to rely on somebody, where normally one would tend to take things for granted. I think you appreciate each other's time more.

—We do a lot of talking. There's so much new all the time.

—Whatever you share together is a shared experience and it brings you a bit closer.

—I'm seeing another side of him that I didn't know was there . . . he seems, I suppose, tender.

Three mothers even reported that their sex life was better as a result of the placement, although the large majority, 86%, did not indicate any improvement or deterioration. One of the three mothers summarized quite cogently why she thought it was better. She said, "Because we love each other more, we love each other more in that way, too."

Finally, the question regarding arguments also indicated little impact, with 83% of the mothers reporting no change for first-placed children and 67% reporting no change for second-placed children. There were a few mothers who said that they argued more since the child had come, a negative impact examined more closely in the next chapter.

In summary, then, the interview data are congruent with the results of the Farber questionnaire, indicating either no change or improvement in marital relations after the placement of the target child. The impression generally formed of these families during the interviews was that they were functioning well, that they were stable and well integrated, and that they were oriented toward children. It is perhaps not surprising, then, that the introduction of a child would not be a major stressful event. Indeed, there is some suggestion that even when a child who is handicapped enters a family, but not by parental choice, those families with high levels of marital stability adjust quite well to what less stable families perceive as traumatic (Friedrich, 1979). Of course, without more elaborate and well-normed measures of the marital relationship, these statements are speculative only. However, it is important to remember that most of these parents were highly motivated to rear a child with a handicap and that the decision to do so was almost always a joint one between husband and wife. This situation alone is undoubtedly indicative of a high level of mutuality in the marriage.

Impact on Siblings

Whenever a new person enters a family, there is always some readjust-ment of the family dynamics to accommodate the needs, demands, and characteristics of the new member. This readjustment is likely to be espe-cially stressful when the new person requires considerable attention that may therefore no longer be available for other family members. There is a substantial psychological literature on the impact of new children on chil-dren already in the family, and it is fairly common knowledge that parents can expect a variety of negative effects such as regression, attention seeking, and attempts to hurt the new child (Dunn, Kendrick, & MacNamee, 1981; McDermott, 1980; Nadelman & Begun, 1982). Some of these behaviors were reported in the present sample and are described in the next chapter. In this chapter, however, the focus is on what parents perceived as the positive impact on children already in the family.

Before turning to the results, however, note that the sample size for these data is somewhat smaller than for the other analyses. First, data are presented only for the first-placed children. Sibling impact for second-placed children is confounded by the first-placed child with retardation who had already joined the family, and thus means something quite differ-ent. Second, because many of the families either had no children in the family or had children of ages inappropriate to some of the questions, the sample size is reduced to approximately 25, varying slightly up or down depending on the specific question.

Overall, mothers perceived that the impact of the placement was quite positive for other children. A global impact question resulted in exactly two-thirds of the mothers reporting that the impact had been positive, with no negative effects. Furthermore, 54% said that other children were hap-pier, 52% that other children were better people, 54% that other children had become more flexible, and 31% that life had become more meaningful for their other children as a result of the placement. In addition, most of the mothers who did not report positive change said that no change had occurred, rather than change in a negative direction.

In addition, 28% of mothers said that the placement had resulted in new activities for children already in the family and 92% said that their other children had benefited because the target child was a companion for them. Exactly one-third of respondents reported that both they and their husbands were closer to their other children as a result of the adoption and 36% thought that they even had *more* spare time for their other children since the new child had entered the family. If this last result seems some-what unbelievable, it can be explained by some mothers giving up work after the target child entered the family and the family reducing their activities not oriented toward children.

These percentages are underscored by the kinds of comments that parents made when they were describing these effects:

—We got to know quite a few handicapped people. You meet every six weeks, all the handicapped from the societies, and because of that our children learn to see different things and I think they're understanding and they're loving, I really do.

—I think the girls have done more. Say when he couldn't walk, they used to pull him along and drag him around. It's really them who got him walking, really. It's probably made them realize that there are other children less well off than themselves.

—We enjoy having him about. The kids like to cuddle him. There's a big argument when they get home from school over whose turn it is to have him. Jeremy likes getting him ready for bed sometimes, apart from doing his nappy. He asked if he could bathe him one night.

—The boys were very curious about girls before. Now their outlook is healthier. And Lionel was never able to build good relations with his brothers. But he's very good with Laura.

—It makes them more aware that there are other children different from them.

—They are learning to be more flexible, more compassionate.

In summary, most respondents thought that the overall effect of the adoption was beneficial for the children already in the family. Their explanations of these benefits centered on two major areas: sheer enjoyment of the new brother or sister and enhanced development of various character traits because of the new child's handicap. This second finding tends to be supported in the literature on the effects children with handicaps have on siblings (Powell & Ogle, 1985, p. 9). Growing up with a brother or sister who is handicapped apparently can lead to compassion and selflessness and puts one at risk for developing the kind of orientation that could lead to a career in the helping professions (Grossman, 1972; Sullivan, 1979).

Social Relations

Thus far, the focus has been on the impact of the adoption on within-family functioning, on examining effects on the individual parents, the marriage, and other children. In addition, the interview explored changes in social functioning outside the immediate family, both with extended family members and with friends and neighbors. The answers to several questions (Appendix A, Q. 125–129) were combined to yield a 9-point social impact scale that could vary from a very negative impact of -4 to a very positive impact of $+4$. For example, a respondent who said that she visited both relatives and friends and neighbors less frequently after the placement, and was less close to someone outside the household and had lost a friend because of the adoption, would have received a -4 on this scale. In contrast, a respondent who said that she visited both relatives and friends and neighbors more frequently since the placement, felt closer to someone outside the household, and had made new friends because of the adoption would have scored a $+4$ on this scale.

The range of scores for both mothers and fathers for the first-adopted child was from -1 to $+3$, with most scores being either 0 or $+1$. The mean for mothers was $+.79$ and the mean for fathers was $+.49$, indicating a slightly positive overall social impact. The data for the second-adopted children were very similar, with a mean of $+.83$ for mothers and $+.55$ for fathers.

Many parents responded that not much had changed in their social lives as a result of the child entering the family. Parents who mentioned positive changes talked about meeting new people and getting involved in new activities as a result of the adoption. Several families mentioned becoming active in organizations that served people with handicaps and meeting new friends through those organizations.

Several respondents mentioned how friendly people were when they discovered the adoption. One mother related an edifying story about a new neighbor who thought at first that their child had been born to them. The neighbor was reserved and nervous around them, this mother said. When she found out that the child had been adopted, her behavior changed completely, and she became outgoing and openly friendly. This respondent realized after that experience how differently people who give birth to children with handicaps may be treated by others.

One father expressed very powerfully the positive social impact on their family. He said, "She's not our baby; she's everybody's baby. We've gone back to the time when you could leave your front door open. Everybody's so friendly. People come knocking on the door, offering help."

In addition to this outpouring of friendliness described by some respondents, others mentioned specific people to whom they felt closer as a result of the adoption. For families without any children before the adopted child, respondents sometimes talked about becoming closer to their friends and relatives who had children because now they had more in common. One couple described feeling closer to their sister/sister-in-law who had given birth to a child with a handicap. And several adoptive mothers reported that they had become closer to their own mothers, who had been extremely generous in their offers of help with the new child.

SUMMARY AND CONCLUSIONS

A variety of measures to assess the impact that adopting a child who is retarded has on the adopting family were examined in this chapter. Although there were occasional reports of negative effects, and in a few families the adoption seems to have been more negative than positive, overall the results indicate remarkably easy adjustment to the presence of the child in the family. This adjustment seems to be in contrast to the typical reactions of families who give birth to children who are handicapped, as described in Chapter 2. These differences between adoptive and birth families, if they are not an artifact of the sampling differences already described, may be a function of many variables, including the way in which the child entered the family, the perception of that event by the family, the characteristics of the family members, and their existing support systems. The present research can only hint at which of these variables are important ones. These variables are discussed more fully in the final chapter. But first, in order to complete the portrait of adoptive families, it is necessary to describe the difficulties of the adoptions. In the next chapter, the focus is on the problems that some families experienced, problems that arose in spite of the family's preparation for, and seeming willingness to rear, a child who is mentally retarded.

Chapter 9

Impact of the Adoption

II. The Crises and the Sorrows

Betty and Victor Campbell had adjusted well to the placement of James, their 3-year-old son who had Down syndrome. In fact, they had adjusted so well that they decided they wanted to adopt another baby as soon as James' adoption was finalized. Because they were working with the same agency and most of their papers were still current, it did not take too many months before Robert, less than a year old, was living with them. The Campbells expected the adjustment to be very easy again, but had not anticipated the difference between taking care of two babies and taking care of one. Betty described her reaction:

> . . . when we first had him, we'd only had him, I think, about a month, and I just didn't feel as though I could wash any more dirty nappies, or, you know, waltz around doing this and that and the other for them. And, at the time, I wasn't very well, you know, it had pulled me down a bit, and at the time he was going through a period of not sleeping and not feeding and losing weight, and all sort of physical problems, really. His foster mother had been to see him, and she's monopolizing the whole day, and he wouldn't settle after she'd gone, and he'd just nonstop scream, and of course, lack of sleep didn't help much.

❑ ❑ ❑

Rochelle Packard, a single woman, had adopted Charles, a child with severe physical and mild mental handicaps. A year later, when she decided that she'd like to try for a second child,

145

both as a companion for Charles and to keep herself busy, she was dissuaded from taking on another child with physical disabilities. "Imagine trying to cope with two wheelchairs," she was told. So, after consideration of several children, she finally chose Thomas, a boy with severe retardation who was only slightly younger than Charles. A year later at the interview, however, Rochelle admitted that it had probably been a mistake. "I should have taken a child with higher intellectual ability, for Charles' sake. Charles tried to treat Thomas as a friend, as an equal. Thomas couldn't understand, and then Charles would shout and start fighting. I questioned whether I had made the right decision." She hastened to add, "I wouldn't let him go now, but I might have made a different decision if I'd known."

❑   ❑   ❑

Irene and Frank Dorsey decided after 9 months that they couldn't go through with David's adoption. He functioned far below what they had expected, what they said that they had been told to expect. His behavior with other children and adults was immature, silly, and childish. He couldn't do the simplest academic tasks, no matter how much they drilled him. "I felt that it was a losing battle. I felt as if we were constantly nagging him," Irene explained. "It's not really much of a life for any of us."

❑   ❑   ❑

Laura and Jonathan Atkinson had three biological children, but had talked about adoption for a long time, even before they had married. When they finally acted on the decision by contacting an agency, they continued to prepare thoroughly by talking to friends and relatives and visiting places where people with handicaps lived and worked. Thus, it was a bit of a surprise to them that they still had such a difficult time when Andrew was actually placed with them. Describing their first meeting, Laura said, "He was not beautiful at all. He hardly had any hair, and his forehead seemed huge." Jonathan added, "We were shocked at his physical appearance." Laura continued, "After we got him, there was a sort of secondary shock in a way. His muscle tone is very poor, and I realized, suddenly, how very little he could actually do."

Elaborating on their reactions during the first weeks and months, Laura described, "We had a period of adjustment probably similar to parents having given birth to a Down's child. We actually came face to face with the reality of it." Jonathan

affirmed Laura's comment and added, "We were having some of the same feelings that a person having a Down's child biologically would have. The first time we saw him, we went home and literally grieved for the child that might have been."
Laura agreed, "It was quite hard to get over that; it was quite strong. Yes, we'd chosen to have him, but it seemed sad that he was marred."

❏   ❏   ❏

Despite the overall positive impact of the placements for most of the adoptive families, the preceding stories and quotations indicate that there were also difficulties. For a very few families, like the Dorseys and Rochelle Packard, the difficulties, the sorrows, and the crises predominated, and the placement was considered to be an error. These families are examined in detail in this chapter.

For the majority of the families, the problems were not extraordinary. Indeed, some of them were predictable reactions to the readjustments necessary when a new person enters the family. As with the Campbells, some caretakers felt overwhelmed with the burden of care required by the child. Betty's description seems not very different from one that we would hear from any mother having to serve the needs of two children, both still in diapers. The concerns that she expressed and the difficulties that she was experiencing were clearly reality crises, objective day-to-day problems arising in the context of caring for the handicapped child.

In contrast, the Atkinsons described a somewhat different set of reactions. By their own admission, at the time of placement they had not yet accepted their child for what he was. Despite their preparation for this child and their willingness to rear him, they were experiencing some of the existential crises that were described in Chapter 2, crises that characterize many of the families who give birth to children with handicaps. In this chapter, both reality and existential crises are described. However, because most of the difficulties that families experienced seemed to be reality-based problems, the focus will be on them. Case study presentations are used for the existential problems because they were atypical of the sample as a whole.

PROBLEMS PRIOR TO PLACEMENT

The Search

Some adopters encountered difficulties right at the outset in searching for a child that they felt they could nurture. Exactly 50% of the families had to contact more than one agency before their first adoption and 29% of them contacted four or more agencies. Although the majority of adopters had very good comments to make about their agencies and the social workers who were involved in their cases, negative sentiments were also expressed. A few families encountered agencies where staff were very discouraging about placing children with handicaps and advised them against it. Other families felt that undue pressure was exerted on them to make a quick decision or to accept a child whom they were not ready to accept. For example, the Brooks reported that their agency wanted an overnight decision after they had seen the child only once. They thought it was "pushing a bit," and initially said no. In fact, Donald Brook felt that even the first visit was scheduled before they were prepared for it. He said it was "emotional blackmail," because "once you'd seen her, it's hard to forget. She touched my face and she smiled. I couldn't walk away."

Similarly, the Traverts reported what they thought was undue pressure. Kenneth Travert, in describing the social worker, said, "She made a very strong pitch." Frances agreed, and added, "She more or less told us that if we turned him down, it was his last chance." In fact, according to the Traverts, when the adoptive child, Peter, was first described, no mention was made of his intellectual deficit or the particular syndrome that had caused it.

So, some families experienced problems even in the search for their child. For most families, however, the waiting time was short and the agency workers were helpful and encouraging. Nonetheless, even with this support many parents described preplacement worries and anxieties that surfaced after they had made the decision to adopt a particular child, but before the child actually came to live with them. Sometimes these anxieties were realistic concerns; sometimes they were not. Sometimes they arose because of the attitudes and behavior of someone outside the family; sometimes they were solely individual perceptions.

Parental Preplacement Worries

Exactly 60% of the respondents admitted that they had experienced worries and anxieties after the child was chosen but before he or she actually came to live with them. Most of these respondents, 64%, realized that their concerns had been unnecessary and that what they had been worried about did not materialize as a problem after the child joined the family. For 25% of the adopted children, however, the worries were realistic and respondents described a variety of difficulties associated with the placement.

These preplacement anxieties spanned a number of different dimensions. Some were very specific concerns relating to the characteristics of the child. For example, one single mother worried about being able to physically lift a teenager who was nonambulatory. Another couple, adopting a child with numerous health problems, were apprehensive about whether the physical health of the child would prevent them from enjoying him. Other concerns were more generally related to being the parent of any handicapped child, as in the case of a few mothers who were giving up work or social activities in order to take care of the child.

Many of the preplacement worries, however, were less present oriented. Some parents reported that they worried about what would happen to the adopted child once he or she became an adult. Several respondents with nonhandicapped children wondered about whether the adopted child would be a burden to these children.

Finally, several respondents reported very general and diffuse anxieties, feelings of self-doubt—were they doing the "right" thing, could they cope. As one mother who typified this reaction said, "In the back of my mind I was always thinking, 'Am I doing the right thing? What have I let myself in for? What would my mum say?'"

What mother did say, or, more generally, the reactions of relatives and significant others, sometimes exacerbated and sometimes ameliorated these preplacement anxieties. Almost one-half, 48%, of the respondents encountered some discouraging attitudes when they first decided to adopt the child. For 29% of the families, these negative attitudes were from relatives, most frequently their own mothers and fathers, who still seemed to want to protect their children from life's vicissitudes. Although all of these respondents obviously went ahead with the adoption anyway, some of them did so with more trepidation than they would have had if others had been uniformly encouraging. Nonetheless, most of the adopters took the attitude that this was their decision and their decision alone. As one mother replied when she was told not to waste her life in taking care of a child with severe mental and physical handicaps, "It's my life."

POSTPLACEMENT DIFFICULTIES

Many families, even those whose global outcome scores were high, experienced some difficulties with adjustment after the child was placed. In fact, on the various interview questions, only five adoptive families reported no negative impact of any kind. Four of these five also showed no negative impact on the Farber questionnaire. The other 37 families, 88% of the sample, reported some problems after the child actually came to live with them. Most of these problems seemed to be reality based, and many of them were short lived. However, as with the biological families of children who are retarded, existential and reality concerns are not easily separable. They are coincident in time and undoubtedly interact with each other in an accelerating fashion, with increases in one causing even greater increases in the other until a crisis is reached. This section describes these adjustment problems, considers their prevalence, and compares them, when relevant, to the corresponding positive impact. Later in this chapter several of the adoptions that had the most negative outcomes are examined; these adoptions experienced problems that seemed to be more clearly in the existential domain.

Impact on Parents and the Parental Relationship

As described in Chapter 8, most families concluded that the adoption had had a positive impact on the family. For a few respondents, however, the impact was rated as negative. Answers to specific questions reveal exactly why this negative assessment was made.

Some respondents thought that the adoption had resulted in a change for the worse in the behavior or personality characteristics of either the mother, the father, or both. Behavior or personality was said to have changed for the worse in 14%, or 8 of the 56 placements. Descriptions of these negative changes focused primarily on temperament or affect, and the behaviors arising from them. For example, several respondents reported that they had felt more irritable or depressed since the adoption and that they thought these feelings caused them to behave in ways that were atypical of them and that they did not like. As Irene Dorsey said, "We used to shout at David and be physical with him, which isn't our nature. We're both very placid people."

These negative effects on behavior and personality were supported by the answers to some specific questions relating to the same domain. In the semi-structured interview, respondents reported that they had more arguments with their spouses after 12% of the adoptions. Similarly, on the Farber questionnaire mothers reported getting angry more easily after 16% of the placements, and fathers after 13% of the placements. Comparable results were found for the question on nervousness. In 16% of the adoptions, mothers reported that they were more nervous after the placement and, in 7% of the placements, fathers reported that they were more nervous. A small minority of mothers and fathers also answered that they worried more. For mothers, this minority represented 15% of the adoptions and for fathers it represented 11% of the adoptions.

Two respondents of the 36 currently married parents thought that their sex life had gotten worse since the placement. And for the six unmarried women in the sample, three answered that it was more difficult for them to maintain an active social life with men. "It's almost impossible, really," said Rochelle Packard, single parent to two adopted children with handicaps.

Despite these negative reports, an even smaller number of respondents stated that they were, overall, unhappier as a result of the placements. In the interview one mother and one father reported being unhappier after the placement of a first-adopted child; two mothers and fathers reported being unhappier after the placement of a second-adopted child. These reports represented three different adoptions. The Farber question on happiness corroborated the reports for two of the adoptions, but not the third. Thus, at most three and possibly only two adoptions resulted in parental unhappiness. All three of these adoptions had composite scores of 4 or lower on the 2- to 6-point scale described in Chapter 8. The two adoptions that resulted in parental unhappiness reported on both the interview and the Farber questionnaire received composite scores of 3 and 2 and global impact scores of 0 or less. They will be among the individual cases that are discussed in detail later in this chapter.

In addition to changes in personality and behavior producing a negative impact on parents, some respondents reported changes in the amount of time that they had to spend with each other or just on their own engaged in leisure activities. For 39% of the adoptions, respondents said that they had less time to spend with their spouse after the child's placement. In addition, after 20% of the adoptions, parents reported that they had had to give up some discretionary activities because of the time demands at home. Although these demands were mostly on the mothers, who were in almost all cases the primary caretakers, in approximately one-quarter of the households mothers reported that their husbands had taken on a greater share of child care and other domestic responsibilities since the child's placement in the home.

Impact on Siblings

Many of the positive outcomes for other children in the family when a child was adopted were examined in Chapter 8. These positive outcomes predominated. However, respondents also described some negative effects for their other children after the adopted child entered the family. Overall, exactly one-third of the families with other children reported some negative effect on those children. Specifically, in 11% of the placements parents reported that children already in the family began demonstrating negative behaviors and personality traits after the child who was handicapped arrived. In 33% of the families with other children, the parents reported that those children expressed some resentment about the newcomer. In 17% of these families, the parents described incidents where the other children hurt the target child. All such incidents had the character, however, of typical sibling battles engaged in by young children.

Some parents admitted that the resentment by other children was based on changes in the household that made the environment less desirable for those children. For example, 22% of the parents assessed that their other children received less attention from them after the adoption. In addition, 17% of the parents believed that they had argued more with their other children since the adopted child's placement. Nonetheless, only one mother and one father thought that they had become less close to their other children because of the adoption.

Sometimes negative effects took place outside the family, but were attributable to the presence of the target child. For 23% of the placements where there were other children already in the home, the parents said that the other children were teased by a nonfamily member because of the adopted child. Although this teasing was regarded as unfortunate by the parents, these same parents were usually proud of their children for the way in which they defended their brother or sister. For example, one mother reported that her nonhandicapped 7-year-old was told by another child, "Your sister looks funny." The reply was, "We don't care—we love her."

Economic Difficulties

In both the United States and Great Britain, economic aid is available to families who adopt children who are retarded. In the United States, aid is provided specifically for families who adopt children with special needs. Regulations regarding the aid are contained in the Adoption Assistance and Child Welfare Act of 1980 (Public Law 96-272) and are interpreted in specific instances by the state where the adoption takes place.

In Great Britain at the time of the study, no subsidies were available exclusively for families who had adopted children with handicaps. However, a variety of subsidies were and are available for persons who are handicapped and their parents or guardians. Parents may receive these benefits regardless of whether the child was born to them or adopted. For example, rate relief, a form of financial assistance, may be given to families who have to make special alterations or additions to their home because of a person's disabilities (Department of Health and Social Security, 1985b). An attendance allowance is paid to disabled people who need frequent attention or supervision from others. Extra subsidies are given for individuals needing care at night as well as during the day (Department of Health and Social Security, 1985a). Many of the adoptive families in this study had received or were receiving some form of economic assistance to help with the care of their children. Nonetheless, 26% reported that they had had to cut back on expenses since the adoption and 19% said that expenses were greater than they had anticipated.

In part, the need to reduce expenses resulted from reduced maternal employment after child placement. Fourteen mothers, 33% of the sample, either stopped working entirely or worked fewer hours after the first adoption. An additional two mothers reduced their paid employment after the second adoption. Although most mothers did not view this work change negatively, a few did talk about reduced income and the changes that that meant for the family.

The families who felt an economic impact described having to be much more careful in what they spent than they had been before the child was placed with them. Discretionary goods and activities such as clothes, cigarettes, liquor, local entertainment, and holidays were sometimes sacrificed. A few respondents, those for whom the target child was their first child, expressed surprise at the cost of certain essential items for children. One mother, for example, said that she was shocked at the price of socks and at how frequently her baby, in the crawling stage, needed new ones. None of the families who reported a negative economic impact seemed to be upset or hostile about these sacrifices, however. Their attitude was generally one of benign acceptance, wherein those who decide to adopt a child must assume financial responsibility for that child.

Social Relations

As described in Chapter 8, the positive impact on social relationships far outweighed the negative. However, a few respondents did report some negative effects. For 8% of the families, contact with relatives was less frequent after the placement, and for 17% of the families, contact with friends and neighbors was less frequent. Respondents attributed most of this reduced frequency to less available time. A few, however, described situations where other people were unwilling or seemed unable to accept the adopted child.

One family, for example, talked at length about the negative reactions of the mother's parents. They were not easily able to accept having a grandchild with retardation, and postponed visiting because of it. When they finally did come, the grandfather withdrew from social contact and refused to hold, touch, or even look at his grandchild. It was many months before his behavior changed.

Only two respondents reported that someone in the family had lost a friend because of the adoption, and in one of these cases it was attributed not to the adopted child's handicap, but to her race. The mother related,

"My eldest boy lost two friends. They didn't want to play with him because he had a colored sister. But he wasn't in any way worried because they weren't really what he called special friends. That was mainly on the basis of color, not a handicap."

Another mother described an incident with one of her friends who was visiting when the adopted child returned from school. The friend froze, seemed extremely uncomfortable, and left soon thereafter, never to return or resume contact in any way. Even for this family, though, the overall impact was positive because the family reported making many new friends and becoming closer to relatives as a result of the adoption.

Difficulties with Professionals

In adopting a child families come into contact with a variety of professionals, including social workers, doctors, health visitors (who, in Great Britain, routinely come to the home after a new child joins the family), teachers, psychologists, and so forth. The majority of the respondents thought that these professionals had been uniformly helpful and had made the adoption and subsequent childrearing easier than it might have been. Some families, however, described one or more professionals with whom they had had difficulties. Although only one respondent said that she thought that no professionals had been helpful, 38% reported having had difficulties with at least one person. There was no tendency to name any particular profession more than any other; teachers, doctors, health visitors, social workers, and various types of therapists were praised and damned with approximately equal frequency.

Most of the complaints focused on the prejudicial attitudes of the professionals and the insensitivity that they displayed in their interactions with the adopted child and the family. One mother, for example, reported that a physician who was doing an eye examination on her child asked, "Any other peculiarities with this mongol?" Another mother said that the reaction of the health visitor, right after the child's placement, was that it was crazy to be adopting a child who was retarded and that children like that should be in institutions.

Some parents believed that many professionals were rigid and sometimes obstructive rather than constructive in their interactions with families. Professionals were sometimes described as dogmatic, supporting the system and the regulations rather than regarding the welfare of the child as foremost. Adoption agencies that would not handle the adoptions, schools that refused to educate the child, and medical personnel who treated the child as an object rather than a person were viewed in this way. In addition, some mothers expressed the feeling that they were regarded as incompetent and dismissed as unimportant rather than treated as valuable resources working toward the goal of an optimal upbringing for the child.

Child Characteristics Associated with Difficulties

Data on positive impact presented in Chapter 8 focused on first-adopted children, but indicated differences between first- and second-adopted children. In a number of instances, more negative results were found for second-adopted children. These results are reviewed in this section, with the cautionary admonitions that the sample size for second adoptions is only 12 and that second-adopted children had been in their adoptive homes a shorter time (17 months) than had first-adopted children (37 months).

In general, second adoptions were more problematic than first adoptions. Table 9-1 summarizes the results for a variety of the interview measures and the combined questions on the Farber questionnaire. Of the nine different maternal assessments of the child, the adoption, and the effects on family members, seven showed a more favorable response for the first-adopted child. Statistical testing was done on the Farber score differences, demonstrating a significantly higher score for Child 1 than for Child 2 ($t = 3.4$, df $= 11$, $p < .01$).

In addition to the measures displayed in Table 9-1, QRS scores were compared for the 10 mothers who had completed questionnaires for both

TABLE 9-1

Comparisons of First- and Second-Child Adoptions—Maternal Assessments

Measure				
Origin[a]	Range[b]	Child 1 score	Child 2 score	Direction of difference
Impact (83-87)	−3 to +3	1.69	1.83	2 > 1
Social impact (125-129)	−4 to +4	.79	.83	2 > 1
Expectations (135)	1 to 3	2.63	2.17	1 > 2
Difficulty in raising (137)	1 to 3	2.34	1.42	1 > 2
Belonging to family (138)	1 to 3	2.65	2.09	1 > 2
Physical abilities (139)	1 to 3	2.44	2.08	1 > 2
Intellectual abilities (140)	1 to 3	2.29	2.00	1 > 2
Good relationships (141)	1 to 3	2.56	2.27	1 > 2
Do it again (142)	1 to 3	2.88	2.58	1 > 2
Farber, Q. 1, 3, 5-10	8 to 25[c]	20.83	17.58	1 > 2

Note. Based on 12 double adopters; $t(11) = 3.4$, $p < .01$.
[a] All numbers in parentheses refer to relevant questions on the semi-structured interview (Appendix A).
[b] For all measures, higher scores indicate more positive outcomes.
[c] For 7 of these 8 questions, possible scores ranged from 1 to 3; for 1 question, possible scores ranged from 1 to 4 (see Appendix C).

TABLE 9-2

**Maternal Holroyd Scores for First- and Second-Adopted Children
in Double Adopting Families (N = 10)**

Category/QRS subscale	Child 1		Child 2		
	X	SD	X	SD	t
Parent problems					
Poor health/mood	1.1	2.2	1.5	2.1	.88
Excess time demands	4.7	2.0	4.1	2.2	−1.33
Negative attitudes	5.1	2.8	6.0	2.9	.94
Overprotection/dependency	3.8	2.5	3.4	1.6	− .50
Lack of social support	4.3	.9	4.4	1.4	.26
Overcommitment/martyrdom	2.7	1.2	2.8	.8	.29
Pessimism	3.3	1.7	3.8	1.5	.68
Family functioning					
Lack of family integration	2.1	1.8	3.8	2.6	3.16*
Limits on family opportunity	.6	1.3	.5	1.3	−1.00
Financial problems	3.5	1.7	3.2	1.3	−1.15
Child problems					
Physical incapacitation	4.5	2.7	5.7	2.2	1.06
Lack of activities	.9	.6	1.1	.7	.80
Occupational limitations	3.5	1.2	3.5	1.7	0.00
Social obtrusiveness	2.1	1.2	2.3	.8	.56
Difficult personality	12.2	3.2	17.6	4.3	4.12*

* $p < .01$

of their adopted children. As Table 9-2 shows, the Holroyd comparisons tend to confirm the conclusions suggested by the other measures. Of the 15 QRS scales, 10 show more favorable scores for Child 1, and only 4 show more favorable scores for Child 2. Separate t tests, however, found that only two of these differences were statistically significant. Mothers felt that there was less family integration with Child 2 and that Child 2 had a more difficult personality.

These data on second-adopted children are suggestive, but clearly need to be replicated. Not all measures showed a difference, and in many cases the differences were very small. In addition, the very small sample size poses problems for generalization. Nonetheless, it may be that the reality burdens in caring for more than one child who is retarded overstress even the most successfully functioning family members. It may also be that only families with the best adaptation to a first child who is retarded even consider adopting a second, and that it is likely that there will be some regression toward the mean. Clearly, it is a subject for additional research and one for which practitioners are in definite need of data (Sinclair, 1985).

In addition to adoption order, the age and gender of the children were examined to determine if either of these characteristics were related to outcome. Table 9-3 presents the means of the 2- to 6-point composite score and the -3 to $+3$ global impact score, converted to a 0- to 6-point scale to facilitate data analysis. For each score, adoptions of younger children were rated more positively than were those of older children, and adoptions of boys were rated more positively than were those of girls. Two-way analyses of variance on these data indicate a significant main effect for gender but not for age for the composite score ($F(df=1, 38) = 5.1, p < .05$), and a significant main effect for age but not for gender for the global impact score ($F(df=1, 38) = 10.7, p < .01$). Neither interaction was statistically significant.

TABLE 9-3

Age and Gender Means for Adoption Outcome

Age	Composite Score		Global Impact Score	
	Boys	Girls	Boys	Girls
≤ 24 months	5.8	5.4	5.6	5.2
> 24 months	5.8	4.8	4.5	4.1

Thus, although both measures showed the same direction of difference, gender and age each yielded statistically reliable results in only one analysis. These data should therefore be considered only as suggestive. In particular, the gender results are suspect because they are discrepant with other research findings. In general, if gender differences are found in adoption studies, they show more positive outcomes for girls than for boys (Nelson, 1985; Raynor, 1980).

On the other hand, the significant effect of age on the global impact score is consistent with other findings that older-child adoptions, especially of children 8 years of age or more, are less successful (Coyne & Brown, 1985; Nelson, 1985). Of course, because age may be correlated with many other factors, this effect, although more frequently found in the literature than the one for gender, still requires further exploration.

One of the correlates of age is preadoptive history. Older children tended to have had more placements, to have been in care longer, and to have been in institutions. In Chapter 7, length of time in care, number of previous placements, and history of institutional residence were combined to describe the quality of the preadoptive environment. Children with the best histories, 0 on this scale, were compared with children with the worst histories, 3 on the scale, on the 2- to 6-point composite scale. The 30 children with good histories had a mean of 5.53 ($SD = .73$), whereas the 20 children with the worst histories had a lower mean of 5.00 ($SD = 1.30$). The difference between these means was significant (t(one-tailed) = 1.86, $df=48, p < .05$).

Caution is warranted in interpreting the age and preadoptive history effects on adjustment. The current research was not designed to examine these specific child characteristics and the sample was not selected with them in mind. Future research interested in age, gender, preadoptive history, or other child characteristics would have to systematically sample for them, carefully controlling for potentially confounding variables such as severity of retardation, number of other handicapping conditions, adoptive family characteristics, and so on.

Summary

Most families, then, experienced at least some problems in the areas of family relations, economic resources, social functioning, and interactions with professionals. Despite these difficulties, though, the impact of the adoption was rated as positive and the adoption was a success in all but a few families. What differentiated these few families from the others? Because there were so few in this study, this question is impossible to answer definitively. However, perhaps examining the worst outcomes in some detail can provide some insights as to the causes of the failures so that future research may be able to explore them in more depth and practitioners may be able to avoid pitfalls in placement and postplacement counseling. In the next section, five case studies are presented. Each of these five adoptions received composite scores of 4 or lower, and mothers did not rate the positive impact more highly than the negative impact.

CASE STUDIES OF NEGATIVE
OUTCOMES

The Dorseys

The Dorseys represented the worst outcome as determined by a variety of measures. They received the lowest possible scores on both the 2- to 6-point composite scale and the 7-point impact scale. In addition, the placement of David with them disrupted, and approximately a year after he came to live with them, he returned to the children's home where he had been living prior to the placement. Indeed, it is serendipitous that this placement was even included in the sample. At the time of referral, David was still living with the Dorseys; by the time the interview was conducted, he had left.

Irene and Frank Dorsey were a middle-class couple who lived in a comfortable, carefully furnished, and spotlessly clean three-bedroom house located in a northwestern suburb of London. Their lives were stable and routine, but they felt that there was something missing. They wanted children. Although there was no diagnosed infertility, they had been married for 6 years and had been trying unsuccessfully to have biological children during most of that time. They first thought about adoption and initially made inquiries in response to a newspaper advertisement. For them, it was clearly a substitute for having biological children. In fact, Irene said, "I thought with having David, it would take my mind off, you know, wanting a child. But I don't think it made any difference really; I still wanted one of my own, even though I'd got David."

David, 11 years old at the time of placement, was classified as educationally subnormal (ESN), with the etiology of his retardation unknown. He was first diagnosed at age 6, when he came to the attention of local authorities because of parental abuse and neglect. He was suffering from what were diagnosed as nonaccidental injuries and was severely malnourished, weighing only 25 pounds (a normal weight for a boy that age is more than 40 pounds). He was removed from the home, put in the hospital for treatment of his injuries and malnutrition, and transferred after several months to the children's home, where he stayed until he was placed with the Dorseys 5 years later.

The Dorseys first learned about David from a photobook. His picture was appealing and he was described as tidy, neat, and educationally slow, rather than retarded. These characteristics fit what the Dorseys had in mind. Cleanliness and tidiness were important to them. They wouldn't have wanted an unkempt child. They also did not see the educational slowness as a permanent disability. Irene said, "We felt that with our encouragement and his teacher's, he would progress. We were hoping that David would eventually grow out of it." Irene went on to describe several children who, she had heard, had gone from an ESN to a normal school.

Their first meeting with David left them with reservations. They were disturbed by some of his behavior at that meeting. He seemed very immature and lacked concentration, talking first about one thing and then another. They also wanted more medical and psychological information about his slowness and were upset that it was not available. These reservations persisted, but they decided to proceed nonetheless.

In retrospect, they realized that this decision was a mistake. They were frustrated in their attempts to teach him skills that he just seemed unable to learn. Irene sighed, "We found it very tiring—wondering whether we could cope much longer." Frank Dorsey added, "If we had known his limits, we wouldn't have taken him." This conclusion was confirmed by their answer to the interviewer's following question: "Do you think that if you had been told when you first inquired about David that he would, at 18, still only be functioning like a 9- or 10-year-old, would you have taken him on?" Frank replied, "No, no, I don't think so. If we knew that whatever we would do wouldn't make any difference, we wouldn't have wanted him." Irene nodded in agreement. At another point she said, reflecting about the decision and what they had learned from it, "I wouldn't take on another ESN child, if I had the choice; I'd be more choosy."

In summary, then, the Dorseys were not prepared for nor did they really want to adopt a child who was retarded. They viewed adoption as a way to replace the child that they had been unable to have biologically. David's ESN diagnosis and lack of definite organic etiology allowed them to believe and hope that his slowness was temporary and could be overcome with diligence and care. This expectation, coupled with a general lack of experience with children and lack of tolerance for disturbance in their routinized life, seemed to be responsible for the breakdown in the placement. Whether more careful preplacement preparation or postplacement counseling would have prevented the disruption cannot be ascertained with the data available in this study. It is possible that they would have, but it is also possible that the Dorseys were a couple with characteristics inappropriate for being parents of a child who is retarded. Certainly, they do not fit the portrait described by Gallagher (1968) when she listed desirable qualities for parents who successfully adopt children with mental retardation. They did not seem exceptionally patient and flexible, knowledgeable about mental retardation or realistic in their expectations for the child, or secure about parenting and accepting a child with limited capabilities.

Dorothy Oppler

The adoption with the second worst outcome as measured by the two global scales was that of a single woman. She said that the adoption had worked out less well than she had expected and that she would not do it again, scoring a 2 on the 2- to 6-point scale. Her answers to questions about impact resulted in a score of -2 on the -3 to $+3$ impact scale. Dorothy Oppler also had very low scores on the Holroyd QRS. In fact, her scores were lower than the mean for the adopted sample on 14 of the 15 scales. The probability that this phenomenon could occur by chance is extremely small, less than .001. Furthermore, her scores were also lower than those for Holroyd's developmentally disabled sample on 14 of the 15 scales, suggesting that she was experiencing even more stress than families with birth children who are handicapped.

Despite their similarly negative outcomes, Dorothy Oppler and the Dorseys represent dramatically different portraits of adopters. Whereas the Dorseys were not experienced with children and were relatively unfamiliar with handicaps and persons who are handicapped, the opposite was true for Dorothy. She was a special education teacher and had done periodic short- and long-term fostering during the previous 8 years. She was also different from the Dorseys in terms of what kind of child she wanted to adopt. While they basically desired a nonhandicapped child, she did not. In fact, Dorothy said explicitly, "I'd like someone no one else would take, somebody that's likely to get left." The only restriction she mentioned in the interview was that she did not want a child with severe emotional problems.

Dorothy did not make a hasty decision about Susan's adoption. She first learned about her from a photo sheet, but at the time was not willing to sacrifice her job or her boyfriend. She saw advertisements for Susan several times during the next year, and finally decided to pursue the adoption. In describing this decision, Dorothy offered the following rationale:

> I've always worked with handicapped people—for 12 years I've worked with handicapped people. And I felt that the chances of her getting a family were quite slim because of her total handicap. And I was in a position, because of my experience and me as a person, I could offer her love and a home, and I had the skills to cope with her handicap, and she was somebody that needed a chance, really, to be given a chance to be part of society. It wasn't love, it wasn't "oh gosh," you know, and it's still not like that at all, it's not. It's just, this is what I can offer, a sheltered accommodation, support, and, call it love, but it's total commitment.

Part of the reason for the difficulties may reside in the child's characteristics. She was one of the oldest and most handicapped of the adoptees. Born with spina bifida, she was nonambulatory, incontinent, and severely mentally retarded. Thus, the burden of care was large, especially for a single caretaker. However, in her interview these daily chores were not what seemed most troubling to Dorothy. Rather, it was what she perceived as Susan's emotional problems, arising from her history of abuse, neglect, and institutionalization. Dorothy admitted that her difficulties in dealing with these problems stemmed at least in part from her own history of battering and neglect. In regard to this existential issue, Dorothy had the following insight:

> I've always been someone who loved to live in peace and harmony; I'm a very calm person. I'm suddenly faced with a child who is a shadow of myself as regards the abuse and bereavement and broken, damaged homelife. That's also quite damaging for me to have to look at.

At several points in the interview, Dorothy made comments similar to the one above. Thus, having to relive parts of her own tortured past in her adopted child resulted in an existential crisis that made this adoption more negative than it might have been with a different child.

Despite the overall negative impact, Dorothy was determined to continue the placement. She expressed her long-term goals in the following way:

> Even if I can only offer weekend care eventually when she's 18, when I'm older and I maybe can't lift her that at least she'll have something. And she'll have a mother who cares, whether I care two days a week or I care seven days a week, and she'll have somebody who will speak for her; she'll have somebody; she'll have a base. I don't use the word love too much because it's quite difficult to love somebody who's so disturbed. But Susan will have a base, and she'll have a name, and she'll belong.

In summary, the data indicate that the negative outcome for Susan's adoption was based on both reality and existential issues. Clearly she was a difficult child to care for, but the adoptive mother's own background, a history that was still very much with her, also seemed to play a role in producing the negative effects. Of course, these existential issues are different in content than they are for the family dealing with the birth of the child with handicaps. Nevertheless, they may operate similarly in terms of increasing stress in the parenting role and producing a crisis that may make it difficult to provide for the child's needs in an optimal way.

Additional Negative Outcomes

The other three adoptions that resulted in scores of 4 or lower on the composite scale and a nonpositive rating on the global impact scale all involved families that had adopted more than one child. In all cases, the adoptions of the other children were viewed more positively and did not represent negative outcomes. In two of the families, the adoption was of a second child and the families thought that they were having more problems with this second child than they had had with the first. In one of the families the problems seemed to stem at least in part from the child's poor health and his prognosis of a short life expectancy because of a congenital heart defect.

In the other of these two families, it was very difficult to ascertain the cause of the negative outcome. The family, still in preadoptive placement, seemed not yet to have made a commitment to the child. They were a couple without biologic children, who had initially explored adoption with the hope of getting a healthy baby. Their familiarity with handicaps led them to accept a child with retardation; the rated outcome of their first adoption was quite positive, with a 5 on the 2- to 6-point composite scale and a +1 on the global impact scale. Despite this success with their first-adopted child, when they decided to adopt again they continued to pursue the adoption of a nonhandicapped child. When this pursuit was unsuccessful, the interviewer's impression was that they "settled" for their second child. It is certainly possible that an incomplete resolution of their desire to rear a "normal" child made the adjustment to their second child more difficult. Perhaps it was only after their second try that they fully accepted that they would not be able to adopt a nonhandicapped child. This analysis is quite speculative and is offered more as a suggestion for future study than as a firm explanation of the current results.

Finally, the negative results for the third family seemed to be conclusively rooted in a reality crisis. This family was experienced in childrearing and with handicap and had both biological and adopted children. The negative outcome experienced was firmly tied, in the parents' descriptions, to the child's characteristics. Diane had one of the worst preadoptive histories of the sample. A victim of abuse by a violent stepfather, the daughter of a woman who was mentally disturbed and mentally retarded, she had lived in 33 different residences before placement with the Ziglers. When she was first placed, she had a mild physical and mental handicap; after placement she developed epilepsy and a progressive and incurable neurological condition believed to be at least partially responsible for the development of violent and uncontrollable behavior. Even so, Nora Zigler hastened to qualify her statements about the negative impact, saying that they had felt quite differently in the early years of the placement, before Diane's deterioration and its subsequent effect on the family.

Existential Crisis with Positive Outcome

The Atkinsons, briefly described at the beginning of this chapter, in some ways represent one of the most interesting of the adoption outcomes. They were extremely forthcoming in their interview and unusually articulate in their description of the difficulties that they had experienced in the first few months of Andrew's placement. They are included in this chapter, but not because of an overall negative outcome. In fact, their score on the composite scale was 5, and on the global impact scale, +2. On the Farber questionnaire, neither Laura nor Jonathan had negative changes indicated, and on the QRS they each fell about in the middle of the total sample. Rather, they are of interest in spite of the positive outcome, because they experienced existential crisis. They seemed to have emerged from this crisis with intact strength and the determination and firm commitment to rear Andrew. Thus, their story may be particularly important and relevant to families who give birth to children with handicaps, families who also suffer existential crises.

It would not have been easy to predict that the Atkinsons would have had difficulties based on their motivation for the adoption. They were both experienced with handicaps and had thought about adoption for a long time before they felt in a position to be able to do it. They were ideologically committed to helping. Laura, who had done volunteer work with persons who were handicapped, said, "I felt they needed a voice, because they hadn't one of their own." The initial idea of adopting a child with a handicap was hers, but Jonathan, discouraging at first ("I thought it was a mad idea"), quite quickly felt comfortable with it.

In addition to their ideological commitment, they felt strong support from their religious faith. This support seemed to derive mostly from a spiritual orientation and an attitude toward prayer as a vehicle towards insight and resolution. Jonathan described that he finally felt comfortable with the decision after a reading from Matthew 25, which he cited as "Inasmuch as you've done this to the least of my brethren, you've done it to me." This reading helped him to remember the importance of brotherhood for all persons, regardless of characteristics, and to recognize his role in sharing the responsibility for another, less genetically fortunate individual.

Despite this motivation and support, they still had many doubts, both when they made the decision to adopt Andrew and after he was placed with them. They worried about the lifelong commitment. They agonized about what it would be like when their son reached adulthood, but finally decided that "other people's grown-up handicapped children may look frightening, but your own handicapped child will be your own handicapped child grown up." These concerns gradually abated and they came to the conclusion that they would be a "normal family with a handicapped child" and not a handicapped family.

Nevertheless, they described many difficulties after the placement. Jonathan said that they tested out all their original decisionmaking, worrying again whether they were doing the right thing. Laura admitted that she was "scared stiff," afraid that she wouldn't be able to cope, worried about the effect on their other children. It was "like expecting a first baby. I was completely thrown when we got him."

Bonding took a long time, according to both Laura and Jonathan. "It took 6 months for us to settle down. It's only recently that he's seemed really ours." Laura continued, "In the first fortnight, I'd be changing his nappy or something and I would suddenly, as it were, come to and think, what on earth am I doing here, changing this strange baby's nappy?" Jonathan affirmed Laura's comments and added, "For a long time I related to him, hopefully with love, because I knew that was what I was supposed to do, but it was a long time before I really began to make a relationship with him and began to cuddle him and lift him up because he was Andrew rather than because he was the baby we'd started to foster." In response to the interviewer's query about whether the difficulty was because of Andrew's being adopted or being handicapped, Jonathan answered, "Both, and specifically because it was an adopted handicapped child. Everyone's congratulating us on receiving our adopted child and we were having very mixed feelings."

In regard to these mixed feelings, both Laura and Jonathan seemed to be experiencing many of the reactions that are typical of the family when a child is born retarded. Indeed, they recognized the similarities themselves. Laura said, "We had a period of adjustment probably similar to parents having given birth to a Down's child. We actually came face to face with the reality of it." Jonathan agreed. "Yes, we were having some of the same feelings that a person having a Down's child biologically would have. The first time we saw him, we went home and literally grieved for the child that might have been." Laura added, "It was quite hard to get over that; it was quite strong. Yes, we'd chosen to have him, but it seemed sad that he was marred."

The existential nature of these concerns is highlighted by the comparison Laura made between Andrew and a baby that she miscarried that would have been Andrew's age. Laura explained, "I grieved for the loss of my normal baby and almost rejected Andrew; I could hardly bear to look at him for a fortnight . . . probably in much the same way that a parent giving birth to a handicapped child is grieving for the loss of her normal child."

Laura also described feeling depressed, a reaction that has been found among the biological parents of children with handicaps (Berry & Zimmerman, 1983; Burden, 1980; Solnit & Stark, 1961). She said that her first reaction in difficulty is to get depressed and that Andrew's placement was no exception. For the first few months, she thought daily of giving up. Andrew seemed to take so much time. One of their other children was having a negative reaction with temper tantrums and other behavior problems. And she so frequently felt frustrated trying to teach Andrew to do things that he resisted. Laura elaborated, "It probably takes two weeks of hard slog during which time you begin to think that he will never, ever do it, and then suddenly, there's a breakthrough, whereas with the other children so many things you just began to realize they were doing it. With walking we have to walk him up and down the room, ten times across the room every day, just to get his legs working. He hates most minutes of it, complains immensely." This depression, then, seemed to have both existential and reality bases to it.

The Atkinsons were initially very sensitive to other people's reactions. Laura said, "When you first get them, you feel so conspicuous. It's all so fresh and new and strange." Jonathan elaborated by telling a story about their first day with Andrew. "On the way home, we went to McDonald's to celebrate. It suddenly hit me that no longer would we ever be able to go into McDonald's without being noticed. Was I really prepared for that? Were we really ready to have that?" The reactions of strangers who stared or avoided even minimal contact were disturbing to them. They were also upset by Laura's parents, who initially rejected Andrew. As a consequence of this rejection, Laura and Jonathan did not feel as close to them as they had felt before the placement.

Despite all these crises, about 9 months after the placement both the Atkinsons felt extremely positive. They said that the adoption had made them happier, had added meaning to their lives, had made them more flexible, had brought them closer to each other, had been responsible for their making new friends and getting involved in new activities, and had contributed positively to Jonathan's worklife by helping him build relationships and become more sensitive to other people's needs. They had no hesitation that they would make the decision to adopt if they had it to do over again. In fact, they had even begun talking about adopting a second child with a handicap.

Thus, existential crises notwithstanding, there seemed little doubt that this was a positive outcome. This case study provides insights, however, into the nature of the adjustment that must be made, an adjustment that may be difficult regardless of the way the child enters the family. It also helps to remind us that existential crisis may be an occasion for growth and development, rather than one for distress and disintegration. The courageous self is one that can create meaning from life's experienced realities (Tillich, 1952). Maturity and a heightened sense of self-esteem and self-confidence, of fidelity and awareness, of values and the possibilities of being may emerge from crisis and conflict (Frankl, 1984; May, 1983). For some families a child who is handicapped may mean a new identity that would not have been achieved without that child. Increasingly, the contributions that such children can make to parents and siblings are being viewed more positively (Turnbull & Behr, 1986), and negative reactions are interpreted in the context of lifespan developmental tasks.

SUMMARY AND CONCLUSIONS

Both existential and reality crises occurred in the adoptive families. For a few of these families, the crises made adjustment very difficult and the overall outcomes were negative. For the other families the benefits outweighed the problems, and overall outcomes were considered positive. Although too few families had negative outcomes for generalizations to be formulated, it did seem that both existential and reality crises were components of the poorer adjustments. On the other hand, as the Atkinson case study illustrates, existential crisis does not necessarily lead to poor adjustment. The important next question, then, is, What other variable or variables are responsible for some families adjusting in spite of crises and others not doing so? In the final chapter this question is addressed by reexamination of some of the findings of the present research in the context of reactions of individuals to stress and crisis.

Chapter 10

Looking Behind, Looking Ahead

Consolidation, Summary, and Predictions

Interviewer: What advice would you consider giving to someone who was considering adopting a child like . . . ?
Responses:
— In the last analysis, all adoption comes to your falling in love with the child . . . you click with him. . . . Whatever is said on paper about any child, although you should bear all this in mind, being realistic, in the end you kind of fall in love with them.
— I think it's a lot easier than you would naturally think. Difficulties that somebody like Frank has work for you in many ways.
— Try to see the more normal side . . . try to look for the positive, more normal aspects rather than dwelling upon the negative aspects, which is what the well-meaning officials often do.
— If they felt they could do it, go ahead. It's a positive thing, but be prepared for the down moments . . . Don't expect all good moments . . . and don't try to go it all alone. Seek contact. A support group and friends are really helpful.
— I would suggest that they get advice from somebody beforehand, somebody like perhaps a social worker, or somebody like that, to point out all the pros and cons of the situation. . . . You've got to just be absolutely sure that you know what you're letting yourself in for . . . if you are not absolutely certain, you'll have a nasty reawakening when she does come.
— We were asked to speak at one of the adoption meetings on having a special-needs child, and we said really that having Heather had been quite a lot easier than we had expected . . . you have to look positively at it, thinking of what they can do.

You must be aware of the disadvantages, but also you should know about the rewards.
— People say, aren't you wonderful, but we don't feel wonderful, because it hasn't been difficult. . . . everything seemed so much better than it might have been.
— I mean, obviously, you can't put roses on it. It's not a bed of roses. You can't tell them that. I mean, you've got to tell them all the bad points before you tell them the good points.
— It really doesn't seem as hard as you might think when you first look at it. If there are problems, as the child grow with you, you adapt.
— But anybody who's thinking of adopting should never think twice about it.

❑   ❑   ❑

Most of the advice that respondents gave to the hypothetical potential adopter reflected the results that were presented in Chapters 8 and 9. Mothers and fathers were encouraging, but their enthusiasm was tempered with the need to be cautious and to be fully prepared for what would be a very important commitment, one that might dramatically alter their lives. The best preparation was in talking to and visiting families with children who are retarded, most adopters stated. This advice was typified by the mother who said, "I wouldn't suggest they read the book, because I think that books can put them off, and I think it's finding out what you can from people who've already got one."

The concluding statements of the interview, then, frequently summarized the overall outcome for the families: positive, but recognizing the reality burdens that are part of the rearing of any child, perhaps especially a child who is mentally handicapped. It was proposed in the beginning of this book that this positive outcome would occur because the families would not suffer the existential crises that birth families suffer with the unexpected entrance of a child who is retarded. This proposition was borne out for most of the adoptive families, but not for all. Some few families did suffer existential crises, sometimes with an overall positive result, as was the case with the Atkinsons, and sometimes with a less positive result, as for Dorothy Oppler, both described in Chapter 9.

Thus, a slightly different model from the one proposed in the introduction seems appropriate to fit the present results. Figure 10-1 depicts this model. It is generalizable to the entry of a child who is handicapped into a family either by birth or by adoption. As soon as the child enters the

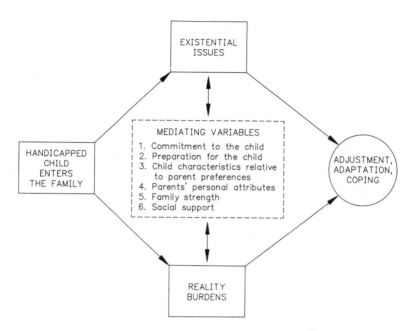

FIGURE 10-1: Adjustment model for families with children who are handicapped. Mediating variables affect the relationship between existential and reality crises.

family, two types of adjustments must be made: Existential issues must be resolved, as depicted in the upper pathway of the model, and reality burdens must be coped with, frequently entailing a time and energy commitment and lifestyle changes that are major adaptational tasks for the family.

In general, the resolution of existential issues is not a major component of the adjustment for adoptive families, but it is important in the adjustment of birth families. There are many reasons for this difference. Some of these reasons are aggregated into a category labeled *mediating variables,* because they are presumed to influence or mediate the resolution of existential issues and the impact of that resolution on the degree of success achieved in coping with reality burdens.

This list of six mediating variables is by no means exhaustive. They were selected for further elaboration because, based on the current research, they are likely to differentiate between parents who adopt children who are handicapped and parents who give birth to children who are handicapped. Therefore, they are also likely to differentiate between those birth parents who successfully cope with a child who is handicapped in the family and those who do not.

MEDIATING VARIABLES

Commitment

If the commitment to the child and the task of childrearing are strong, existential issues are not likely to play a prominent role in the adjustment process. Adoptive families go through a process of decisionmaking and voluntarily commit themselves to the child; that commitment is present when the child enters the family. In contrast, the birth family, although perhaps committed to childrearing in general, is not committed to and does not expect a child with a handicap. Thus, birth parents are likely to ask the existential question "Why me?"—sometimes over and over again—as they rail against the perceived injustice of life's events. One adoptive mother summarized this different quite precisely when she said, "When you're talking about fostering or adopting a mentally handicapped child, it is a completely different relationship. You chose the child; you took it because you felt you could do something for it, whereas the poor mother is presented with this child . . . completely different altogether."

Preparation

Not only is the commitment to the child likely to be greater when the child is adopted, but so is the preparation. Adoptive families are likely to be familiar with handicaps even before they adopt; certainly by the time the child enters the family they are familiar with the particular child's needs and characteristics. In contrast, for the birth family the entrance of the child is an unexpected event. Although they are prepared for a child, they are not prepared for one who may have needs very different from those of a normal infant. They may know little about handicaps in general and nothing about this particular handicap.

This lack of preparation may precipitate existential crises centered around a lack of self-confidence and a perceived inability to cope. As described in Chapter 9, even many of the adoptive mothers, who as a group were highly experienced childrearers, were nervous and apprehensive before the child entered the family, wondering about whether they could cope. Birth parents are much less prepared. In addition, as described in Chapter 2, after the birth professionals are frequently unskilled and inept in providing the kind of services and information that will best prepare parents for the reality burdens that lie ahead. This lack of preparation and existential crises that it causes may make the reality burdens seem worse than they are, thus further eroding self-confidence and precipitating even greater existential crises.

Child/Family Fit

The characteristics of the child relative to the characteristics and life-styles of other family members will undoubtedly influence the degree of existential crisis experienced. Despite the flexibility of the adoptive families in this study, almost all of them said that there were some types of children that they could not or would not accept. As described in Chapter 6, there was no uniformity to these restrictions. A child rejected by one family might be the same child sought by another.

Birth families, of course, are not able to pick and choose among available children. They must accept whoever is born to them, regardless of the fit between the child and their lifestyle. Some studies have found significant influences of type or severity of handicap condition on adjustment outcome, but others have not (Beckman-Bell, 1981; Byrne & Cunningham, 1985; Fried-rich, 1979). There may be a relationship not as a main effect, but as an interaction between child characteristics and family characteristics. The notion of fit between child and parent temperament and personality has gained prominence in recent years in the developmental literature (Belsky, 1984). This mediating variable is a specific instance of that more general relationship.

Parental Personal Attributes

In addition to a fit between family and child characteristics, there are some parental personal attributes that undoubtedly ameliorate the experi-ence of existential crises. The current research was not designed to delineate the personalities of the men and women who adopted children with mental retardation. No measure of personality was included in the interview or questionnaires. Nonetheless, there is extraordinary face validity that these adoptive parents were a select group, both self-selected and agency selected. For the most part, they seemed easygoing, flexible, patient and tolerant, child oriented, and energetic. It is quite possible that they were selected for some or all of these characteristics. In contrast, the birth of a child who is handicapped is likely to be a random event in regard to personality attributes. Therefore, the adoptive parent may be much better able to cope with both existential issues and reality burdens simply by virtue of these personality features.

Family Strength

In addition to individual attributes that may make coping easier for the adoptive parents than for the birth parents, marital and family strength can also influence adjustment, adaptation, and coping. Previous research (Farber, 1960a; Friedrich, 1979) has found that marital integration may be a reasonably good predictor of how well a family copes with the birth of a child who is handicapped. Again, although this study included no formal measure of marital harmony or marital integration, these men and women were less likely to be divorced than the average and were remarkably consensual, at least with respect to the decision to adopt—only one mother and three fathers were initially negative about the idea of adopting a child when the other spouse proposed it.

Support and mutuality within the family are likely to ease the existential concerns that parents might feel. In the case of the adoptive parents, because the decision to adopt was a joint one, when and if reality burdens threatened family happiness, responsibility was also more likely to be joint. In contrast, in the birth family guilt for the handicap may be assigned to only one of the parents. This guilt contributes to the existential crisis and may undermine the strength of the family, making caretaking tasks more burdensome.

Social Support

Just as support within the nuclear family is important for good adjustment, social support outside the family can also be a critical factor. This support may be from formal institutions such as those providing social, medical, and educational services, or from extended family, friends, and parent groups organized around the child. The adoptive family is already tied into the social service network via the adoption agency and it receives a variety of services, both pre- and post-adoptive placement. Many services are also available to birth families, but they do not always know about them or understand how to become eligible for them. Whereas the adoptive family has a ready-made liaison—the adoption worker—for the provision of other services, the birth family frequently feels informationally deprived (Matheny & Vernick, 1969), overwhelmed by an intricate and intermeshed series of regulations that seem impossible to disentangle. Even some of the adoptive families in the current study railed against what they saw as obstructionist attitudes instead of optimal social support systems. And these families, by virtue of their preparation, education, and already established links with social services, would have been far better able to negotiate these networks than would birth parents.

Informal support may be as important as formal support in facilitating adjustment. The attitudes of others are undoubtedly significant in determining the resolution of existential issues. For the birth family, neighbors, friends, extended family members, and colleagues all may be embarrassed and ill at ease and may avoid dealing with what they perceive as a tragic event. In contrast, the family who adopts a child who is handicapped is regarded positively, greeted with enthusiasm and wonder. Over and over again, respondents described how everyone would tell them how special they were, how wonderful they were. Although they would usually say that they did not consider themselves particularly special, ultimately the high esteem in which they were being held by others must have increased their own feelings of well-being. Thus, for the adoptive family initial existential changes may be in a positive direction, whereas in the birth families they are more likely to be in a negative direction.

This difference was portrayed most graphically in the story told by one adoptive mother and related in Chapter 8. This family had moved soon after adopting their baby, who had Down syndrome. A new neighbor, described by the adoptive mother as aloof and ill at ease in her occasional interactions, finally discovered that the baby had been adopted. Her behavior toward the family changed dramatically, becoming friendly and admiring. She no longer acted in a manner that would lead to the family's social isolation.

This kind of isolation is frequently experienced by the birth family, as described in Chapter 2. It is sometimes self-imposed, sometimes of external origin, probably most often a combination of these. Regardless of its origin, isolation means decreased social support and, as a result, intensified existential crises. It can also directly increase reality burdens by making it less likely that caretaking will be shared among those members of the social network that could help out by giving respite to the primary caretakers.

This model, then, proposes two important components to the adjustment of an individual or family: the existential component and the reality component. Although they are separated in the model, they are of course interrelated, and the mediating variables just discussed are part of that interrelationship. This model and the variables that it specifies have important implications for both research and practice.

IMPLICATIONS, SUGGESTIONS
AND PREDICTIONS

Research

Research that focuses on the adaptation to a child with a handicap as a unitary event, occurring only at birth, presents a deceptively simple view of the dynamic and complex nature of adjustment. Similarly, research that measures only existential concomitants, or only reality burdens, is likely to produce a one-dimensional description of what is a multidimensional series of events. It has become increasingly clear in recent years that longitudinal research is necessary (Gallagher, Beckman, & Cross, 1983; Glidden, 1986), because the nature of the event is chronic and changes over time. Adaptation to an infant with Down syndrome is not the same as adaptation to a teenager with Down syndrome, despite the certainty of many adoptive parents that you grow with the problems. Ultimate conclusions must await data derived from continuous and repeated examinations of families throughout the duration of their lifespans. For example, the sample from the current study is being contacted for follow-up 3 to 4 years after the first interview to determine adjustment in the longer term. This type of research is virtually nonexistent in this domain and should be the highest priority for future investigators.

Similarly, univariate research that explores only a small component of the total adjustment process is at best fragmentary, and at worst misleading. For example, early studies in the adjustment to the birth of children with handicaps tended to focus on the immediate existential crises that were precipitated. As a result of this narrow focus, investigators adopted a negative bias that is only now being revealed and corrected. Although the amount is still small, there is some research that has been designed to look for—and has found—positive effects. For example, as described in Chapter 2, Darling (1979) concluded that the long-term adjustment of families was far more positive than negative. And currently, in research that is still in the exploratory stages, Turnbull and Behr (1986) are developing an instrument designed to measure positive effects in birth families of children with handicaps. Their checklist includes such items as making friends, being tolerant and sensitive, giving and receiving love, personal growth, being patient, and learning about disabilities.

The current research on adoptive families lies very much in this new orientation. By examining families most likely to have positive outcomes, such research provides a very detailed picture of what those positive effects can be. As explored in depth in Chapter 8, these benefits span all members of the family unit and cross diverse areas of functioning. Future researchers should be able to extract many of these elements for investigation in birth families as well as in other adoptive families. By looking for and finding rewards in the rearing of children with handicaps, investigators may be able to elucidate the nature and course of stress and adaptation. Such elaboration and clarification have implications not only for additional research and theory, but also for practice.

Practice

The current research relates to practice in two fields—adoption and exceptionality—and, of course, to their intersection, the adoption of children with handicaps. Although children with handicaps are being adopted in larger numbers than ever before, there are still thousands of children with developmental disabilities in foster care. Many of these children wait for years, sometimes their entire childhood, because of a failure to find permanent homes for them (Hardy, 1984). Reducing the numbers of children in what has been called *foster care drift*, moving from one short-term care home to another, has become a high priority in contemporary adoption policy. Permanent placement planning was formally assisted on the federal level by the passage of Public Law 96-272, the Adoption Assistance and Child Welfare Act of 1980. This law authorized federal contributions to the adoption subsidies for children with special needs that many states had begun to provide.

Although adoption of children with handicaps would seem to be a decided improvement over foster care, federal and state initiatives have been launched with little in the way of substantive data on the outcomes of such adoptions. The present study, along with some other recent research (Marx, 1985; Nelson, 1985), empirically supports the positive view that proponents had previously taken on faith. At least in terms of parent adjustment and family functioning, the large majority of these adoptions seem remarkably successful. Thus, adoption workers can move forward with the knowledge that the placements they make have a high probability of positive outcomes.

In addition, the current research findings are consistent with those of other studies in portraying the family likely to adopt a child with a handicap as middle-class, experienced with childrearing, familiar with handicapping conditions, and motivated by a wide variety of beliefs and events. These motivations include a humanistic or religious view of the importance of caring for others in need, an already existing attachment to the child, and a desire to start or enlarge a family, sometimes without the ability to do so biologically. Based on the number of *double adopters*, families who adopt more than one child who is handicapped, adoption specialists should look to families with whom they have already placed children for additional placement opportunities (Sinclair, 1985). Workers should be mindful, however, that there may be more adjustment difficulties with placements subsequent to the first.

These current findings are also relevant to practice involving services to birth families of children with handicaps. By understanding the rewards to be gained from rearing a child who is handicapped, professionals can begin to emphasize those rewards in working with birth families. Currently, counselors usually help birth parents adjust to a tragic event. A reorientation based on the findings described in this book would interpret this same event not as tragic, but as an opportunity for existential growth. Knowing that there are possibilities of strengthening the marriage, of enhancing the development of compassion and tolerance in both the parents and siblings, and of developing pride in the child's accomplishments makes the counselor's job very different than it would otherwise be.

Although the counselor should not put "roses on it," in the words of one adoptive parent, this reinterpretation is easier to do in present Western society. The 1960s, 1970s, and 1980s saw attitudes toward persons with disabilities change. With these changing attitudes came policy changes such as normalization and deinstitutionalization in living arrangements and mainstreaming in educational settings. In the United States, as a result of parent advocacy efforts and a few powerful political leaders, legislation and executive mandate created a spectrum of services that made it far easier to care in the home for a child with severe handicaps. Thus, the counselor can correctly advise the family that its members need not be isolated, that the reality burdens can be eased, and that the birth of a child who is handicapped need not signal the birth of a family that is handicapped. Although no one would actively wish to give birth to a child who is disabled, it is possible to develop the kind of love and commitment that would lead to the following comments recorded by Darling (1979, pp. 168-169):

—She's my whole world.
—It's hard to imagine life without Julie. She's part of the family. She's as much one of our family as any of them.
—She's my baby, and I love her and I wouldn't trade her for another child.
—I would want another Down's child. I wouldn't have said that a year ago. . . . So many [normal] kids turn out rotten. . . . She'll never turn on us.

This last mother may well find herself at an adoption agency some day, making inquiries about the availability of a child with Down syndrome! What remains somewhat obscure, however, is what causes some families to develop that commitment along with positive long-term adjustment, while other families relinquish the child or suffer severe existential crises and subsequent poor adjustment. Research is only beginning to probe the variables that may be important in predicting these differences. Certainly, the discovery of these variables is a high priority for future investigation.

Future Emphases

The present research, in describing people who made voluntary commitment to rearing children who are retarded, offers some preliminary guesses at what some of these variables are. The mediating variables specified earlier in the chapter are good starting points for future research. Because the present study had no comparison group of birth families, however, its results are only speculative with regard to the critical variables and the role that existential crises and their resolution may play in long-term adjustment.

A next step, then, would be a comparison of adoptive and biological families, matched on demographic and handicap characteristics. This study would explore the entry of the child into the family and assess the degree of existential crisis experienced. The relationship of the crisis to current adjustment would be measured. Other measures of parental and family functioning would help to clarify what variables influence the quality of the adjustment to the specified stressor of a child who is handicapped.

This research should be longitudinal. As mentioned earlier in this chapter, most research with families suffers from taking only a temporal cross-section of their lives. Although this time-bound approach is understandable—after all, longitudinal research is difficult to do—it is far from optimal. Increasingly, researchers are calling for a longitudinal design as the only one that can portray the nature of the adjustment process. This process is dynamic, changing over time with internal changes in the family as well as external changes in society (Gallagher et al., 1983; Turnbull, Summers, & Brotherson, 1986). The current results should strengthen this view, emphasizing the importance of finding out how these families fare in the future.

Finally, because the current research relates to *adoption* of children who are handicapped, it is relevant to future research in adoption. In this domain, it adds to a small body of work that indicates that adoption of children who are handicapped is generally successful. However, some adoptions disrupt and others seem to be problematic. The present sample had too few negative outcomes to warrant more than speculation as to the reasons, speculation that was presented in Chapter 9. Certainly, future work in this area must focus on the less successful families, attempting to diagnose, and with an aim toward predicting, and therefore preventing, failure. And this research, too, must be longitudinal. Ultimately, the impact of an event such as the entry of a child who is handicapped into a family cannot be understood unless the family is followed through its life cycle, with its adjustment measured as the child enters school, reaches adolescence, possibly leaves home. Many of these adoptive families talked about future adjustments that they knew they would have to make. Some of them expressed apprehension about how they might deal with an adult retarded son or daughter, or what provisions might be necessary when they become too old or sickly to care for a still dependent family member.

Thus, the story is far from over and, although happy endings seemed to be the rule for these adoptive families, long-term adjustment and its relationship to short-term adjustment will not be known without longitudinal data. The mother who said, "But anybody who's thinking of adopting should never think twice about it," had adopted a baby girl and was interviewed when her daughter was still only a toddler. It remains to be seen whether she will reiterate her advice in another 5, or 10, or 15 years as she has to adjust to different realities and resolve other existential issues.

FINAL SUMMARY

This book describes research that explored the experiences of 42 families who had adopted or were long-term fostering 56 children with mental retardation. The parents were mostly middle class and economically comfortable. They were better educated than average, with the majority of mothers and fathers having had some college or university course work. Most of the adoptive parents were married, and the majority already had children in the family, either full biological children, stepchildren, or previously adopted children. Their motivations to adopt a child with retardation were varied, but predisposing factors that characterized many of the families were experience with handicapping conditions and with adoption or fostering, empathy with needy children, wanting a particular child or children in general, and a commitment to religious or humanitarian values.

All of the families adopted their children with the aid of one or more adoption agencies, and most of the parents spoke very positively about the agency workers who had facilitated the adoption. Nonetheless, there was substantial variability in the experience of the adoption process. Some adopters contacted many agencies before a placement was made, and others worked with the first and only agency they contacted. Sometimes placement was very rapid, and other times it was quite slow. Some families already knew the child that they were adopting; others first "met" him or her in a photograph and made a commitment with very little information about the child's characteristics or prognosis for development.

The children themselves were very different, although almost all of them were retarded because of an organic pathology such as Down syndrome or brain damage. Their ages ranged from newborn to mid-teens and their previous histories sometimes included many foster and institutional placements. Many of the children had medical, physical, sensory, or emotional handicaps in addition to their mental retardation. The majority of the children were available for adoption because of their handicaps, but for most of the others, parental abuse, neglect, or inability to cope led to involuntary or voluntary surrender of the child.

The results of the adoptions for the families were overwhelmingly positive. Mothers and fathers generally reported a rapid adjustment to the presence of the child in the family and described benefits in terms of increased parental happiness, marital closeness and positive impact on siblings and social relations. In almost all of the adoptions, the respondents said that they would do it again. Only one placement had disrupted, and only one other mother reported that she would not adopt her child if she had the opportunity to remake her decision.

Despite the very positive results, there were some negative outcomes. In 5 of the 56 placements the outcome seemed more negative than positive; in some of the other families there were difficulties despite the overall good result. Sometimes these difficulties were the result of existential crises experienced despite the preparation and seeming readiness of the family for the child. In other cases, problems seemed to stem directly from reality crises, crises precipitated by a child requiring extraordinary caretaking efforts.

The results of the research were interpreted in the context of general adjustment in the family to a child who is handicapped. A model was proposed to aid in that interpretation. This model differentiates between the existential and reality crises that occur with the presence of a child who is handicapped. It also specifies the relationship between existential and reality crises and suggests variables that mediate that relationship. The model should be heuristic in guiding future research, research that will be most useful if it is multidimensional and longitudinal.

References

Adams, C. R. (1951). *Preparing for marriage: A guide to marital and sexual adjustment.* New York: E. P. Dutton.

Alstein, H., & Simon, R. (1981) *Transracial adoption: A follow-up.* Lexington, MA: Lexington Books.

Ballard, R. (1978). Help for coping with the unthinkable. *Developmental Medicine and Child Neurology, 20,* 517–521.

Beckman, P. J. (1983). Influence of selected child characteristics on stress in families of handicapped infants. *American Journal of Mental Deficiency, 88,* 150–156.

Beckman-Bell, P. (1981). Child-related stress in families of handicapped children. *Topics in Early Childhood Special Education, 1(3),* 45–53.

Belmont, J. M. (1971). Medical-behavioral research in retardation. In N. R. Ellis (Ed.), *International review of research in mental retardation* (Vol. 5, pp. 1–81). New York: Academic Press.

Belsky, J. (1980). Child maltreatment: An ecological integration. *American Psychologist, 35,* 320–335.

Belsky, J. (1984). The determinants of parenting: A process model. *Child Development, 55,* 83–96.

Berman, C. (1974). *We take this child: A candid look at modern adoption.* Garden City, NY: Doubleday.

Bernheimer, L. P., Young, M. S., & Winton, P. J. (1983). Stress over time: Parents with young handicapped children. *Journal of Developmental and Behavioral Pediatrics, 4,* 177–181.

Berry, J. O., & Zimmerman, W. M. (1983). The stage model revisited. *Rehabilitation Literature, 44,* 275–279.

Bigner, J., Jacobsen, C., Miller, T., & Turner, J. G. (1982). The value of children for farm families. *Psychological Reports, 50,* 793–794.

Blacher, J. (1984). Sequential stages of parental adjustment to the birth of a child with handicaps: Fact or artifact? *Mental Retardation, 22,* 55–68.

Blatt, B., & Kaplan, F. (1966). *Christmas in purgatory.* Boston: Allyn and Bacon.

Bohman, M. (1970). *Adopted children and their families.* Stockholm: Proprius.

Booth, T. A. (1978). From normal baby to handicapped child: Unravelling the idea of subnormality in families of mentally handicapped children. *Sociology, 12,* 203–221.

Bowden , L. (1984). Adoption of mentally handicapped children. *Adoption and Fostering, 8,* 38–43.

Bowlby, J. (1951). *Maternal care and mental health.* Geneva: World Health Organization.

Bowlby, J. (1969). *Attachment and loss* (Vols. I & II). New York: Basic Books.

Bradt, J. O. (1980). The family with young children. In E. A. Carter and M. McGoldrick (Eds.), *The family life cycle: A framework for family therapy* (pp. 121–146). New York: Gardner.

Bray, N. M., Coleman, J. M., & Bracken, M. B. (1981). Critical events in parenting handicapped children. *Journal of the Division for Early Childhood, 3,* 26–33.

Britain 1985, an official handbook. (1985). London: Her Majesty's Stationery Office.

Brodzinsky, D. M., Pappas, C., Singer, L. M., & Braff, A. M. (1981). Children's conception of adoption: A preliminary investigation. *Journal of Pediatric Psychology, 6,* 177–189.

Bruininks, R. H., Hauber, F. A., & Kudla, M. J. (1980). National survey of community residential facilities: A profile of facilities and residents in 1977. *American Journal of Mental Deficiency, 84,* 470–478.

Buck, P. S. (1950). *The child who never grew.* New York: John Day.

Buck, P. S. (1964). *Children for adoption.* New York: Random House.

Buckle, J. R. (1984). The extra costs of mentally handicapped living. *International Journal of Rehabilitation Research, 7,* 78–80.

Burden, R. L. (1978). An approach to the evaluation of early intervention projects with mothers of severely handicapped children: The attitude dimension. *Child Care, Health, and Development, 4,* 171–181.

Burden, R. L. (1980). Measuring the effects of stress on the mothers of handicapped infants: Must depression always follow? *Child Care, Health, and Development, 6,* 111–125.

Byrne, E. A., & Cunningham, C. C. (1985). The effects of mentally handicapped children on families: A conceptual review. *Journal of Child Psychology and Psychiatry and Allied Disciplines, 26,* 847–864.

Callan, V. J., & Gallois, C. (1983). Perceptions about having children: Are daughters different from their mothers? *Journal of Marriage and the Family, 45,* 607–612.

Children's Home Society of California. (1984). *The changing picture of adoption.* Los Angeles: Author.

Churchill, S. R., Carlson, B., & Nybell, L. (Eds.). (1979). *No child is unadoptable.* Beverly Hills: Sage Publications.

Classification of occupations. (1970). London: Her Majesty's Stationery Office.

Coyne, A., & Brown, M. E. (1985). Developmentally disabled children can be adopted. *Child Welfare, 64,* 607–615.

Cunningham, C. C., Morgan, P. A., & McGucken, R. B. (1984). Down's syndrome: Is dissatisfaction with disclosure of diagnosis inevitable? *Developmental Medicine and Child Neurology, 26,* 33–39.

Cunningham, C. C., & Sloper, T. (1977). Parents of Down syndrome babies: Their early needs. *Child Care, Health, and Development, 3,* 325–347.

Darling, R. B. (1979). *Families against society: A study of reactions to children with birth defects.* Beverly Hills: Sage Publications.

DeLeon, J., & Westerberg, J. (1980). *Who adopts retarded children?* Unpublished manuscript.

Department of Health and Social Security. (1985a). *Attendance allowance: Cash help for disabled people who need a lot of attention or supervision* (N.I. 205). Norcross, Blackpool: Author.

Department of Health and Social Security. (1985b). *Which benefit?* (FB. 2). Norcross, Blackpool: Author.

Department of International Economic and Social Affairs. (1985). *Demographic yearbook 1983.* New York: United Nations.

Dickerson, M. U. (1982). New challenges for parents of the mentally retarded in the 1980's. *Exceptional Child, 29,* 5–12.

Drotar, D., Baskiewicz, A., Irvin, N., Kennell, J., & Klaus, M. (1975). The adaptation of parents to the birth of an infant with a congenital malformation: A hypothetical model. *Pediatrics, 56,* 710–717.

Dunlap, W. R., & Hollinsworth, J. (1977). How does a handicapped child affect the family? Implications for practitioners. *Family Coordinator, 26,* 286–293.

Dunn, J., Kendrick, C., & MacNamee, R. (1981). Reaction of first-born children to the birth of a sibling: Mothers' reports. *Journal of Child Psychology and Psychiatry, 22,* 1–18.

Dworetzky, J. P. (1984). *Introduction to child development* (2nd ed.). St. Paul: West.

Eheart, B. K., & Ciccone, J. (1982). Special needs of low-income mothers of developmentally delayed children. *American Journal of Mental Deficiency, 87,* 26–33.

Farber, B. (1959). Effects of a severely mentally retarded child on family integration. *Monographs of the Society for Research in Child Development, 24* (2, Whole No. 71).

Farber, B. (1960a). Family organization and crises: Maintenance of integration in families with a severely mentally retarded child. *Monographs of the Society for Research in Child Development, 25* (1, Whole No. 75).

Farber, B. (1960b). Perceptions of crisis and related variables in the impact of a retarded child on the mother. *Journal of Health and Human Behavior, 1,* 108-118.

Farran, D. C., Metzger, J., & Sparling, J. (1986). Immediate and continuing adaptations in parents of handicapped children. In J. J. Gallagher and P. M. Vietze (Eds.), *Families of handicapped persons: Research, programs, and policy issues* (pp. 143–163). Baltimore: Paul Brookes.

Fawcett, J. T. (1978). The value and cost of the first child. In W. B. Miller and L. F. Newman (Eds.), *The first child and family formation* (pp. 244–265). Chapel Hill: Carolina Population Center, University of North Carolina.

Featherstone, H. (1980). *A difference in the family.* New York: Penguin.

Firth, M., Gardner-Medwin, D., Hosking, G., & Wilkinson, E. (1983). Interviews with parents of boys suffering from Duchenne muscular dystrophy. *Developmental Medicine and Child Neurology, 25,* 466–471.

Fossen, A. (1983). Supportive work with parents of disabled children: A questionnaire study from Frambu Health Centre, Norway. *School Psychology International, 4,* 233–228.

Frankl, V. E. (1984). *Man's search for meaning* (3rd ed.). New York: Simon & Schuster.

Franklin, D. S., & Massarik, F. (1969a). The adoption of children with medical conditions: Part I: Process and outcome. *Child Welfare, 48,* 459–467.

Franklin, D. S., & Massarik, F. (1969b). The adoption of children with medical conditions: Part II: The families today. *Child Welfare, 48,* 533–539.

Friedrich, W. N. (1979). Predictors of the coping behavior of mothers of handicapped children. *Journal of Consulting and Clinical Psychology, 47,* 1140-1141.

Friedrich, W. N., & Friedrich, W. L. (1981). Psychosocial assets of parents of handi-capped and nonhandicapped children. *American Journal of Mental Deficiency, 85,* 551–553.

Frodi, A. M. (1981). Contribution of infant characteristics to child abuse. *American Journal of Mental Deficiency, 85,* 341–349.

Gallagher, J. J., Beckman, P., & Cross, A. H. (1983). Families of handicapped children: Source of stress and its amelioration. *Exceptional Children, 50,* 10–19.

Gallagher, J. J., Cross, A., & Scharfman, W. (1981). Parental adaptation to a young handicapped child: The father's role. *Journal of the Division for Early Childhood, 3,* 3–14.

Gallagher, U. M. (1968). The adoption of mentally retarded children. *Children, 15,* 17–21.

Gath, A. (1977). The impact of an abnormal child upon the parents. *British Journal of Psychiatry, 130,* 405–410.

Gath, A. (1983). Mentally retarded children in substitute and natural families. *Adoption and Fostering, 7,* 35–40.

Gath, A., & Gumley, D. (1984). Down's syndrome and the family: Follow-up of children first seen in infancy. *Developmental Medicine and Child Neurology, 26,* 500–508.

Gershenson, C. P. (1984). *Race and ethnicity of children in state foster care systems* (Child Welfare Research Notes #7). Washington, DC: Administration for Children, Youth, and Families.

Glidden, L. M. (1986). Families who adopt mentally retarded children: Who, why, and what happens. In J. J. Gallagher and P. M. Vietze (Eds.), *Families of handicapped persons: Research, programs, and policy issues* (pp. 129–142). Baltimore: Paul Brookes.

Gordeuk, A. (1976). Motherhood and a less than perfect child: A literary review. *Maternal-Child Nursing Journal, 5,* 57–68.

Graliker, B. V., Parmelee, A. H., & Koch, R. (1959). Attitude study of parents of mentally retarded children: Two initial reactions and concerns of parents to a diagnosis of mental retardation. *Pediatrics, 24,* 819–821.

Grossman, F. K. (1972). *Brothers and sisters of retarded children.* Syracuse, NY: Syracuse University Press.

Grossman, H. J. (Ed.). (1983). *Manual on terminology and classification in mental retar-dation.* Washington, DC: American Association on Mental Deficiency.

Halpern, R., & Parker-Crawford, F. (1982). Young handicapped children and their families: Patterns of interaction with human service institutions. *Infant Mental Health Journal, 3,* 51–63.

Hardy, D. R. (1984). Adoption of children with special needs. *American Psychologist, 39,* 901–904.

Hill, R. (1949). *Families under stress.* New York: Harper & Row.

Hill, R. (1958). Generic features of families under stress. *Social Casework, 39,* 139–150.

Hockey, A. (1980). Evaluation of adoption of the intellectually handicapped: A retrospective analysis of 137 cases. *Journal of Mental Deficiency Research, 24,* 187–202.

Hoffman, L. W. (1978). Effects of the first child on the woman's role. In W. B. Miller and L. F. Newman (Eds.), *The first child and family formation,* (pp. 340–367). Chapel Hill: Carolina Population Center, University of North Carolina.

Hoffman, L. W., & Hoffman, M. L. (1973). The value of children to parents. In J. T. Fawcett (Ed.), *Psychological perspectives on population* (pp. 19–76). New York: Basic Books.

Holt, K. S. (1958). The home care of severely retarded children. *Pediatrics, 22,* 744–755.

Holroyd, J., (1974). The Questionnaire on Resources and Stress: An instrument to measure family response to a handicapped family member. *Journal of Community Psychology* , 2, 92–94.

Holroyd, J. (1985). Questionnaire on Resources and Stress manual. Unpublished manuscript. University of California, Los Angeles, Neuropsychiatric Institute.

Holroyd, J., & Guthrie, D. (1979). Stress in families of children with neuromuscular disease. *Journal of Clinical Psychology, 35,* 734–739.

Horn, J. M. (1983). The Texas adoption project: Adopted children and their intellectual resemblance to biological and adoptive parents. *Child Development, 54,* 268–275.

Houser, B. B., Berkman, S. L., & Beckman, L. J. (1984). The relative rewards and costs of childlessness for older women. *Psychology of Women Quarterly, 8,* 395–398.

Huber, C. H. (1979). Parents of the handicapped child: Facilitating acceptance through group counseling. *Personnel and Guidance Journal, 57,* 267–269.

Jackson, P. L. (1974). Chronic grief. *American Journal of Nursing, 74,* 1288–1291.

Jaffee, B., & Fanshel, D. (1970). *How they fared in adoption: A follow-up study.* New York: Columbia University Press.

Jervis, G. (1975). Biomedical types of mental deficiency. In M. F. Reiser (Ed.), *American handbook of psychiatry: Vol. IV. Organic disorders and psychosomatic medicine* (pp. 463–474). New York: Basic Books.

Jones, L. A. (1979). Census-based prevalence estimates for mental retardation. *Mental Retardation, 17,* 199–201.

Kennedy, J. F. (1970). Maternal reactions to the birth of a defective baby. *Social Casework, 51,* 410–416.

Kirk, H. D. (1964). *Shared fate: A theory of adoption and mental health.* New York: Free Press.

Kirk, H. D. (1981). *Adoptive kinship: A modern institution in need of reform.* Toronto: Butterworths.

Koch, R., Graliker, B. V., Sands, R., & Parmelee, A. H. (1959). Attitude study of parents with mentally retarded children: I. Evaluation of parental satisfaction with the medical care of a retarded child. *Pediatrics, 23,* 582–584.

Korfnitzer, M. (1952). *Child adoption in the modern world.* London: Putnam.

Krisheff, C. H. (1977). Adoption agency services for the retarded. *Mental Retardation, 15(1),* 38–39.

Lamb, M. E. (Ed.). (1981). *The role of the father in child development* (revised). New York: Wiley.

Leavy, M. L. (1954). *The law of adoption* (2nd ed.). New York: Oceana.

Leyendecker, C. H. (1982). Psychological effects of mutual handicap upon the family. *International Journal of Rehabilitation Research, 5,* 533–537.

Lipton, H. L., & Svarstad, B. (1977). Sources of variation in clinicians' communication to parents about mental retardation. *American Journal of Mental Deficiency, 82,* 155–161.

Lyon, S., & Preis, A. (1983). Working with families of severely handicapped persons. In M. Seligman (Ed.), *The family with a handicapped child: Understanding and treatment* (pp. 203–232). New York: Grune & Stratton.

MacDonald, W. S., & Oden, C. W.., Jr. (1978). *Moose, a very special person.* Minneapolis: Winston.

MacMillan, D. L. (1982). *Mental retardation in school and society* (2nd ed.). Boston: Little, Brown.

Mandelbaum, A. (1967). The group process in helping parents of retarded children. *Children, 14,* 227–232.

Marx, J. P. (1985, May). *Adoption of children with handicaps: An important component in developmental services.* Paper presented at the meeting of the American Association on Mental Deficiency, Philadelphia, PA.

Massie, R., & Massie, S. (1973). *Journey.* New York: Warner.

Matheny, A. P., Jr., & Vernick, J. (1969). Parents of the mentally retarded child: Emotionally overwhelmed or informationally deprived. *Journal of Pediatrics, 74,* 953–959.

May, R. (1983). *The discovery of being.* New York: Norton.

Maza, P. L. (1983). *Characteristics of children free for adoption* (Child Welfare Research Notes #2). Washington, DC: Administration for Children, Youth, and Families.

McCubbin, H., & Patterson, J. (1983). Family stress adaptation to crises: A double ABCX model of family behavior. In H. McCubbin and J. Patterson (Eds.), *Social stresses and the family: Advances and developments in family stress theory and research* (pp. 39–60). New York: Haworth Press.

McDermott, J. F., Jr. (1980). *Raising Cain (and Abel too): The parents' book of sibling rivalry.* New York: Wyden.

McGown, M. P. (1982). Guidance for parents of a handicapped child. *Child Care, Health, and Development, 8,* 295–302.

Meier, J. H., & Sloan, M. P. (1984). The severely handicapped and child abuse. In J. Blacher (Ed.). *Severely handicapped young children and their families* (pp. 247–272). Orlando: Academic Press.

Miller, L. G. (1969). Helping parents cope with the retarded child. *Northwest Medicine, 68,* 542–547.

Miller, W. B. (1983). Chance, choice, and the future of reproduction. *American Psychologist, 38,* 1198–1205.

Mintzer, D., Als, H., Tronick, E. Z., & Brazelton, T. B. (1985). Parenting a child with a birth defect: The regulation of self-esteem. *Zero to Three: Bulletin of the National Center for Clinical Infant Programs, 5,* 1–8.

Murdoch, J. C. (1984a). Experience of the mothers of Down's syndrome and spina bifida children on going home from hospital in Scotland 1971–1981. *Journal of Mental Deficiency Research, 28,* 123–127.

Murdoch, J. C. (1984b). Immediate post-natal management of the mothers of Down's syndrome and spina bifida children in Scotland 1971-1981. *Journal of Mental Deficiency Research, 28* 67–72.

Nadelman, L., & Begun, A. (1982). The effect of the newborn on the older sibling: Mothers' questionnaires. In M. E. Lamb and B. Sutton-Smith (Eds.), *Sibling relationships: Their nature and significance across the lifespan* (pp. 13–37). Hillsdale, NJ: Erlbaum.

Nardella, M. T., Sulzbacher, S. I., & Worthington-Roberts, B. S. (1983). Activity levels of persons with Prader-Willi syndrome. *American Journal of Mental Deficiency, 87*, 498–505.

National Committee for Adoption. (1985). *Adoption factbook: United States data issues, regulations and resources.* Washington, DC: Author.

Nelson, K. A. (1985). *On the frontier of adoption: A study of special-needs adoptive families.* New York: Child Welfare League of America.

Nirje, B. (1969). The normalization principle and its human management implications. In R. B. Kugel and W. Wolfensberger (Eds.), *Changing patterns in residential services for the mentally retarded* (pp. 231–240). Washington, DC: U.S. Government Printing Office.

Olshansky, S. (1962). Chronic sorrow: A response to having a mentally defective child. *Social Casework, 43*, 191–194.

Parke, R. D. (1981). *Fathers.* Cambridge: Harvard University Press.

Parks, M. (1977). Parental reactions to the birth of a handicapped child. *Health and Social Work, 2*, 51–66.

Patterson, J. M., & McCubbin, H. I. (1983). Chronic illness: Family stress and coping. In C. R. Figley and H. I. McCubbin (Eds.), *Stress and the family: Vol. II: Coping with catastrophe* (pp. 21–36). New York: Brunner/Mazel.

Payne-Price, A. C. (1981). Etic variations on fosterage and adoption. *Anthropological Quarterly, 54*, 134–145.

Plomin, R., & DeFries, J. C. (1983). The Colorado Adoption Project. *Child Development, 54*, 276–289.

Powell, T. H., & Ogle, P. A. (1985). *Brothers and sisters—A special part of exceptional children.* Baltimore: Paul Brookes.

Paznanski, E. O. (1984). Emotional issues in raising handicapped children. *Rehabilitation Literature, 45*, 214–219.

Price-Bonham, S., & Addison, S. (1978). Families and mentally retarded children: Emphasis on the father. *Family Coordinator, 27*, 221–230.

Raynor, L. (1970). *Adoption of non-white children: The experience of a British adoption project.* London: George Allen & Unwin.

Raynor, L. (1980). *The adopted child comes of age.* London: George Allen & Unwin.

Rivera, G. (1972). *Willowbrook: A report on how it is and why it doesn't have to be that way.* New York: Random House.

Robinson, N. M., & Robinson, H. B. (1976). *The mentally retarded child: A psychological approach* (2nd ed.). New York: McGraw-Hill.

Roos, P. (1985). Parents of mentally retarded children—Misunderstood and mistreated. In H. R. Turnbull, III and A. P. Turnbull (Eds.), *Parents speak out, then and now* (2nd ed.) (pp. 245–257). Columbus: Charles Merrill.

Roskies, E. (1972). *Abnormality and normality: The mothering of thalidomide children.* Ithaca: Cornell University Press.

Ross, J., & Kahan, J. P. (1983). Children by choice or by chance: The perceived effects of parity. *Sex Roles, 9*, 69–77.

R. S. T. in Quebec. (1985, July 1). Dear Ann Landers [Letter to Ann Landers]. *Washington Post*, p. D8.

Rubin, A. L., & Rubin, R. L. (1980). The effects of physician counseling technique on parent reactions to mental retardation diagnosis. *Child Psychiatry and Human Development, 10*, 213–221.

Rutter, M. (1979). Maternal deprivation, 1972–1978: New findings, new concepts, new approaches. *Child Development, 50,* 283–305.

Salisbury, C. L. (1985). Internal consistency of the short-form of the Questionnaire on Resources and Stress. *American Journal of Mental Deficiency, 89,* 610–616.

Saperstein, S. (1984, July 24). Adoption: White couple battles for black three-year-old. *Washington Post,* pp. B1, B3.

Saperstein, S. (1984, August 4). White couple wins fight to adopt black child. *Washington Post,* pp. B1, B5.

Scarr, S., & Weinberg, R. A. (1983). The Minnesota adoption studies: Genetic differences and malleability. *Child Development, 54,* 260–267.

Schild, S. (1971). The family of the retarded child. In R. Koch and J. C. Dobson (Eds.), *The mentally retarded child and his family* (pp. 431–442). New York: Brunner/ Mazel.

Schonell, F. J., & Rorke, M. (1960). A second survey of the effects of a subnormal child on the family unit. *American Journal of Mental Deficiency, 64,* 862–868.

Schonell, F. J., & Watts, B. H. (1956). A first survey of the effects of a subnormal child on the family unit. *American Journal of Mental Deficiency, 61,* 210–219.

Searl, S. J. (1978). Stages of parent reaction. *The Exceptional Parent, 8,* 127–129.

Sieffert, A. (1978). Parents' initial reaction to having a mentally retarded child: A concept and model for social workers. *Clinical Social Work Journal, 6,* 33–43.

Silcock, A. (1984). Crises in parents of prematures: An Australian study. *British Journal of Developmental Psychology, 2,* 257–268.

Sinclair, L. (1985). Multiple placements of mentally handicapped children. *Adoption and Fostering, 9(4),* 37–40.

Sloper, P., Cunningham, C. C., & Arnljotsdottir, M. (1983). Parental reactions to early intervention with their Down's syndrome infants. *Child Care, Health, and Development, 9,* 357–376.

Social Trends, No. 15. (1985). London: Her Majesty's Stationery Office.

Solnit, A. J., & Stark, M. H. (1961). Mourning and the birth of a defective child. *Psychoanalytic Study of the Child, 16,* 523–537.

Spitz, R. A. (1946). Anaclitic depression. *Psychoanalytic Study of the Child, 2,* 313–342.

Springer, A., & Steele, M. W. (1980). Effects of physicians' early parental counseling on rearing of Down syndrome children. *American Journal of Mental Deficiency, 85,* 1–5.

Stone, N. W., & Chesney, B. H. (1978). Attachment behaviors in handicapped infants. *Mental Retardation, 16,* 8–12.

Sugarman, M. (1977). Paranatal influences on maternal-infant attachment. *American Journal of Orthopsychiatry, 47,* 407–421.

Sullivan, R. (1979). Siblings of autistic children. *Journal of Autism and Developmental Disorders, 9,* 287–298.

Tillich, P. (1952). *The courage to be.* New Haven: Yale University Press.

Trainer, M. (1975, September 25). He's lucky, this little boy. *Washington Post,* p. VA2.

Trout, M. D. (1983). Birth of a sick or handicapped infant: Impact on the family. *Child Welfare, 62,* 337–348.

Turnbull, A. P., & Behr, S. K., (1986, May). *Positive contributions that persons with mental retardation make to their families.* Paper presented at the meeting of the American Association on Mental Deficiency, Denver, CO.

Turnbull, A. P., Summers, J. A., & Brotherson, M. J. (1986). Family life cycle: Theoretical and empirical implications and future directions for families with mentally retarded members. In J. J. Gallagher and P. M. Vietze (Eds.), *Families of handicapped persons: Research, programs, and policy issues* (pp. 45–67). Baltimore: Paul Brookes.

Tyler, N. B., & Kogan, K. L. (1977). Reduction of stress between mothers and their handicapped children. *American Journal of Occupational Therapy, 31,* 151–155.

U.S. Bureau of the Census. (1986). *Statistical abstract of the United States: 1987* (107th ed.). Washington, DC: Author.

Waisbren, S. E. (1980). Parents' reactions after the birth of a developmentally disabled child. *American Journal of Mental Deficiency, 84,* 345–351.

Wikler, L. M. (1986). Family stress theory and research on families of children with mental retardation. In J. J. Gallagher and P. M. Vietze (Eds.), *Families of handicapped persons: Research, programs, and policy issues* (pp. 167–195). Baltimore: Paul Brookes.

Wikler, L., Wasow, M., & Hatfield, E. (1981). Chronic sorrow revisited: Parent versus professional depiction of the adjustment of parents of mentally retarded children. *American Journal of Orthopsychiatry, 51,* 63–79.

Winton, P., & Turnbull, A. (1981). Parent involvement as viewed by parents of preschool handicapped children. *Topics in Early Childhood Education, 1,* 11–19.

Wishart, M. C., Bidder, R. T., & Gray, O. P. (1980). Parental responses to their developmentally delayed children and the South Glamorgan Home Advisory Service. *Child Care, Health, and Development, 6,* 361–376.

Wittenborn, J. R. (1957). *The placement of adoptive children.* Springfield, IL: Charles C Thomas.

Wolfensberger, W. (1967). Counseling parents of the mentally retarded. In A. A. Baumeister (Ed.), *Mental retardation: Appraisal, education, and rehabilatation* (pp.217–240). Chicago: Aldine.

Wolfensberger, W. (1972). *The principle of normalization in human services.* Toronto: National Institute on Mental Retardation.

Wolkind, S., & Kozaruk, A. (1983). *Children with special needs: A review of children with medical problems placed by the Adoption Resource Exchange from 1974–77.* Report to the Department of Health and Social Services. London: Family Research Unit, London Hospital Medical College, March 1983.

Wolkomir, B. (1947). The unadoptable baby achieves adoption. *Child Welfare League of America Bulletin, 26,* 1–7.

Wright, L. S. (1976). Chronic grief: The anguish of being an exceptional parent. *Exceptional Child, 23,* 160–169.

Zimmerman, S. L. (1984). The mental retardation family subsidy program: Its effects on families with a mentally handicapped child. *Family Relations, 33,* 105–118.

Appendix A

Semi-Structured
Interview

SECTION I: PREADOPTION
MOTIVATION

We're trying to get a picture of how people decide to adopt a child. My first questions will be about you and your family before _____ came to live with you.

1. About how long before _____ came to live with you did you first think about adopting?

2. Try to remember back then and tell me as best you can how you first thought about adopting.

[Questions 3 and 4 explore further.]

5. When you first thought about adoption, did you have in mind a child with particular characteristics? What were they?

[Questions 6–10 explore further.]

11. Many people change their attitudes about adopting from when they first think about it until the time they actually adopt. They may think differently about characteristics of the child, about how the child might fit into their family, etc. From the time that you first thought about adoption until the time _____ came to live with you, would you say that your attitudes had changed?

4. A great deal
3. Somewhat
2. Very little
1. Not at all

Will you describe the most important changes?

12. Different people have different reasons for wanting to adopt children. Sometimes one person has several reasons for wanting to ad∩ppt.

Acknowledgement. In creating the interview schedule, I relied on portions of two other schedules that were used in previous adoption research. These schedules are unpublished, but the research results based on them appear in Nelson (1985) and Wolkind and Kozaruk (1983).

Try to think back to the time you decided you might want to adopt
a child. What were the reasons that influenced you to adopt?

13. When people make important decisions, they frequently talk to others
about what they are planning to do. Other than each other and the
agency, whom did you talk to about adopting?

[Questions 14 and 15 explore further.]

[Questions 16–32 explore information specific to the adoption of the target
child, including agency referrals, agency role, and initial positive and negative attitudes.]

33. I'm sure you realize that not everyone would be willing to raise a
child with _____'s condition. Why do you think you were willing,
that you wanted to do this?

34. What do you think are the most important characteristics for parents
of a child like _____.?

[Questions 35 and 36 explore further.]

SECTION II:
SOCIODEMOGRAPHIC
INFORMATION

[Questions 37–77 focus on family, education, work, and religious variables.]

SECTION III: ADJUSTMENT AND
PRESENT FUNCTIONING

Whenever someone enters or leaves a family, the family may change
in many ways. Some of the changes may be for the better and some may
be for the worse. My next questions concern these changes; they are about
the positive and negative impact that _____'s adoption has had on your
family.

78. Just before _____ came to live with you, but after you knew that
s/he was coming, did you have any worries, apprehensions, uncer-
tainties?

79. Did these worries turn out to be realistic? Did you have any of the
problems you thought you might? Describe:

[Questions 80–82 explore further.]

83. Now, I want to ask you specifically about the positive impact of your
adopting _____ .
By "positive impact," I mean the benefits of the adoption for your
family, or the ways that it has changed things in your family for the
better. Has adopting _____ had a positive impact on your family
or has it changed things in your family for the better in any way?

84. Has the impact been very positive or somewhat positive?
85. Even when there is a positive impact there can be a negative one as well. Has adopting _____ had a negative impact on your family or has it changed things in your family for the worse in any way?
86. Has the impact been very negative or somewhat negative?
87. Overall, has the positive impact been greater than the negative, has the negative impact been greater than the positive, or have the positives and negatives been about equal?
88. Has the adoption made any family members happier, or not?
89. Has the adoption made any family members unhappier, or not?
90. Has adopting made family members better people in any way?
91. Has the adoption added meaning to the lives of any family members?
92. Because of the adoption, do any family members have less meaning in their lives?
93. Has adopting _____ had a negative effect on any family member's behavior or personality?
94. Overall, has the adoption made family members more flexible? By "flexible" I mean able to adapt or change as circumstances around you change.
95. Has the adoption made any family members less flexible?
96. Do you (or your husband/wife) work longer hours, or have you taken on an extra job to help pay for _____'s expenses?
97. Have (either of) you started working shorter hours or have you stopped working in order to take care of him/her/them?
98. Has the adoption had any other positive or negative effects on your (or your husband's/wife's) work life?
99. Have expenses for _____ made it necessary for your family to cut back on money for other things?
100. Have you received any allowances because of _____'s expenses?
101. Because of the adoption, has anyone given up plans to continue with or go back to school?
102. Because of adopting _____, do any family members feel that they do not have enough spare time?
103. Has anyone developed new spare-time interests or activities because of the adoption?
104. Does anyone enjoy spare time more because of adopting _____?
105. Does anyone now enjoy spare time less?
106. For your other child/ren, has having _____ as a member of the family been: a good experience, a bad experience, both good and bad, or has it had no effect?
107. Is/Are _____ (a) friend/s or companion/s to (either/any of) your other child/children?
108. (Does your other child) (Do either/any of your children) resent _____?

109. Except accidentally or during play, does _____ ever physically hurt (either/any of) your other child/ren?

110. Except accidentally or during play, (does your other child) (do either/any of your other children) ever physically hurt _____?

111. (Does your other child) (Do either/any of your children) ever get teased about _____ by other children at school or from the neighborhood?

112. Because of the adoption, are you (and your husband/wife) closer to your other child/ren, less close, or has the adoption had no effect on this?

113. Because of the adoption, do you (and your husband/wife) have more arguments with your other children, fewer arguments, or has the adoption had no effect on this?

114. (Does your other child) (Do any of your other children) feel that they don't get as much of your time as they used to?

115. Did _____'s adoption have anything to do with your (separation) (divorce)?

116. Because of the adoption, do you find it easier or more difficult to meet and get to know members of the opposite sex, or does adoption have no effect on this?

117. Has adopting _____ had any effect on how close you and your husband/wife are?

118. Has the adoption had any effect on the amount of time you and your husband/wife have to do things together, just the two of you?

119. Has the adoption had any effect on how many arguments you and your husband/wife have?

120. Has adopting _____ had any effect on your sex life?

121. Has the adoption changed in any way, whether you or your husband/wife has the more say in important family decisions?

122. Has adopting _____ changed in any way how household responsibilities are divided in your family?

[Question 123 explores further.]

124. During the last six months, about how often have you and other family members visited relatives? Would you say: daily, weekly, monthly, less than monthly, or never?

125. If you think back to the six months before _____ started to live with you, did your family visit relatives: more often, about as often, or less often?

126. Have any family members become less close to anyone outside the household because of adopting _____?

127. Because of the adoption, have any family members become closer to anyone outside the household?

128. Have any family members made new friends because of _____?

129. Has anyone lost friends, or does anyone consider himself no longer a friend to someone because of the adoption?

130. You've undoubtedly met a lot of professionals, e.g., social workers, doctors, psychologists, teachers, as a result of adopting _____. Overall, would you say these people had been helpful to you?

[Questions 121–133 explore further.]

134. If you compare your experiences with _____ to' those with your other child/ren, how have your experiences with _____ been different?

135. All things considered, has _____'s adoption worked out: Better than you expected, about as well as you expected, or less well?

136. I'd like to ask about some specific ways in which _____'s adoption might have turned out differently than you expected. Compared to what you expected, back when you were first considering legally adopting _____, has taking care of him/her been: More expensive, less expensive, or about as expensive?

137. Compared to what you expected, has _____ been more difficult to raise, less difficult, or about as difficult?

138. As far as _____'s feeling that s/he belongs to your family and is with you to stay, has it taken him/her more time than you expected to feel this way, less time, or about as much time?

139. Compared to what you expected back when you were first considering adopting _____, are his/her physical abilities about as good as you expected them to be, not as good, or are they actually better than you expected them to be?

140. Are his/her/their intellectual, or mental, abilities about as good as you expected them to be?

141. Is his/her ability to make good relationships with people: about as good as you expected them to be, not as good, or are they actually better than you expected them to be?

142. Thinking back over your entire experience with _____, and all the good times and the bad times—if you had it to do over again, do you think you'd adopt _____, would you not adopt him/her, or are you unsure?

143. What advice would you give to someone who was considering adopting a child like _____?

Appendix B

Questionnaire on Resources and Stress

1. _____ demands that others do things for him/her more than is necessary.
2. _____ understands the idea of time.
3. Because _____ is the kind of person he/she is, he/she can handle his/her situation better than another person could.
4. _____ is cared for equally by all members of our family.
5. It will take us three years or more to pay off our debt.
6. A member of my family has had to give up education (or a job) because of _____ .
7. One of the things I appreciate in _____ is he/she is independent.
8. Members of the family share in the care of _____ .
9. _____ would not resent being left at home while the family went on vacation.
10. Members of our family praise each other's accomplishments.
11. _____ has a pleasing personality.
12. I do not attend very many meetings (PTA, church, etc.).
13. I know _____'s condition will improve.
14. _____ does not have problems with seeing or hearing.
15. Even if people don't look at _____ , I am always wondering what they might think.
16. I take on responsibility for _____ because I know how to deal with him/her.
17. _____ has some unusual habits which draw attention.
18. In our house the whole family eats dinner together.
19. The doctor sees _____ at least once a month.

Acknowledgement. From "The Questionnaire on Resources and Stress: An Instrument to Measure Family Response to a Handicapped Family Member" by J. Holroyd, 1974, *Journal of Community Psychiatry, 2,*(pp. 92-94). The Questionnaire on Resources and Stress was adapted by permission of the author and reprinted by permission of the publisher. Copyright 1987 by Clinical Psychology Publishing Company, Inc. Respondents had to indicate true or false for each item.

20. I usually do not have to take _____ with me when I go out.
21. There is more than one wage-earner in our family.
22. _____ is a very capable, well functioning person despite his/her other problems.
23. I always watch to make sure _____ does not do physical harm to himself/herself or others.
24. The special opportunities needed by _____ are available in our community.
25. Our house is comfortably arranged to meet _____'s needs without making it difficult for other members of the family.
26. Money from the government or an organization pays for part of our medical costs.
27. _____ would be in danger if he/she could get out of the house or yard.
28. I feel that our family situation will get better.
29. Medicine does not have to be given to _____ at a set time.
30. _____ doesn't communicate with others of his/her age group.
31. People who don't have the problems we have don't have the rewards we have either.
32. Other members of the family have to do without things because of _____ .
33. _____'s problems or illness do not stand in the way of our family progress.
34. When others are around _____ I cannot relax; I am always on guard.
35. If _____ were more pleasant to be with it would be easier to care for him/her.
36. Thinking about the future makes me sad.
37. Much of the time I think about _____ dying.
38. If I knew when _____ would die I wouldn't worry so much.
39. I don't worry too much about _____'s health.
40. Our family agrees on important matters.
41. Professionals (nurses, etc.) in an institution would understand _____ better than I do.
42. When _____ is not well, I can't go out.
43. I am afraid that by limiting _____'s activities he/she will not develop on his/her own.
44. Our family's income has dropped over the past 5 years.
45. The constant demands for care for _____ limit growth and development of someone else in our family.
46. _____ feels that I am the only one who understands him/her.
47. In his/her own way _____ brings as much pleasure to our family as the other members.

48. I worry about what will happen to _____ when I can no longer take care of him/her.
49. I think in the future _____ will take up more and more of my time.
50. I am able to leave _____ alone in the house for an hour or more.
51. I fear the day when other members of the family leave home and I am left alone with _____ .
52. It would be better for _____ if our house could be remodeled.
53. A counselor or a teacher sees _____ at least once a month.
54. I get out of the house to do something interesting at least once a week.
55. I am very careful about asking _____ to do things which might be too hard for him/her.
56. The attitude of our family makes it impossible for _____ to live with us any longer.
57. I would rather be caring for _____ than doing some other kind of work.
58. _____ is limited in the kind of work he/she can do to make a living.
59. I have accepted the fact that _____ might have to live out his/her life in some special setting (i.e., hospital, institution, foster home).
60. I have given up things I have really wanted to do in order to care for _____ .
61. My family argues about how to care for _____ .
62. _____ is able to fit into the family social group.
63. Some members of my family don't like the way I do things.
64. I would not want the family to go on vacation and leave _____ at home.
65. At times I fear _____ will not be able to function in society if he/she is out of our house.
66. It is difficult for me to stand back and watch _____'s condition get worse.
67. In the future our family's social life will suffer because of increased responsibilities and financial pressure.
68. It doesn't make any difference to _____ if he/she is at home or in a hospital.
69. _____ knows the difference between strangers and friends.
70. I am afraid that other members of the family will be hurt because they are related to _____ .
71. There is no way we can possibly keep _____ in our house.
72. People should take care of their own.
73. One of us has had to pass up a chance for a job because _____ could not be removed from a clinic or a special school, etc.
74. I would rather help _____ do something than have him/her fail and feel badly.

75. _____ has always lived with our family.
76. I cannot manage _____ .
77. Sometimes I avoid taking _____ out in public.
78. _____ is on a special diet.
79. Many people simply don't understand what it is like to live with _____ .
80. Every member of our family has had to do without things because of money spent on _____ .
81. _____ can feed himself/herself.
82. I tend to do things for _____ that he/she can do himself/herself.
83. When we go on vacation, I'm not afraid to leave _____ for any length of time.
84. As the time passes I think it will take more and more to care for _____ .
85. I belong to organizations which help with problems I have with _____ .
86. There have been serious emotional problems for someone in our family.
87. Our relatives have been very helpful.
88. We have discussed what will happen when _____ dies.
89. It is easier for me to do something for _____ than to let him/her do it himself/herself and make a mess.
90. _____ is easy to manage most of the time.
91. I don't think that _____ depends too much on me or other members of the family.
92. It is not necessary for _____ to go up or down steps in our house.
93. I feel that I must protect _____ from the remarks of children.
94. We can afford to pay for the care _____ needs.
95. Just talking about problems with close friends makes life easier.
96. I can never leave the house because of _____ .
97. I am happy when I watch the development and achievements of _____ .
98. It bothers me that _____ will always be this way.
99. No one in our family drinks alcohol too much.
100. The community is used to people like _____ .
101. _____ uses special equipment because of his/her handicap.
102. _____ has a handicap which prevents him/her from improving.
103. _____ is sometimes too sexual.
104. _____ has a lot of pain.
105. I feel tense whenever I take _____ out in public.
106. _____ is easy to live with.
107. The doctor sees _____ at least once a year.
108. _____ eats his/her meals with other members of the family.

109. Wheelchairs or walkers have been used in our house.
110. An electricity failure would endanger _____'s life or health.
111. Caring for _____ has been a financial burden for our family.
112. _____ made a good income at one time.
113. Some friends are very helpful when it comes to _____ .
114. I worry that _____ may sense that he/she does not have long to live.
115. _____ will not do something for himself/herself if he/she knows someone will do it for him/her.
116. I can go visit with friends whenever I want.
117. Members of the family show no interest in what happens to _____ .
118. We enjoy _____ more and more as a person.
119. We have changed our house because of _____ .
120. Taking _____ on a vacation spoils pleasure for the whole family.
121. The family does as many things together now as we ever did.
122. _____ knows his/her own address.
123. _____ gets along very well with others.
124. _____ is aware of who he/she is (for example, male 14 years old).
125. _____ prevents any communication within our family.
126. Someone in our family turns against _____ when his/her friends are around.
127. Sometimes I need to get away from the house.
128. I get upset with the way my life is going.
129. Sometimes I feel very embarrassed because of _____ .
130. Having to care for _____ has enriched our family life.
131. Neighbors want us to move because of _____ .
132. I respect _____'s judgment about what he/she can do.
133. _____ doesn't do as much as he/she should be able to do.
134. Our family has been on welfare.
135. We have discussed what will happen if _____ lives longer than we do.
136. _____ is truly accepted by the family.
137. A bed that raises and lowers has made things easier.
138. We take _____ along when we go out.
139. It makes me feel good to know I can take care of _____ .
140. Others do for _____ what he/she could do for himself/herself.
141. Because of _____ our family has never enjoyed a meal.
142. I hate to see _____ try to do something and fail.
143. _____ is accepted by other members of the family.
144. I fear _____ might get hurt while playing games or sports.
145. It is difficult to communicate with _____ because he/she has difficulty understanding what is being said to him/her.
146. _____ spends time at a special day center or in special classes at school.

147. _____ is very anxious most of the time.
148. _____'s health is not getting worse.
149. There is no special government program to help _____ .
150. I have no time to give the other members of the family.
151. Our family is quite religious.
152. In our family _____ takes an active part in family affairs.
153. There are many places where we can enjoy ourselves as a family when _____ comes along.
154. It is hard to think of enough things to keep _____ busy.
155. _____ is over protected.
156. Our family income is more than average.
157. Some of our family do not bring friends into the home because of _____ .
158. I try to get _____ to take care of himself/herself.
159. Caring for _____ gives one a feeling of worth.
160. We have discussed his/her death with _____ .
161. _____ is able to take part in games or sports.
162. One of us has had to pass up a chance for a job because _____ could not be left without someone to watch him/her.
163. We think _____ will live longer in an institution.
164. _____ has too much time on his/her hands.
165. There is an organization for families who share our problems.
166. I am disappointed that _____ does not lead a normal life.
167. We spend up to 25 percent of our income on medical care (or care for _____).
168. Time drags for _____ — especially free time.
169. I worry about how our family will adjust after _____ is no longer with us.
170. The part that worries me most about _____ going on his/her own is his/her ability to make a living.
171. _____ resents being treated as a handicapped person.
172. _____ can't pay attention very long.
173. I worry about what will be done with _____ when he/she gets older.
174. If _____ were healthier, it would be easier to go away for a holiday.
175. Compared to others, we spend a lot of money on medical costs.
176. I get almost too tired to enjoy myself.
177. _____ has things to entertain him/her (TV, radio) in his/her room.
178. We owe a great deal of money.
179. _____ is depressed most of the time.
180. If I were healthier, it would be easier to care for _____ .
181. Most persons in public places indicate they don't want _____ around.
182. _____ can get around the neighborhood quite easily.

183. _____ wants more freedom than he/she has.
184. One of the things I appreciate about _____ is his/her confidence.
185. I don't mind when people look at _____ .
186. Whenever I leave the house I am worried about what's going on at home.
187. In our family _____ plays as an important role as other members.
188. _____ will never be any brighter than now.
189. One of the things I appreciate about _____ is his/her ability to recognize his/her own limits.
190. I believe _____ should go places as often as others in the family.
191. I am not embarrassed when others question me about _____'s condition.
192. There is a lot of anger and resentment in our family.
193. If _____ could get around better we would do more as a family.
194. Our family has managed to save money or make investments.
195. We own or are buying our own home.
196. Information and encouragement is available to those who seek it.
197. We get special funds because of _____'s problem.
198. One of the things I enjoy about _____ is his/her sense of humor.
199. We can have no luxuries.
200. I have enough time to myself.
201. _____ is able to go to the bathroom alone.
202. I am afraid _____ will not get the individual attention, affection, and care that he/she is used to if he/she goes somewhere else to live.
203. I have too much responsibility.
204. No member of the family pities _____ too much.
205. _____ cannot remember what he/she says from one moment to the next.
206. _____ is better off in our home than somewhere else.
207. _____ can describe himself/herself as a person.
208. Others in the family should help care for _____ .
209. A nurse sometimes works in our home.
210. Relatives have done more harm than good when it comes to _____ .
211. I am afraid that as _____ gets older it will be harder to manage him/her.
212. It is easy to keep _____ entertained.
213. It makes me feel worthwhile to help _____ .
214. _____ wants to do things for himself/herself.
215. In the future _____ will be more able to help himself/herself.
216. _____ needs a walker or a wheelchair.
217. I have become more understanding in my relationships with people as a result of _____ .

218. The constant demands to care for _____ limit my growth and development.
219. _____ cannot get any better.
220. _____ is very tense in strange surroundings.
221. It is easy to communicate with _____ .
222. I feel sad when I think of _____ .
223. Our family should do more together.
224. I have had to give up a chance for a job because of _____ .
225. _____ accepts himself/herself as a person.
226. Outside activities would be easier without _____ .
227. Our relatives give us much help.
228. I enjoy church.
229. Caring for _____ puts a strain on me.
230. I often worry about what will happen to _____ when I no longer can take care of him/her.
231. _____ can use the bus to go wherever he/she wants.
232. People can't understand what _____ tries to say.
233. If it were not for _____ things would be better.
234. I feel that _____ would prefer a professional (nurse, day care helper, etc.) to care for him/her rather than a member of our family.
235. Some members of the family resent _____ .
236. Members of our family get to do the same kinds of things other families do.
237. _____ embarrasses others in our family.
238. My happiness goes up and down with _____'s behavior.
239. _____ uses the phone frequently.
240. _____ has many things to keep him/her busy.
241. Sometimes the demands _____ makes drive me out of my mind.
242. I had high hopes for _____'s future.
243. _____ could do more for himself/herself.
244. My family understands the problems I have.
245. It is easy to do too much for _____ .
246. _____ appreciates the interest others show in him/her.
247. It is easier for our family to do things with people we know than with strangers.
248. I am pleased when others see my care of _____ is important.
249. We can hardly make ends meet.
250. _____ rarely has nightmares.
251. I don't try to shelter _____ from life's difficulties.
252. Members of my family are able to discuss personal problems.
253. I often have the desire to protect _____ .
254. I am as healthy as I ever was.
255. _____ does not dress right.

256. Most of _____'s care falls on me.
257. No one can ever understand what I go through.
258. We have household help (cleaning woman, nurse, etc.).
259. It is fortunate how _____ has adjusted to life.
260. _____ accepts his/her handicap.
261. _____ has his/her own room.
262. _____ is very irritable.
263. We have lost most of our friends because of _____ .
264. _____ has an attractive, clean appearance.
265. _____ can ride a bus.
266. _____ will always be a problem to us.
267. _____ is able to express his/her feelings to others.
268. It is easy for me to relax.
269. _____ has to use a bedpan or a diaper.
270. I rarely feel blue.
271. We have good laundry facilities at home.
272. _____ can walk without help.
273. _____ needs help in the bathroom.
274. I have chances to carry on interests outside the home.
275. It bothers me to see _____ in pain.
276. Every cloud has a silver lining.
277. I like myself as a person.
278. I am worried much of the time.
279. _____ has a strongly defiant personality.
280. Because _____ uses special equipment and facilities, it is difficult to take him/her out.
281. One of the things I appreciate about _____ is his/her sensitivity to others.
282. Others have offered to share the load in caring for _____ .
283. _____ likes to follow the same schedule all the time.
284. _____'s needs come first.
285. _____ attracts attention.

Appendix C

Changes Since the _____**Placement**

In what ways do you think you have changed since _____ was placed with you? Please tick one in each of the questions below.

1. I've become (more patient _____ , less patient _____ , about as patient _____) as I was before.
2. I plan more for the future _____ ; I live more from day to day _____ ; I plan about as much as I did before _____ .
3. I make friends (more easily _____ , less easily _____ , about as easily _____) as I used to.
4. I've become (more deeply religious _____ , less religious _____ , about as religious _____) as I was before.
5. I worry (more _____ , less _____ , about as much _____) as I did before.
6. I've become (more nervous _____ , less nervous _____ , about as nervous _____) as I was before.
7. I get angry (more easily _____ , less easily _____ , about as easily _____) as I did before.
8. In general, I've become (more unhappy _____ , happier _____ , about as happy _____) as I was before.
9. In general, I feel I've changed for the better _____ , changed for the worse _____ , in some respects I've changed for the better and in some for the worse _____ , I haven't changed at all _____ .
10. In general, I get along (better _____ , less well _____ , about as well _____) with my husband/wife as before.

Acknowledgement. From "Effects of a Severely Mentally Retarded Child on Family Integration" by B. Farber, 1959, *Monographs of the Society for Research in Child Development, 24*, (2, Whole No. 71). Copyright 1959 by the Society for Research in Child Development, Inc. Adapted by permission.